The French Revolution 1787–1804

Now in its fourth edition, P.M. Jones's *The French Revolution* has been extensively revised and incorporates the most recent research on race, religion, gender and citizens' rights. It also covers, in detail, the colonial repercussions of the revolution in both the Caribbean and the Indian Ocean.

Written with the needs of students in mind, this volume recounts the dramatic years from 1787 to 1804 when the *ancien régime* was replaced by a constitutional monarchy and then a republic. Jones covers the difficulties facing King Louis XVI in the run up to the attack on the Bastille, and explains how the revolution led to the creation of the First French Empire by France's most successful General – Napoleon Bonaparte. Wherever possible, the actions and reactions of ordinary men and women who found themselves caught up in the turmoil are recorded. By analysing the revolution's significance for both Europe and the world beyond, the concluding section sets the revolution in a global context.

With study aids such as a chronology, who's who, glossary and an enlarged selection of documents to allow for research and discussion, this book remains a useful tool for students interested in politics, culture and society during the French Revolution.

P.M. Jones is Emeritus Professor of French History at the University of Birmingham. Previous publications include *The Peasantry in the French Revolution* (1988), *Reform and Revolution in France: the Politics of Transition, 1774–1791* (1995), *The French Revolution in Social and Political Perspective* (1996) and *Liberty and Locality in Revolutionary France: Six Villages Compared, 1760–1820* (2003).

Seminar Studies

History is the narrative constructed by historians from traces left by the past. Historical enquiry is often driven by contemporary issues and, in consequence, historical narratives are constantly reconsidered, reconstructed and reshaped. The fact that different historians have different perspectives on issues means that there is often controversy and no universally agreed version of past events. *Seminar Studies* was designed to bridge the gap between current research and debate, and the broad, popular general surveys that often date rapidly.

The volumes in the series are written by historians who are not only familiar with the latest research and current debates concerning their topic, but who have themselves contributed to our understanding of the subject. The books are intended to provide the reader with a clear introduction to a major topic in history. They provide both a narrative of events and a critical analysis of contemporary interpretations. They include the kinds of tools generally omitted from specialist monographs: a chronology of events, a glossary of terms and brief biographies of 'who's who'. They also include bibliographical essays in order to guide students to the literature on various aspects of the subject. Students and teachers alike will find that the selection of documents will stimulate the discussion and offer insight into the raw materials used by historians in their attempt to understand the past.

Clive Emsley and Gordon Martel
Series Editors

The French Revolution
1787–1804

Fourth edition

P.M. Jones

Routledge
Taylor & Francis Group

LONDON AND NEW YORK

Fourth edition published 2022
by Routledge
2 Park Square, Milton Park, Abingdon, Oxon OX14 4RN

and by Routledge
605 Third Avenue, New York, NY 10158

Routledge is an imprint of the Taylor & Francis Group, an informa business

© 2022 P. M. Jones

First edition published by Pearson Education Limited 2003

Third edition published by Routledge 2016

British Library Cataloguing-in-Publication Data
A catalogue record for this book is available from the British Library

Library of Congress Cataloging-in-Publication Data
Names: Jones, Peter, 1949- author.
Title: The French Revolution, 1787-1804 / P.M. Jones.
Description: Fourth edition. | Abingdon, Oxon ; New York,
NY : Routledge, [2022] |
Series: Seminar studies | Includes bibliographical references and index.
Identifiers: LCCN 2021014498 | ISBN 9780367741341 (hbk) |
ISBN 9780367741327 (pbk) | ISBN 9781003156185 (ebk)
Subjects: LCSH: France--History--Revolution, 1789-1799.
Classification: LCC DC148 .J574 2022 | DDC 944.04--dc23
LC record available at https://lccn.loc.gov/2021014498

ISBN: 978-0-367-74134-1 (hbk)
ISBN: 978-0-367-74132-7 (pbk)
ISBN: 978-1-003-15618-5 (ebk)

DOI: 10.4324/9781003156185

Typeset in Sabon
by Taylor & Francis Books

Contents

Illustrations

Figures

Maps

Map 0.1 Administrative geography of France before 1789
Key to provinces:

1 Brittany	13 Nivernais	25 Limousin
2 Normandy	14 Burgundy	26 Auvergne
3 Picardy	15 Lorraine	27 Languedoc
4 Artois	16 Alsace	28 Dauphiné
5 Flanders and Hainaut	17 Franche-Comté	29 Comtat Venaissin
6 Champagne	18 Lyonnais	30 Provence
7 Ile-de-France	19 Bourbonnais	31 Roussillon
8 Maine	20 Berry	32 Foix
9 Anjou	21 Marche	33 Béarn
10 Poitou	22 Saintonge and Angoumois	34 Corse
11 Touraine	23 Aunis	
12 Orléanais	24 Gascony and Guyenne	

Map 0.2 Administrative geography of France after 1789

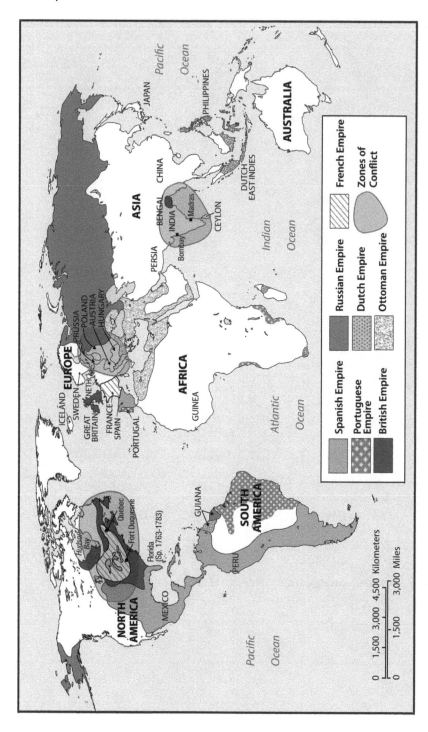

Map 0.3 The global Seven Years War (1756–63) with major battle zones

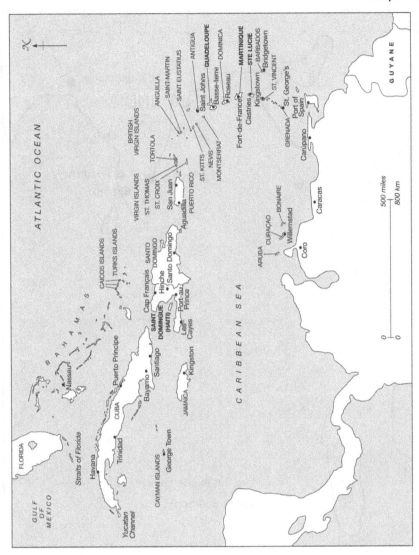

Map 0.4 France's Caribbean colonies (French territory in 1789 in bold text)

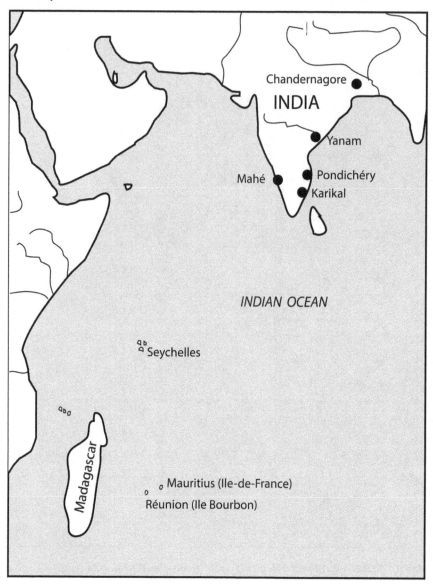

Map 0.5 France's Indian Ocean territories in 1789

Map 0.6 A Grande Nation (French republic and the sister republics)

Chronology

1763

10 February   Treaty of Paris ending the Seven Years War.

December   Fiscal crisis, Laverdy is appointed Controller General.

1766   Lorraine is ceded to France.

1774

10 May   Death of Louis XV.

24 August   Turgot is appointed Controller General.

1775

11 June   Coronation of Louis XVI, grandson of Louis XV.

1776

12 May   Turgot is dismissed.

1777

29 June   Necker is appointed Director General of Finance.

1778

February   France enters an alliance with the American colonists.

10 July   France declares war on Britain.

1781

January   Publication of Necker's *Compte rendu au roi*.

19 May   Necker is dismissed.

1782

July   A third *vingtième* applicable to the years 1783–86 is introduced.

1783

3 September   Peace is agreed between France, the American colonists, Spain and Great Britain.

2 November   Calonne is appointed Controller General.

1785

10 November	France signs a treaty of alliance with Holland.

1786

17 August	Death of King Frederick the Great of Prussia.
20 August	Calonne submits to the king a package of sweeping reforms.
26 August	A trade treaty ('the Eden Treaty') is signed between France and Britain.

1787

13 February	Death of Vergennes.
22 February	Opening session of the Assembly of Notables.
8 April	Calonne is dismissed.
1 May	Loménie de Brienne is appointed *chef du Conseil royal des finances* (subsequently Principal Minister).
25 May	Dissolution of the Assembly of Notables.
June/July	Provincial Assemblies reform goes ahead, as does grain trade deregulation (allowing exports), and the conversion of the *corvée* into a monetary tax.
August	Prospect of a new Russo-Turkish war.
6 August	King enforces registration of the land tax and stamp duty reforms by means of a *lit de justice*.
15 August	Parlement of Paris is exiled to Troyes.
17 August	Ottoman Empire declares war on Russia
September/ October	Foreign policy crisis triggered by civil war in the United Provinces; Prussia sends in troops in support of the Stadholder and the Orangeists.
28 September	Return of the Parlement of Paris from Troyes.
19–20 November	King agrees to call an Estates General by 1792. Enforced registration of a 420 million *livres* loan. The Duke of Orleans is exiled and two *parlementaires* are arrested.

1788

3 May	The Parlement of Paris publishes a statement regarding the 'fundamental laws' of the kingdom.
8 May	Lamoignon, the Keeper of the Seals, issues the 'May Edicts'.
7 June	'Day of the Tiles' in Grenoble.
5 July	Loménie de Brienne agrees to call an Estates General for the following year
13 July	Violent hail storms imperil the harvest in northern France.

16 August	Admission of partial bankruptcy.
25 August	Loménie de Brienne is dismissed. Lamoignon, the Keeper of the Seals, also retires a few days later.
26 August	Necker is appointed Director General of Finance (again) and agrees to a meeting of the Estates General in January (subsequently delayed until May) 1789.
25 September	Restored to office, the Parlement of Paris declares in favour of the 1614 model for the Estates General.
6 November	A second Assembly of Notables is convened and deliberates inconclusively for five weeks.
12 December	Memorandum of the Princes of the Blood.
27 December	Procedures for the convocation of the Estates General are agreed.

1789

February/ March	Rural unrest in Franche-Comté, Dauphiné and Provence.
March/April	The drawing up of *cahiers de doléances*.
5 May	Opening session of the Estates General.
4 June	Death of the heir apparent.
17 June	The deputies of the Third Estate rename themselves the 'National Assembly'.
20 June	Tennis Court Oath is sworn.
23 June	In a *séance royale*, Louis XVI tries to wrest the initiative from the Third Estate.
11 July	Necker is dismissed (again).
12–17 July	Paris rises in revolt; the Bastille fortress is taken by force.
16 July	Necker is recalled.
22 July	Murders of Bertier, intendant of Paris, and Foulon, mayor.
late July/ August	Great Fear; uprisings in many provinces.
4–11 August	Decrees abolishing the feudal regime.
10 August	Decree instituting the National Guard.
27 August	Promulgation of the Declaration of the Rights of Man and the Citizen.
11 September	National Assembly votes for a 'suspensive' rather than an 'absolute' royal veto over legislation.
5–6 October	March to Versailles; return of royal family to Paris.

2 November	National Assembly votes to nationalize the property of the Church.
14 November	Necker's speech reporting a 170 million *livres* deficit.

1790

February/ March	Elections take place to create the new municipalities.
4 February	Rapturous support for Louis XVI when he attends the National Assembly.
13 February	Decree prescribes the closure of monasteries.
26 February	Decree reorganizing France into departments.
13 April	National Assembly declines to make Catholicism the religion of state.
30 April	'Address to the French People' announcing that the *assignat* would 'serve as money'.
22 May	National Assembly repudiates wars of conquest.
19 June	Decree abolishing hereditary nobility and titles.
12 July	Civil Constitution of the Clergy is voted.
14 July	Fête de la Fédération; celebration of the first anniversary of the revolution.
4 September	Resignation of Necker.
16–24 August	Decree reorganizing the judiciary.
October/ November	Start of disturbances among slaves and free blacks in Saint-Domingue.
27 November	Decree imposing an oath on the clergy.

1791

January	New tax system takes effect.
10 March	Pope condemns the Civil Constitution of the Clergy; links with the Holy See are severed.
2 April	Death of Mirabeau.
18 April	Royal family is stopped from leaving Paris for Saint-Cloud.
May	French forces occupy Avignon and the Comtat Venaissin.
15 May	Reubell's motion to extend some civil and political rights to the colonies.
20–21 June	Royal night-time flight from Paris.
16–17 July	Petitioning and a 'massacre' in the Champ de Mars.
22 August	Slave revolt in Saint-Domingue.

27 August	Declaration of Pillnitz is issued.
14 September	Louis XVI accepts the new constitution; annexation of Avignon and the Comtat Venaissin.
27 September	Citizenship is granted to Ashkenazi Jews.
1 October	First session of the Legislative Assembly.
9 November	Measures against *émigrés* (vetoed by the king).
29 November	Measures against non-oath-swearing priests (vetoed by the king).
December	Arguments for war begin to be debated in the Jacobin Club.

1792

1 January	Legislative Assembly decrees the beginning of the 'era of liberty'.
18 January	Comte de Provence is excluded from the regency.
January/ February	Sugar and coffee disturbances in Paris.
9 February	First measure to seize *émigré* property.
4 April	Decree granting full rights to 'free blacks'.
20 April	War is declared on Austria.
May	Reports of military setbacks reach Paris.
21 May	Prussia declares war on France.
27 May	Deportation of non-oath-swearing priests is voted (vetoed by the king).
20 June	Armed demonstration in the Tuileries Palace by the Paris Sections.
28 June	Manœuvres by General Lafayette against Parisian 'agitators'.
11 July	Legislative Assembly declares 'the fatherland in danger'.
25 July	Publication of the Brunswick Manifesto.
10 August	Insurrection in Paris; deposition of Louis XVI.
2–6 September	Massacres in the prisons of Paris.
20 September	Victory over the Prussians and the *émigrés* at the battle of Valmy.
21 September	National Convention votes to abolish the monarchy and to declare France a republic.
6 November	French victory against the Austrians at the battle of Jemappes.
11 December	Start of the trial of the king.

1793

21 January	Execution of Louis XVI.
1 February	France declares war on Britain and Holland.
24 February	Decree to recruit an additional 300,000 troops.
7 March	France declares war on Spain.
9 March	Despatch of *représentants en mission* to the departments.
10–11 March	Start of the uprising of the Vendée.
18 March	French suffer a reverse at the battle of Neerwinden.
4 April	Defection of General Dumouriez to the Austrians.
6 April	Establishment of the Committee of Public Safety.
31 May–2 June	Mobilization of the Sections of Paris; expulsion of Girondin deputies from the Convention.
June/July/ August	'Federalist' revolts in the departments.
24 June	Constitution of 1793 is approved.
27 August	Toulon is surrendered to the British fleet of Admiral Hood.
5–6 September	Pressure is exerted on the Convention by the *sans-culottes* in order to secure implementation of the 'popular programme'.
17 September	Law of Suspects is passed.
29 September	Law of the General Maximum is passed.
10 October	Decree on 'Revolutionary Government'; the Constitution of 1793 is put into abeyance until peacetime conditions prevail.
16 October	Execution of Marie-Antoinette.
30 October	Closure of women's political clubs.
31 October	Execution of twenty leading Girondin deputies.
10 November	Dechristianization in Paris; cathedral of Notre Dame becomes a Temple of Reason.
4 December	Passing of the Law of 14 Frimaire II formalizing 'Revolutionary Government'.
5 December	First issue of *Le Vieux Cordelier* appears; start of the Indulgents Campaign.

1794

4 February	Abolition of slavery in French colonies.
18 February	Festival of the Abolition of Slavery in Notre Dame cathedral, Paris.

13–24 March	Arrest and execution of the Hébertists.
5 April	Execution of Danton, Desmoulins, Delacroix, Philippeaux and the *pourris*.
7 May	Decree establishing the Cult of the Supreme Being.
8 June	Festival of the Supreme Being is held in Paris.
10 June	Law of 22 Prairial II increases the conviction rate of the Revolutionary Tribunal.
26 June	French victory against the Austrians and the Dutch at the battle of Fleurus.
27 July	*Coup* of 9 Thermidor; overthrow of Robespierre and his allies.
August/ September	Relaxation of the Terror.
12 November	Closure of the Paris Jacobin Club.
8 December	The 75 deputies who had protested at the expulsion of the Girondins return to their seats in the Convention.
24 December	Repeal of the Law of the General Maximum.
1795	
21 February	Formal separation of Church and State.
April/May	Start of the 'White' Terror against revolutionary personnel in southern France.
1-2 April	Crowds from the Sections invade the Convention to demand bread.
5 April	Signing of the peace treaty of Basle with Prussia.
16 May	Withdrawal of *assignats* from circulation.
23 May	Exclusion of women from the assemblies of the Paris Sections.
8 June	Death of the son of Louis XVI (styled 'Louis XVII' by the *émigrés*).
24 June	Publication of the Declaration from Verona.
27 June	*Emigré* forces land in Quiberon Bay (southern Brittany) with the assistance of British warships.
22 August	Constitution of 1795 is approved.
22–30 August	Two-Thirds decrees.
October	Elections in progress to replace the National Convention.
3 November	The Executive Directory takes office.
16 November	Opening of the Pantheon Club.

1796

19 February	Production of *assignats* ceases.
26 February	The Executive Directory orders the closure of the Pantheon Club and all neo-Jacobin societies.
2 March	Bonaparte is appointed general-in-chief of the Army of Italy.
30 March	Gracchus Babeuf's 'Conspiracy of the Equals' takes shape.
April/May	French forces win a succession of battles against the Piedmontese and the Austrians in Italy.
10 May	Babeuf is arrested.
16 October	General Bonaparte sets up the Cispadane Republic (subsequently merged into the Cisalpine Republic).
December	General Hoche's naval expedition to Ireland ends in failure.

1797

March/April	Significant royalist gains in the 'Year Five' elections to the legislative Councils.
18 April	Peace negotiations with Austria begin at Leoben.
27 May	Execution of Babeuf and his comrade Darthé.
9 July	General Bonaparte sets up the Cisalpine Republic.
24 August	Repeal of the laws of 1792 and 1793 against non-oath-swearing clergy.
4 September	*Coup* of 18 Fructidor V; two Directors are removed; elections in 49 departments are annulled and 177 deputies are purged from the Councils.
8 September	Merlin de Douai and François de Neufchâteau replace Carnot and Barthélemy as Directors.
30 September	Partial bankruptcy; two-thirds of the national debt is repudiated.
15 October	France signs the Treaty of Campo Formio with Austria.
12 November	Centralized tax-collecting institutions are established in each department.

1798

15 February	Proclamation of the Roman Republic.
March/April	The neo-Jacobins make gains in the elections to the legislative Councils.
11 May	*Coup* of 22 Floréal VI; the election results of neo-Jacobins and other 'firm republicans' are set aside.
19 May	General Bonaparte sets off on a naval expedition (to Egypt).

1 August	French expeditionary fleet is destroyed in Aboukir Bay by Rear-Admiral Nelson (battle of the Nile).
August	Second unsuccessful attempt by French forces to invade Ireland.
5 September	*Loi Jourdan*; general conscription is introduced.

1799

12 March	France declares war on Austria (War of the Second Coalition).
April	Legislative elections turn to the advantage of the neo-Jacobins.
9 May	Sieyès is elected to the Directory in the place of Reubell.
June/September	War crisis; France loses nearly all of her conquests in Italy and Germany.
18 June	*Coup* of 30 Prairial VII; the Councils force through a purge of the Executive Directory.
5–20 August	Royalist uprising in the southwest.
25–30 September	Military situation is stabilized by the French victory over the Austrians and Russians at the second battle of Zurich.
9 October	General Bonaparte returns to France from Egypt.
9–10 November	*Coup* of 18–19 Brumaire VIII; Executive Directory is overthrown and replaced by a 'Consulate'.
24 December	Adoption of the Constitution of the Year Eight.

1800

17 February	Law providing for the administrative reorganization of France; establishment of the prefects.
2 March	Partial amnesty for *émigrés*.
14 June	General Bonaparte defeats the Austrians at the battle of Marengo.
3 December	General Moreau defeats the Austrians at the battle of Hohenlinden.
24 December	Opera House (*machine infernale*) plot; Bonaparte narrowly escapes with his life.

1801

8 February	Peace signed with the Austrians at Lunéville.
18 February	Law establishing special tribunals to try cases of brigandage without juries or appeal.
15 July	The Concordat with Pope Pius VII is signed.

23 July	Discussions on the Civil Code begin.
1802	
25 March	Peace with Britain is signed at Amiens.
27 April	Decree maintaining or reinstating slavery in France's colonies.
May	Establishment of the Legion of Honour.
2 August	Proclamation of the Life Consulate.
1803	
28 March–7 April	Introduction of a new decimal currency.
18 May	Britain declares war on France.
1804	
1 January	Declaration of the independent republic of Haiti (formerly Saint-Domingue).
9 March	Arrest of the royalist plotter, Cadoudal.
15 March	Promulgation of the Civil Code.
21 March	Execution of the Duc d'Enghien.
2 December	Coronation of Napoleon Bonaparte as Emperor of the French.

Who's who

Amar, Jean-Baptiste-André: Montagnard deputy and member of the Committee of General Security from June 1793; he would be involved in the pre-emptive strike against Robespierre on 27 July 1794; arrested, in turn, by the Thermidorians, he was held for a time and then amnestied; in 1796 he was implicated in the abortive Conspiracy of the Equals.

Babeuf, François-Noel called 'Gracchus': Hailing from a modest rural background, he made a name for himself as a radical journalist and utopian communist; arrested in May 1796 whilst preparing a *coup* against the Directory as a participant in the Conspiracy of the Equals, he was put on trial and executed.

Barentin, Charles-Louis-François de Paule de: Replaced Lamoignon as Keeper of the Seals in September 1788 having made a name for himself in the Assembly of Notables; a conservative opponent of Necker; resigned after the taking of the Bastille and soon emigrated.

Barnave, Antoine: Barrister from Grenoble who played a prominent role in the Dauphiné revolt; a leading member of the patriot party from 1789–91; increasingly moderate in outlook thereafter, his constitutional royalist sympathies would result in imprisonment and execution in November 1793.

Barras, Paul, Vicomte de: A disreputable army officer who was drawn into revolutionary politics for the pickings it offered; elected to the Convention, he was responsible for brutal repression in Marseilles and Toulon in the autumn of 1793; played a key role in the *coup* against Robespierre in July 1794; returned to the Council of Five Hundred in October 1795; served as a Director from 1795–99; forced out of politics after Brumaire.

Belley, Jean-Baptiste: Ex-slave from Saint-Domingue and first black deputy (in the Convention and then the Council of Five Hundred).

Bertin, Henri Léonard Jean-Baptiste: Controller General, 1759–63 and Secretary of State for Agriculture, 1763–80.

Billaud-Varenne, Jacques Nicolas: A schoolmaster turned lawyer, he first attracted attention as a radical member of the Cordeliers and Jacobin Clubs;

elected to the Convention in 1792 and to the Committee of Public Safety in September 1793, he acted as a spokesman for the extreme left; survived Thermidor, but was deported as a terrorist in 1795 and never returned to France.

Breteuil, Louis-Auguste Le Tonnelier, Baron de: Aristocrat, soldier and diplomat; briefly became prime minister in July 1789 following the dismissal of Necker.

Brienne, Etienne Charles de Loménie de: Archbishop of Toulouse and Principal Minister, 1787–88.

Brissot, Jacques Pierre: A writer, journalist and campaigner against slavery, he was elected to the Legislative Assembly and then the Convention. One of the leaders of the Girondin group of deputies; expelled from the Convention and executed in October 1793.

Buzot, François: From a legal background, he came to notice as a patriot deputy in the National Assembly; elected to the Convention, his hostility to the Paris Commune and the Sections launched him into a short-lived career as a Girondin and a Federalist; escaped arrest and execution only by means of suicide.

Cadoudal, Georges: One of the men who led the royalist rebels of the Vendée in 1793; subsequently involved in the *chouan* insurgency and the Quiberon Bay landings of June 1795; emigrated to Britain following the pacification of the west; participated in the 'second *chouannerie*' of 1799–1800; involved in the Opera House plot against Bonaparte of December 1800; returned to Paris for another covert operation against the First Consul in August 1803; betrayed and taken prisoner, he was executed on 25 June 1804.

Calonne, Charles Alexandre de: Controller General, 1783–87.

Carrier, Jean-Baptiste: A former Cordeliers Club militant, he would be elected to the Convention in 1792; known chiefly as the hard-line Montagnard deputy who was responsible for the mass drownings in Nantes after the crushing of the Vendée revolt, he would be recalled after Thermidor, put on trial and executed in December 1794.

Castries, Charles Gabriel de la Croix, Marquis de: Minister for the Navy, 1780–87.

Chaumette, Pierre Gaspard called 'Anaxagoras': A club militant and notorious atheist who rose to power as an official of the Paris Commune; organized the Festival of Reason in Notre Dame cathedral on 10 November 1793; spoke at the Festival of the Abolition of Slavery in February 1794; arrested as a Hébertist 'conspirator' and executed in April 1794.

Collot d'Herbois, Jean Marie: Settled in Paris following a theatrical career in the provinces; involved in the uprising of 10 August 1792; elected to the Convention and taken into the Committee of Public Safety following pressure from the Sections in September 1793; responsible for the savage repression in Lyons; conspired against Robespierre on 26–27 July 1794; deported as a terrorist in April 1795.

Couthon, Georges: A lawyer from Clermont-Ferrand who became a close ally of Robespierre in the Convention; despite disablement, which confined him to a wheelchair, he undertook a number of missions; elected to the Committee of Public Safety in May 1793; fell victim to the Thermidor *coup* which resulted in his execution on 28 July 1794.

Danton, Georges: A lawyer by training who came to prominence as a Cordeliers Club militant; deeply implicated in the uprising of 10 August 1792 from which he emerged to become Minister of Justice; a Montagnard deputy from 1792 until his execution in April 1794.

Desmoulins, Camille: Radical journalist, pamphleteer and Cordeliers Club militant, 1789–92; Montagnard deputy from 1792 until his execution in April 1794.

Dumouriez, Charles François du Périer: A professional soldier whose career blossomed into politics after 1789; briefly a government minister in the spring of 1792 before taking command of the Army of the North; victor at Valmy and Jemappes; loser at Neerwinden (18 March 1793); emigrated in April 1793 after a fruitless bid to lead his forces against Paris.

Fouché, Joseph: A member of the Oratorian teaching order in Nantes before the revolution; elected to the Convention in 1792; carried out a number of important missions, notably one that initiated the wave of church closures in the departments; recalled to Paris in order to answer for his activities in Lyons and elsewhere in April 1794; conspired against Robespierre, but survived the reaction after Thermidor; despatched as ambassador to the Cisalpine Republic in September 1798; returned to Paris in 1799 and was made Minister of Police following the Brumaire *coup*.

Frederick William II: King of Prussia; ruled 1786–97.

Hébert, Jacques René: An artisan by background, he found his metier as the publisher of the scurrilous journal *Le Père Duchesne*; militant of the Cordeliers Club in 1792; to the fore in a number of insurrections, or near-insurrections; a dechristianizer married to a former nun, he was targeted by the Indulgents in late 1793 and early 1794; executed March 1794.

Lafayette, Marie Joseph Paul Roch Yves Gilbert Motier, Marquis de: Wealthy nobleman with liberal leanings who had fought in the War of American Independence; member of the Assembly of Notables in 1787; appointed commander of the National Guard of Paris in July 1789; appointed to an army command early in 1792; tried unsuccessfully to persuade the Legislative Assembly to act against the Jacobin Club in July 1792; defected to the Austrians in August 1792.

Lamoignon, Chrétien François de, Marquis de Bâville: Keeper of the Seals, 1787–88.

La Révellière-Lépeaux, Louis Marie: A patriot of 1789 vintage who made his name in the Jacobin Club of Angers; his national career as a deputy in the Convention was marred by association with the Gironde, and he only came to prominence after Thermidor; elected to the Council of Elders in October 1795, and to the Directory the following month; an architect of the Fructidor purge and pillar of the regime, he remained in office until June 1799; played no part in the public life of the Consulate; declined to take the oath of allegiance to the Emperor.

Leopold II: Archduke of Austria and Habsburg Emperor; ruled 1790–92.

Lepoutre, Pierre-François: elected as one of four Third Estate deputies to represent the *bailliage* of Lille in the Estates General. He never spoke in public and is known chiefly for his correspondence.

Loménie de Brienne: see **Brienne.**

Louis XV: King of France; ruled 1715–74.

Louis XVI: King of France; ruled 1774–92 (deposed).

Louis XVIII: Self-proclaimed accession 1795; ruled as King of France 1814–23.

Malesherbes, Guillaume Chrétien de Lamoignon de: Twice minister of Louis XVI in 1775–76 and 1787–88; volunteered to defend the king during his trial; executed in April 1794.

Marat, Jean-Paul: A physician by training, he edited the uncompromisingly violent and democratic journal *L'Ami du Peuple*; implicated in the September Massacres, he was nonetheless elected to the Convention; assassinated by Charlotte Corday in July 1793.

Marie-Antoinette: Queen of France, 1774–91.

Maupeou, René Nicolas Charles Augustin de: Chancellor, 1768–90.

Merlin de Douai, Philippe-Antoine: A deputy to the Estates General, National Assembly and then the Convention whose legal expertise brought him to public notice; chief architect of the legislation on the abolition of feudalism in 1790; completed a number of missions during the Terror; helped to negotiate the Treaty of Basle with Prussia in April 1795; elected to the Council of Elders in October 1795; served several stints as a minister; became a Director in September 1797, after the Fructidor *coup*; resigned just before Brumaire and retired from public life.

Mirabeau, Honoré Gabriel Riqueti, Comte de: A prominent constitutional monarchist deputy whose promising career was cut short by an early death in 1791; although a noble, he represented the Third Estate of Aix-en-Provence in the Estates General; is remembered for his act of public defiance after the royal session (*séance royale*) of 23 June 1789 and for the advice he conveyed to the royal family in 1790–91.

Miromesnil, Armand Thomas Hue de: Keeper of the Seals, 1774–87.

Moreau, Jean Victor: Participated in the Breton pre-revolution as a law student in 1788; joined the colours in 1791; promoted briefly to command the Army of the North in October 1794; in charge of the Army of the Rhine and the Moselle in 1796–97; victor at Hohenlinden in December 1800; returned to Paris, but became estranged from Bonaparte; accused of links with the *émigrés* and Pichegru and arrested; in self-imposed exile from 1804 to 1813.

Necker, Jacques: Finance Minister, 1776–81; 1788–89; 1789–90.

Noailles, Louis Marie, Vicomte de: Nobleman who served under his brother-in-law Lafayette during the American War of Independence; elected to the Estates General, he is chiefly remembered for his role on the night of 4 August 1789.

Palloy, Pierre-François: one of the capital's biggest building contractors, his men began to demolish the Bastille without waiting for authorisation.

Pétion, Jérôme: Trained as a lawyer, he came to notice as one of the most radical 'patriot party' deputies in the National Assembly and subsequently the Convention; was mayor of Paris at the time of the uprising of 10 August 1792; died a Girondin fugitive during the Terror.

Pichegru, Charles: Of humble background, he made his way in the army; promoted to a command position in the Army of the Rhine in October 1793; converted to royalism in 1795; elected to the Council of Five Hundred, but the chance of a political career was blocked by the Fructidor *coup*; threatened with deportation, he fled abroad and thereafter worked with the *émigrés* for a Bourbon restoration; arrested in Paris on 28 February 1804, he was found dead in his prison cell on 5 April 1804.

Reubell, Jean-François: A lawyer from Alsace who served in most of the revolutionary Assemblies; a Director from the inception of the regime until May 1799; retired from public life after Brumaire.

Robespierre, Maximilien: A provincial lawyer who came to notice because of his unswervingly democratic opinions in the National Assembly; Montagnard deputy in the Convention from 1792; powerful member of the Committee of Public Safety; toppled in a *coup* on 27 July 1794 and executed the following day.

Roux, Jacques: A priest and militant member of the Cordeliers Club; spokesman of the *enragés*; imprisoned in September 1793 and committed suicide.

Saint-Just, Louis Antoine de: An austere comrade-in-arms of Robespierre; elected to the Convention where he made his maiden speech on the subject of the trial of the king in November 1792; member of the Committee of Public Safety from May 1793; carried out several missions as a political commissar attached to the armies; defended Robespierre unflinchingly during the Thermidor crisis and was duly executed on 28 July 1794.

Santerre, Antoine Joseph: A brewer by trade, he was involved in both the assault on the Bastille and the uprising of 10 August 1792; became a commander of the Paris National Guard.

Ségur, Philippe Henri, Marquis de: Secretary for War, 1780–87.

Sieyès, Emmanuel Joseph: Clergyman (*abbé*) and writer who in 1789 emerged as one of the main theoreticians of revolution. Author of *What is the Third Estate?*, he went on to become a legislator and a Director.

Terray, Jean Marie, abbé: Controller General, 1769–74.

Thibaudeau, Antoine: An obscure member of the Convention who rose to prominence after Thermidor when he spurred on the tide of political reaction; elected to the Council of Five Hundred in October 1795; accepted the Brumaire *coup*; briefly prefect of the Gironde in 1800; appointed to the Council of State in September 1800 where he was involved in drafting the Civil Code.

Toussaint Louverture, François-Dominique: Ex-slave; leader of the 1791 uprising in Saint-Domingue and the most effective general of the Haitian Revolution.

Turgot, Anne Robert Jacques: Controller General, 1774–76.

Turreau, Louis-Marie: A career soldier before the revolution; appointed to the rank of general in September 1793; remembered chiefly for his brutal pacification of the Vendée.

Vadier, Marc Guillaume Alexis: Despite a parliamentary career between 1789 and 1791, only came to prominence following his election to the Convention; aligned himself firmly against the Gironde; key member of the Committee of General Security from September 1793; an extreme anti-clerical, he joined the plot against Robespierre but was denounced in turn for his role in the Terror; sentenced to deportation in April 1795, but went into hiding; survived to become a neo-Jacobin stalwart under the Directory.

Vergennes, Charles Gravier, Comte de: Foreign Secretary, 1774–87.

Voltaire, François Marie Arouet de: Author and *philosophe*.

Part I

1 The setting

France in the eighteenth century was a powerful country which dominated Europe – a fact that the descent into turmoil and revolution from 1787 should not be allowed to obscure. By comparison with her neighbours, she achieved territorial unity quite quickly and definitively; even at the start of the century the so-called 'hexagon' featured recognizably on the map. In fact, once the absorption of Lorraine had been completed in 1766, the frontiers of the **Bourbon** kingdom would resemble closely those of the present-day Fifth Republic. France was a large, compact and well-populated state then. With perhaps 21.5 million inhabitants in 1700 and over 29 million by the century's end, she bestrode the Continent. Great Britain (England, Wales and Scotland) and Prussia (10.5 million and about 10 million respectively in 1800) were small countries by comparison. Only the Austrian Habsburg Empire (about 20 million) and the unmeasured and largely untapped resources of the Russian Empire appeared to offer a counterweight. A fifth of all Europeans were born French (compared with under one-tenth today). Historians looking for an explanation of the train of events from 1787 often dwell on the ramshackle aspects of the Bourbon state, but not so contemporaries. By the standards of Europe in the second half of the eighteenth century, France was a prospering and effectively administered country whose rulers possessed an enviable (if still inadequate) capacity to extract tax revenue from their subjects.

Bourbon rule was based on compromise and a large measure of consent – at least until the summer of 1787. Although styled 'absolute monarchs', **Louis XV** and his grandson **Louis XVI** were nothing of the sort in practice. They ruled – or rather their agents governed – by means of elaborate and repeated exercises in negotiation. It would therefore be more accurate to describe the monarchy as a hybrid type of government which sought consensus, but displayed a readiness to resort to coercion if necessary. Yet the pure theory of Bourbon rule remained completely innocent of this day-to-day reality. At his coronation in 1775 Louis XVI, like Louis XV before him, swore an oath not to his subjects but to God Almighty. The fundamental laws of the kingdom allowed no distinction to be made between the body of the nation and the person of the monarch and woe betide anyone who pretended otherwise [**Doc. 1**]. Only in 1791 would Louis XVI accept formally the principle of contractual monarchy in the shape of the oath of allegiance to the constitution drawn up by the National Assembly.

DOI: 10.4324/9781003156185-2

With whom did the monarch and his agents in the provinces negotiate, before 1787? *Ancien régime* France was a corporate society held together by a framework of hierarchy. This is another way of saying that mere individuals did not count for very much unless clustered together into legally recognized interest groups known as 'orders' or 'estates' of the realm. It was with such groupings that the king and his officials negotiated. Individuals might lay claim to corporate status by virtue of a common possession (noble blood, for instance); or an affinity (membership of the same professional body); or common access to certain privileges; or else by virtue of a common geographical origin. For example, all Bretons, whether high or low-born, believed that they were set apart from other French men and women – and with good reason. Yet all these relationships presupposed an unceasing round of negotiation, and it was thanks to the skills of successive monarchs and their servitors in this sphere that the so-called *ancien régime* persisted and prospered for as long as it did.

In common with most large European states of the period, France's population was divided into three supposedly functional categories: clerics who prayed, nobles who fought and commoners who worked. Known as the **First, Second** and **Third Estates** respectively, each grouping was reinforced with rights and responsibilities. In the case of the clergy and the nobility, the exemptions and immunities they enjoyed far outweighed any duties attaching to their status by the end of the *ancien régime*, whereas the Third Estate was chiefly defined not by rights but by the responsibilities its members were expected to shoulder. Indeed, the clergy and the nobility would come to be referred to as the 'privileged orders' when the struggle to reform the structures of absolute monarchy began in earnest in 1787. Nobody knows for certain how many nobles there were on the eve of the Revolution. Estimates range from 120,000 to 400,000, although the lower figure – corresponding to roughly 28,000 families (140,000 individuals) – is likely to be the more accurate. They represented about 0.5 per cent of the total population (Dewald, 2019: 916). The clergy, by contrast, are easier to count and cannot have numbered more than 125,000 individuals (59,500 priests and curates; 5,000 non-beneficed persons; 23,000 monks; and 37,000 nuns). By process of deduction, therefore, the Third Estate must have totalled around 27,475,000 or 98 per cent of the population. The *abbé* **Sieyès**'s notorious pamphlet *What is the Third Estate?* [**Doc. 4**], which would be published at the start of 1789 just as preparations for the meeting of the Estates General were getting under way, scarcely fell short of the mark, therefore.

However, a three-part classification that lumped together the vast majority of French men and women, whether rich or poor, town or country dwellers, in the lowest tier had little use in practice. Only during the crisis of transition from absolute to contractual monarchy (see Chapter 2) was explicit reference made to the 'society of orders'. The corporate texture of the *ancien régime* found expression in far more meaningful ways. Although united in the physical sense, pre-revolutionary France was honeycombed with overlapping jurisdictions and privileges which conferred advantages on one group of individuals, or group of territories, at the expense of another. The *philosophe* **Voltaire** once quipped that a long-distance traveller would change law codes more often than he changed his post-horses. An overstatement no doubt, but the fact remains that the *ancien régime* had evolved on the principle of 'particularism' – that is to say, an exaggerated respect for diversity and vested interests. Reformers had long talked of the need for a streamlined hierarchy of courts, uniform machinery of local government, an integrated and universal tax regime, a common system of weights and measures, the eradication of road and river tolls and so forth. Yet none of these things existed prior to 1787. Litigants had to cope with a bewildering array of law tribunals: some seigneurial, some royal, with others belonging to the admiralty, the forest authority, the salt administration and even the Catholic Church. Merchants intent on moving goods around the country encountered toll gates nearly every step of the way: more than 2,000 customs barriers still impeded inland road and river traffic at the end of the *ancien régime*. Consumers paid more or less for salt depending on where they lived; even farmers could be restricted by regulations as to the crops they might grow. The cultivation of the tobacco plant, for instance, was confined to certain 'privileged' provinces within the realm.

The price charged for salt varied because the kingdom was divided into different tax assessment zones. In no other sphere, in fact, is the diversity and particularism that lay at the heart of the *ancien régime* more apparent. Individuals who were classed as clergymen or as nobles paid little direct tax. Their contributions to the common good were made in other ways. Yet beneath this straightforward – if increasingly contested – attribution of roles and responsibilities, we find a picture of great incoherence. The privilege of exemption from taxation could be attached to persons, but it could also be attached to whole provinces. No inhabitant of Brittany – irrespective of formal status – paid tax on salt (the **gabelle**) and the inhabitants of Poitou, Flanders, the Artois and several other territories were similarly exempt. By contrast, an inhabitant of the provinces of Maine, Normandy or Picardy (see Map 0.1) might well be required to pay up to ten times the market rate for this indispensable commodity. In an age in which governments relied increasingly on revenue generated by indirect taxation (duties charged on items of everyday use or consumption), such discrepancies would not pass unnoticed. Yet the mechanisms which had evolved for the assessment and collection of taxes on incomes and property were scarcely uniform across the country either. In theory only members of the Third Estate were liable to the **taille** – the main direct tax on which the monarchy had relied for centuries. But in the south, where land surfaces as well as households bore the label 'noble' or 'commoner', members of the Second Estate could find themselves paying the *taille* if they owned any 'commoner' land. As for the Church, it managed to avoid almost entirely any form of income tax on its very considerable assets (urban buildings and about 6 per cent of the land surface).

It goes without saying that different territories also paid direct tax at different rates, and some were exempted altogether. Inhabitants of Paris, Rouen, Bordeaux and several other privileged towns enjoyed block immunity from the *taille*, a situation that also prevailed across Brittany, Flanders and the Artois.

All three of these provinces numbered among the *pays d'états* – regions making up a large quarter of the kingdom in which local assemblies or Estates (*états*) continued to meet at the end of the *ancien régime*. Most were to be found at the extremities of the country – a fact that provides an important clue as to the nature and extent of royal authority in the eighteenth century. As the power of the Valois and then the Bourbon monarchs expanded, territories were added to the core kingdom on a pledge that their distinctive characteristics as once-independent duchies and fiefdoms would be respected. Thus Brittany retained its hearth tax (*fouage*) in place of the *taille* and remained outside the scope of the salt tax, while Provence (acquired in 1481) was assured that its antique 'constitution' would never be put aside.

Such assurances, offered in abundance by Louis XVI's predecessors, represented so many barriers to the full exercise of absolute monarchy. The larger of the *pays d'états* (Brittany, Burgundy, Languedoc), indeed, had even retained their powerful organs of regional government. In matters of taxation, as in so much else, the king and his ministers were obliged to negotiate with these bodies and to offer compromises in order to get their business through. The corporate status of the **Gallican Church** likewise prompted the monarch to adopt a posture of compromise. Until the very end of the *ancien régime*, the clergy were able to insist that any financial assistance they might provide towards the running costs of the state be treated as a 'voluntary grant' (*don gratuit*).

So many misunderstandings cling to the image of absolute monarchy that it is necessary to dwell upon these restraints. However, it is important also to keep matters in proportion: Bourbon France was admired by contemporary commentators precisely for the progress she had made in overcoming provincial separatism and the studied resistance of private interest groups. No other continental European state had yet escaped the bonds of late medieval and Renaissance monarchy, and all were envious of the success of their larger and apparently much stronger neighbour. The sour reactions of some English travellers who tempered their admiration for the Palace and Park of Versailles with references to the 'arbitrary' power of absolute monarchy were definitely a minority view.

Yet the fact remains that French governments experienced increasing difficulty in tapping into the tax-paying capacity of a country whose wealth and population were plainly expanding in the second half of the eighteenth century. Moreover, the anxiety of ministers was heightened by the knowledge that the costs involved in maintaining the status of a Great Power were starting to spiral out of control. France had been defeated in the global Seven Years War of 1756–63 (see Map 0.3), both on land and at sea, and paid a hefty price in terms of the loss of overseas territories (save perhaps in the Caribbean). True, she remained the most powerful state on the Continent even after the signing of the Treaty of Paris in 1763, but for how much longer, commentators asked themselves.

As the Seven Years War drew to a conclusion, governments all over Europe turned to reform. Whether the reform initiatives took the shape of measures to rationalize the machinery of state, to liberalize trade, to curtail immunities, to release unproductive assets from the '**dead hand**' of the Church, to bring new land into cultivation, or to improve fiscal record-keeping, the spoken or unspoken motivation was nearly always the need to increase the flow of tax revenue. The pressure to compete on the international stage was well-nigh irresistible. France considered herself the 'arbiter of Europe'; that is to say the state whose foreign policy objectives claimed priority on the Continent, if not always on the high seas. For such a position to be acknowledged, however, required resources (armies, fleets and commercial advantages aggressively pursued). In effect, therefore, the power of the Bourbons was linked not only to domestic factors, but also to their capacity to exert global reach via international trade.

Sustained by colonial possessions in the Caribbean and the Indian Ocean (see Maps 0.4 and 0.5) as well as a valuable trading monopoly with the Turkish Empire, overseas commerce prospered as never before. In fact, it tripled in volume between 1716 and 1787. The pearl in this economic crown was Saint-Domingue which had overtaken the British colony of Jamaica since the peace settlement of 1763 to become the premier sugar-producing island in the Caribbean (Burnard and Garrigus, 2016: 35–36). But France's relaunched East India Company was making fat profits for its investors from territories in the Indian Ocean during the closing years of the *ancien régime* as well. If Great Power status was now dependent on empire and trade, commercial success relied in turn on finance raised in global capital markets. Viewed from this angle, however, the prized 'arbiter' status looked less secure. Louis XVI's long-serving Foreign Secretary, the **Comte de Vergennes**, was well aware that the success of his diplomatic ambitions in the 1770s and 1780s would hinge on France remaining solvent.

War started up again in 1778 – this time France was an ally of the American colonists in their armed bid for independence from Britain. The aim was to obtain redress for the setbacks of the Seven Years War, and to convert the young American republic into a profitable trading partner. However, the only clear-cut domestic outcome of the conflict was a sharp escalation in the frictions generated by the drive to modernize absolute monarchy. **Jacques Necker**, the far-sighted banker, whose rise and fall was encompassed by the American War, knew better than anyone the price to be paid for international rivalry. 'Many states have turned into vast military barracks', he observed in 1784, 'and the steady augmentation in disciplined armies has led to a proportional rise in taxes' (Kwass, 1994: 376).

The dilemma facing servants of the Crown in what would prove to be the last decade of the *ancien régime* can thus be summarized as follows. Should His Most Christian Majesty Louis XVI abdicate the role of arbiter of Europe? This was an unthinkable proposition; therefore the state would have to change. But change in which direction? Doing nothing was not an option since the future was mortgaged by virtue of the need to service and hopefully repay war debts. The tax 'take' from the country at large was almost certainly in decline as a percentage of national wealth in the course of the eighteenth century in any case. Contrary to the beliefs of contemporaries and some historians, *ancien-régime* France cannot be regarded as an overtaxed state, but rather one in which taxes were badly assessed, badly distributed and expensive to collect. What, then, were the options? A streamlined – that is to say, authentic –

absolute monarchy was probably the outcome favoured by Louis XVI who, unlike his grandfather, took an intelligent if fluctuating interest in matters of government. It was certainly the solution preferred by ministers such as **Terray, Maupeou, Calonne, Vergennes, Lamoignon** and **Barentin**. An alternative option, which would not have displeased the grandees of the Court and influential figures in the **Provincial Estates** and the **Parlements**, was a return to the organic roots of kingly power: a kind of aristocratic or **conciliar monarchy** from which all traces of absolutism were removed. Even though it is difficult to imagine how a dispersal of authority to largely tax-exempt elites would have served to strengthen the fiscal sinews of central government, such a course of action had powerful advocates (**Miromesnil, Castries, Ségur**) in the royal councils of the 1780s. A third scenario would be to make a move towards contractual – that is to say, quasi-liberal – constitutional monarchy on the reasonable assumption that some kind of partnership with affluent, educated and politically docile commoners would bring fresh ideas and hitherto underexploited resources to the business of government. We may guess that **Turgot, Malesherbes** and Necker entertained hopes that the Bourbon monarchy might develop in this direction, but the only minister actually to try to achieve this outcome would be **Loménie de Brienne**.

While the Parlement of Rouen had been ritually humiliated in 1766 when it dared to assert the existence of a body called the 'nation' that was separate from that of the monarch [**Doc. 1**], there are grounds for supposing that by the 1780s absolute monarchy was indeed inching towards a form of contract government. Louis XVI may not yet have been prepared to swear an oath to his people, but the pretention that politics was the '*secret du roi*' (the private preserve of the king) had become unsustainable. There were two reasons for this development which, although closely connected, are best examined separately.

Enlightened thinking was making inroads and in the case of the most literate and articulate social groups in the kingdom, equipping them with arguments – and a political language – with which to berate the government and, by extension, the monarchy. No doubt a 'public opinion' of some sort had long existed, but hitherto it had taken its cue from the Court. Now political events became a topic of conversation – even at street level in Paris (Farge, 1994). Inheritance records for the 1750s show that in the capital 13 per cent of wage labourers and 20 per cent of domestic servants had some access to book knowledge (Burrows, 2015: 78–79). Chancellor Maupeou's decision, in a rare display of coercive power, to have done with one source of opposition to the Crown and in 1771 to truncate the Parlements caused many to reconsider the relationships on which absolute monarchy had been built. Participation in the American War after 1778 would produce a similar intellectual ferment. In 1786, the British ambassador to the Court of Versailles reported that France's intervention on the side of the American colonists had raised a spirit 'of discussion of public matters which did not exist before' (Browning ed., 1909: 147). No less significant was the fact that Louis XVI's ministers now felt it necessary to justify their policies and where possible to secure support for them by actively canvassing public opinion.

Figure 1.1 The Port au Blé and the Pont Notre-Dame, 1782
© Musee de la Ville de Paris, Musee Carnavalet, Paris, France/Bridgeman

The second reason for the shift is to do with the nature of the Bourbon government itself. Some historians prefer to stress its medieval or Renaissance features and the centrality of the Court as 'the nerve centre of the realm' (Campbell, 2013: 17). Every minister, we are told, was first and foremost a courtier. Others, by contrast, are more impressed by its modernity, in terms of both institutions and ways of thinking, even if they acknowledge the continuing relevance of courtiers competing for influence and sinecures (Félix, 2015: 60–62). Most would agree on two things, however. The neat picture drawn by Alexis de Tocqueville (1969: 41–69), which has the monarchy progressively depriving corporate bodies of their rights and privileges in an onward march towards centralization, does not do justice to the complexity of the *ancien régime*. Moreover, it is largely accepted that the evolution of the institutions of government towards modernity did accelerate after 1750, or thereabouts. Indeed, it has been claimed that 'French politics broke out of the absolutist mould' (Baker ed., 1987: xvi) around the mid-century point as censorship was eased.

But this is to go too far and too fast, if only for the reasons already given. A more streamlined version of absolute monarchy remained a reasonable political option even as late as 1787. The point to grasp is that no one – and least of all the personnel of government – was content with the status quo after about 1760. It should not cause surprise, therefore, to discover that the main promotors and consumers of Enlightenment ideas were government ministers and their advisors. Nearly all the great reform projects of the age (grain trade liberalization; agricultural enclosure; the secularization of the monasteries; the commutation of feudal dues; religious toleration; internal customs abolition; the universal land tax, etc.) were gestated in the offices of the **Contrôle Général**. This sprawling administration was the closest the Bourbon monarchs ever came to developing a civil service.

A more efficient and far-reaching tax system, if nothing else, presupposed a significant increase in the bureaucratic weaponry of government. An example can be found in the anxiety of ministers to place new across-the-board taxes (the *capitation* and the *vingtièmes*) in the hands of professional administrators who could be controlled from the centre. Such taxes were the key to financial recovery after the strains and stresses of the Seven Years War because they applied to all and sundry (with the sole exception of the clergy). Yet everyone knew that self-assessment would soon erode their yield. Aware of what was at stake, Jacques Necker, who headed the Contrôle Général as the Director General of Finance between 1777 and 1781, fought long and hard to ensure that his officials would not be hampered in their work of asset verification. When his conciliatory offer to allow local landowners to become involved in the activities of the inspectors was spurned by the Parlement of Paris, he went ahead with the reform nonetheless.

Such reforms, pursued admittedly in a somewhat staccato fashion throughout the 1770s and early 1780s, fostered a new, utilitarian ethic within government as the Enlightenment debate came to focus more and more on useful knowledge (Bond, 2021). The old lubricants of politics – nepotism, cronyism, clientism, pluralism and even **venality of office** – started to look increasingly out of place. Some historians employ the phrase 'administrative monarchy' in order to capture this transition (Jones, 1995: 46; Félix, 2015: 62). The label directs our attention to the growth of forms of interventionism with wider objectives than the mere collection of tax. Administrative monarchy was not hostile to power sharing, but the elites whose energies it wished to harness were not necessarily those ensconced in the corporate bodies of the realm who normally expected to be consulted. Whether this ethic of administrative monarchy would have transformed Louis XVI into a constitutional ruler in the fullness of time is an interesting question, but one which was overtaken by the events of 1787–89 before it could be answered.

Taxation was a problem that would not go away. In 1764 – that is to say, just after the ending of the Seven Years War – nearly half of the French government's annual revenue had to be earmarked in order to meet interest payments on debt. Or to put it another way, the accumulated capital value of the state debt was equivalent to about six and a half years of income. By 1788 – the last complete year of the old regime – loan servicing charges were still eating up 50 per cent of a (much larger) revenue flow, but the accumulated debt had risen to 5,000 million *livres*, or the equivalent of eight years of income. Much of the reason for the deterioration stemmed from the fact that the monarchy had chosen to meet its liabilities in the aftermath of the Seven Years and American Wars by issuing *rentes viagères* (lifetime annuities). In return for one-off capital payments into the royal treasury investors received generous twice-yearly sums in interest over many decades. As the Comte d'Antraigues observed, borrowing of this sort 'devours the future' (Spang, 2015: 16).

No one in possession of these facts could doubt that France was facing a structural weakness in her public finances and mounting public concern about her long-term creditworthiness. Yet we should not rush to the conclusion that financial imprudence alone condemned the *ancien régime*. Some historians think that the debt problem could have been managed had it not been for outside shocks that undermined France's Great Power claim. There was no lack of sensible advice on offer, it is true. Before 1750, scarcely one or two works a year had been published on the subject of finance and political economy. However, in the decade that witnessed the conclusion to the Seven Years War, 61 books and pamphlets appeared, and the 1780s witnessed a veritable flood of printed material on taxation and related topics. Between 1780 and 1789, 243 works were published (Félix, 1999: 20). Much of this advice was politically unpalatable, of course, and it is here that we touch upon the main paradox of Bourbon rule. Far from having been consolidated on the ruins of particularism and 'privilege', absolute monarchy coexisted with these older forms of power sharing. It even drew strength from them.

'Privilege' (literally, private law) was intrinsic to the *ancien régime*. The term can be expanded to cover rights of immunity, exemption, independent jurisdiction and self-government, as well as the more familiar concept of non-liability to direct taxation. However, it also expressed an approach to economic development according to which ministers allowed exceptions to the usual rules and regulations applying to trade so as to encourage entrepreneurs. The Jewish merchants of Bordeaux and protestant manufacturers who had transferred their wealth-creating activities to France benefited from this kind of 'privilege' (Horn, 2015: 168–203)

The eighteenth-century mind often conceived of these special rights as 'liberties', and when this word was used in negotiations with the Crown it usually signaled a defence of the institution of privilege. But this was not necessarily a 'selfish' defence: individuals and corporate bodies genuinely believed that if their 'freedoms' were taken away, the country would be rendered vulnerable to tyranny and despotism. Perhaps it was not such an unreasonable assumption in view of the absence of any other channel for representation within the state. Indeed, there are grounds for supposing that the officials of absolute monarchy shared this view too, which enormously complicated their duties. A senior servitor of the monarchy such as a provincial **intendant** might enjoy personal privilege (as a near tax-exempt noble); might feel an obligation to defend corporate privilege (by virtue of his family connections, his profession or his geographical roots); and yet still be required to police and, wherever possible, curtail the ramifications of privilege as a direct employee of the Crown.

Viewed from Versailles or Paris, privilege was both a hindrance and a help, then. It hindered the programme of national recovery inasmuch as the reforms mooted in the 1760s and 1770s nearly always involved a challenge to corporate rights and immunities. Most obviously, the tax privileges enjoyed by the clergy and the nobility along with certain provinces sheltered some of the most affluent groups in society from the spiralling cost of the burdens of state. It could also be a help, though. For all the modernizing ambitions located at the heart of government, the absolute monarchy could scarcely manage without privilege. There were three main reasons for this. Corporate bodies provided a fairly efficient system of local government which the monarchy was either unable or unwilling to furnish from its own resources. Such bodies, moreover, collected revenue for the government, and did so in a manner that was generally thought to be more equitable and 'enlightened' than that employed by the monarchy's own direct tax collectors. Third, and most important, the existence of corporate bodies did more to assist than to hinder the creditworthiness of the state. As royal finances became ever more finely balanced, loan monies were raised increasingly on the economic strength of institutions such as the Provincial Estates or the **Hôtel de Ville** of Paris.

To have dispensed with privilege in a clean-sweep reform would have been a huge gamble, therefore. Hence the cautious – not to say contradictory – spectacle of ministers of the Crown chipping away at immunities for fiscal reasons, while consolidating and even extending other forms of privilege, such as office-holding or commercial protection – also for pecuniary reasons. With uniformity on the agenda, and equality waiting in the wings, such a policy was inherently difficult to manage of course. There would come a time when the monarchy risked losing control. The exasperation of elites when faced with a revenue-hungry government is not difficult to understand. Nobody likes to pay additional tax, particularly when the reasons for the increase are left unclear. In the eighteenth century, kings were still expected to finance the business of government largely from their own pockets: taxes could be raised for special needs as long as they were of fixed duration and yield. Yet the *capitation*, first introduced in 1695, had become a permanent, near-universal tax, and by the 1770s it looked as though the *ving-tièmes* were heading in the same direction. However, there was also an issue of principle at stake for the three-tier separation of *ancien-régime* society into 'estates' turned ultimately on the question of exemptions. Direct taxation was demeaning and to be liable to it was an unmistakable sign of baseness. Bringing the clergy and the nobility – not to mention various other groups – into the tax net might make perfect economic sense, but the social implications were huge.

Nevertheless, the Bourbon monarchs clearly did enjoy some success in taxing elites during the course of the eighteenth century. No doubt this was the chief reason why they were so admired by neighbouring rulers who had long entertained similar ambitions. Historians tend to differ on how much success was achieved, though. Indeed, some question whether privilege really lay at the root of the tax problem at all (Norberg, 1994: 253–98). Yet the comments of contemporaries suggest that reform in this area still had a long way to go. Turgot, the future Controller General, remarked in 1767 that the *capitation* paid by the nobility was exceedingly modest (Hincker, 1971: 27), and in 1787 the Duke of Orleans admitted that his standard practice had been to strike deals with the intendants, enabling him to pay in tax 'more or less what I please' (Jones, 1995: 64). Members of the Second Estate may not have contributed very much then, but, equally, it is certain that they had never paid more than at the end of the *ancien régime*. First minister Bertin's proposal for an all-embracing land tax (**subvention territoriale**) in 1763 had prompted an outcry and was swiftly withdrawn. But Chancellor Maupeou's blow against the Parlements in 1771 opened a window of opportunity for the *abbé* Terray – the man who was now in charge of the royal finances. In 1771, he succeeded in making the first *vingtième* a permanent tax and the second was extended until 1781. A third *vingtième*, dating back to the latter part of the Seven Years War, would also be reintroduced in 1782.

The American colonists' slogan 'no taxation without representation' applied to France as well, and the body that considered itself to be the guardian of the corporate structures of the kingdom was the Parlement of Paris. In 1776 it informed Louis XVI that all his subjects were linked together in a great chain of being 'divided into as many different *corps* as there are different estates in the realm' [Doc. 2]. Yet despite its name the Parlement of Paris was not a representative assembly, but a court of law which judged on appeal cases emanating from subordinate courts in a jurisdiction covering a large third of the kingdom. Jurisdiction in the remaining two-thirds was parcelled out between twelve other Parlements. This is to understate its role, however. The Parlement of Paris also possessed regulatory powers, a recording power and a power of 'remonstrance'. Unless and until royal edicts and declarations had been transcribed into the registers of the Parlement, they lacked the force of law in the territory over which it exercised jurisdiction. Moreover, the 'sovereign courts', as they were collectively known, were entitled to formulate criticisms ('remonstrances') of the laws submitted to them for registration. This could amount to a power of veto on the royal will, although in most cases magisterial doubts and misgivings were smoothed away by negotiation. In cases of utter stalemate, however, the king could resort to a constitutional device known as a Bed of Justice (*lit de justice*) by which he commanded registration by virtue of his physical presence before the Parlement.

On his accession in 1774, Louis XVI reversed the policy pursued by his grandfather and by chancellor Maupeou, and restored to the Parlements their ancient powers and prerogatives. It was a popular, if unfortunate, move in view of subsequent events. Historians tend to judge the Parlements rather harshly, arguing in effect that they were chiefly responsible for the breakdown of the *ancien régime*. In a tenacious defence of privilege – not least their own – they lost sight of the larger array of problems facing the monarchy. Yet this was not how public opinion viewed their stance. **Parlementaire** resistance to the royal will enjoyed huge support among the educated classes and it was maintained almost to the end.

We are bound to ask why, and the answer is unequivocal. The Parlement of Paris, in common with the other so-called sovereign courts, was able to pose successfully as the champion of established law at a time when the absolute monarchy appeared heedless of the knock-on consequences of its reform agenda. By the 1780s, the issue had become one of consent to taxation, and to go along with the government's reform proposals without any checks and balances looked to many observers like the shortest possible route to despotism. Jacques Necker was no longer in power by this time (he fell in 1781, following the publication of the controversial **Compte rendu au roi** which denied the existence of a budget deficit). His cautious **Provincial Assemblies** initiative which might have provided a solution to the conundrum of 'no taxation without representation' was on hold and the partisans of a streamlined version of absolute monarchy had the upper hand once more.

The extent to which these debates reverberated in the country at large is difficult to estimate. Research has not turned up much evidence of proto-revolutionary thinking before 1787 and there is disagreement among historians over the consumption of books and its probable impact (Burrows, 2015: 74–85). In a town such as Dijon, where perhaps two-fifths of householders enjoyed privileges of some description, personal involvement in the weighty constitutional questions of the day seems likely. After all, Dijon was the seat of the ancient Parlement of Burgundy. However, most towns – indeed, most large towns – were not seats. Located hundreds of miles away from the nerve centres of power, regional capitals such as Nantes, Bordeaux, Marseilles and Lyons had rather different preoccupations. The merchant elites of Bordeaux, for instance, were far more concerned about the state of the trading economy than the state of politics in the council chambers of Versailles, or at least they had yet to make a connection between the two. Commenting, somewhat gleefully, on the setbacks to have hit this port city since the conclusion of the American War, the British ambassador reported in 1784 a spate of bankruptcies and not a single American vessel seen in harbour since the previous year (Browning ed., 1909: 15).

Should we therefore link the escalating political problems of the 1780s to a larger crisis of the urban and rural economy? France was a rich land by eighteenth-century standards as her large and expanding population indicated. From the 1750s the country enjoyed a long period of growth and it lasted until the late 1770s. Thereafter a recession set in which was followed by a much sharper domestic downturn between 1786 and 1789.

Yet this growth seems to have been shallow-rooted. The onset of a revolution would quickly knock it off course. Overseas and particularly colonial trade had boomed, notwithstanding periodic bouts of trans-global conflict embroiling European states. Between 1787 and 1791 France overtook Great Britain in the transportation of enslaved black Africans to the Caribbean, and it is also likely that she dispatched more vessels around the Cape of Good Hope and into the Indian Ocean than either the Dutch or the British (Hunt, 2013: 35–36). However, there are few signs that the considerable commercial wealth generated by the port cities was providing much of a stimulus to the vast hinterland of rural France. At best oceanic trade stimulated the proto-industrial economy of the western seaboard (Daudin, 2011: 372–439, 449). The agricultural economy continued to develop in accordance with its own internal rhythms of change (Tarrade, 1972: 777–78; 784). In a large and climatically diverse country, harvest shortfall remained a depressingly commonplace occurrence. There were six inter-regional dearths in the eighteenth century – seven if we count the famine linked to the currency collapse of 1794–95. Each produced ripples in the industrial sector. High bread prices immediately depressed demand for manufactured goods as royal officials frequently noted. However, we cannot say for certain that the troubled economic outlook after 1776, or thereabouts, played a role in the growth of tension between absolute monarchy and its critics. The *ancien régime* did not die of a weak, or poorly integrated, economy. Only during what proved to be the last act of the drama – in 1788–89 – is it reasonable to argue that a decade of mounting economic difficulties began to weigh heavily in the political balance. By this date, elite resistance to the designs of the monarchy had begun to draw in support from the lower classes of both town and country.

Even as late as 1788 then, very few if any ordinary French men and women would have been aware that a 'revolution' was in the offing. In fact, it seems unlikely that the majority would have been equipped with a vocabulary enabling them even to think in these terms. While the word 'revolution' was certainly in more frequent use at the end of the *ancien régime* than at the start of the eighteenth century, it carried no clear connotation of social and political upheaval (Tackett, 2009: 531–54). Historians know better of course, or like to think they do. But hindsight knowledge of what would come next is not as much of a help as it might seem. Despite its impressive longevity, the *ancien régime* stands condemned because it ultimately failed. For researchers reliant on a Marxist analytical approach, the socio-political order which Louis XV bequeathed to his grandson in 1774 could not have survived for the reason that it was unable to contain and give voice to the powerful economic forces that were now reshaping the kingdom. A great deal of archival investigation undertaken during the middle decades of the twentieth century by Georges Lefebvre (1947) and Albert Soboul (1974) documents this mismatch. Whilst effective in explaining the socio-economic fissures that would open up when the crisis began in earnest, their findings cannot shed much light on the process by which the monarchy was weakened by the actions of its own elites.

It is true that perceptive contemporaries had been remarking on the build-up of tensions within the kingdom since the 1760s, if not earlier. Yet crises had come and gone at intervals without any major institutional and social breakdown. Why, we might reasonably ask, did absolute monarchy manage to ride out the perils of the year 1763, only to succumb to those of 1788? After seven years of warfare conducted on a truly global scale, France had undoubtedly faced a substantial debt mountain in 1763 and a dramatically widening budget deficit. However, the 'political' ingredient that might have converted this fiscal disarray into an explosive force was lacking. Not so in 1787–88 as we shall see in the next chapter. It is therefore necessary to supplement long-standing explanations of the descent into revolution which are rooted in a systemic crisis of the *ancien régime*, with the more recent reassessments undertaken by François Furet (1981), Keith Baker (ed., 1990), William Doyle (1999) and others. Their researches enable us to understand rather better the role played by public opinion in the life cycle of the maturing absolute monarchy. Crucially, they explain how 'opinion' could be transformed into an ideology of resistance as ministers outlined yet another round of reforms to cope with an all-too-familiar and predictable crisis of budgetary over-spend and revenue shortfall.

Part II

2   Reform or revolution, 1787–89?

The final crisis that the *ancien régime* went through was essentially man-made, then. Indeed, it was triggered in large measure by the needs and actions of the monarchy. If the Bourbons had refrained from foreign-policy entanglements which required heavy war expenditures, it is possible that the budgetary problem could have been contained within existing structures. This was not to be, and Alexis de Tocqueville's dictum which holds that the most dangerous moment for an authoritarian government occurs when it embarks on reform was framed precisely to accommodate the situation in which France now found herself (1969, Headlam edn: 182).

Yet no one *knew* that the country's governing system was entering its death throes at the start of 1787. A few commentators reached for the word 'revolution' in order to describe what was happening as early as the preceding autumn, but they used the term imprecisely and with little sense of what it might mean. For instance, the Paris bookseller-publisher Nicolas Ruault confided in a letter to his brother that a frightful revolution was in the offing (Ruault, 1976: 79). But 'revolution' – in this context – can be understood as the superlative of 'reform'. Even as late as the spring of 1789, it is likely that the majority of thinking men and women had little inkling of what lay in store. This chapter traces the sequence of events that led from reform to revolution. It explains why reform from above failed to win sufficient support in the country at large, and how this failure helped to unleash forces that would cause the *ancien régime* to fall to pieces within a short space of time.

Gripping the nettle of reform

After two decades of stop–go reform efforts, it is clear that by 1783 Louis XVI's most senior officials were keenly aware of the gravity of the situation facing the country. The window of opportunity to carry out meaningful reform would not remain open for very much longer – if only because the third *vingtième* tax was scheduled to expire in 1787, the year in which the contract for the collection of indirect taxes was also due for renewal. Even the most loyal servants of the Crown were coming to the realization that only by reining in foreign policy ambitions and commitments and curtailing exemptions from taxation could the power of

DOI: 10.4324/9781003156185-4

absolute monarchy be preserved intact. Charles Alexandre de Calonne, the Controller General, numbered among them. It is true that he continued to spend on a lavish scale in order to sustain the confidence of international lenders, but he could not have been unaware of the difficulties that lay ahead. After a period of calm, relations between ministers and the Parlement of Paris were becoming strained again, too – another reason for action sooner rather than later.

Calonne's diminishing freedom of manœuvre can be traced in the reports despatched from the British embassy in Paris. Daniel Hailes, the chargé d'affaires, noted in August 1785 that recent attempts to secure a loan of 125 million *livres* had proved 'very unsuccessful'. Another, floated in December to the tune of 80 million *livres*, ran into similar difficulties – particularly after registration was refused by the Parlement. 'M. de Calonne must have now nearly exhausted all his resources', reported Hailes, 'and it seems next to impossible that he should remain in office. The expenses of Government have exceeded its income near 160 millions of *livres* this year' (Browning ed., 1909: 44, 86). Nevertheless, Calonne tried, in April 1786, to raise 30 million *livres* via a lottery and a further 24 million on the strength of the credit rating of the Paris Hôtel de Ville.

In fact, 1786 was the last year in which the *ancien régime* exhibited an outward appearance of normality. Yet Calonne knew that both his own position and that of the monarchy had become precarious, and in August he obtained the king's assent to a thoroughgoing financial recovery programme. Its key element was the proposal for a universal land tax. The new levy would apply to all owners of land, irrespective of rank; it would not be susceptible to reduction via negotiation; and it would replace the two remaining *vingtième* taxes. This was the proposal, packaged with numerous other reforms, which was put before a specially convened Assembly of Notables in February 1787. The Notables were a hand-picked body of dignitaries whose endorsement of the reforms would, it was hoped, deflect and deter any obstructionist behaviour on the part of the Parlement of Paris. Unfortunately, they were not very well picked (too few members of the Third Estate), nor were they especially compliant. Commentators likened their summoning to the calling of a 'national assembly' (Jones, 1995: 116) which was not at all Calonne's intention, if scarcely surprising. After all, the dignitaries were informed that the country had a colossal public debt requiring extraordinary measures to resolve. This misapprehension reveals the extent to which the government was beginning to lose its grip on opinion among the educated.

A whole package of reforms, albeit somewhat hastily cobbled together, was submitted to the Notables for their consideration. Nearly everything the package contained (deregulation of the corn trade; conversion of the road-building *corvée* into a monetary tax; reform of local government; reform of the *taille*; redemption of the clerical debt, etc.) had been talked about incessantly for several decades. Nevertheless, Calonne made no bones about the need for swift and far-reaching action. In addition to the largely unfunded debt, he disclosed for the first time that government spending was outstripping tax receipts by a wide margin. This deficit, he suggested, was attributable to the American War and, more particularly, to Necker's financial mismanagement of France's intervention in that conflict, which had cost about four years' revenue from tax receipts. In reality, the deficit went back much further – to the Seven Years War and beyond. For a minister with powerful enemies at Court, it was scarcely a statesmanlike move to antagonize in this way Necker's numerous friends within the Assembly.

That being said, the Notables were not incapable of responding to the apparent urgency of the situation. They endorsed the proposals regarding the grain trade, the *corvée* and even the *taille*, and raised no serious objections to the scheme for a uniform and consultative system of local government. On the other hand, they declared themselves not qualified to approve any new financial impositions. Both the universal land tax and the proposal for a wider duty to be levied on stamped documents were open-ended, they noted, and therefore gave rise to objections of a 'constitutional' nature. As for the suggestions as to how the Church might clear its accumulated debts, these amounted to a frontal attack on property. The king who, despite some misgivings, had pledged his support for reform the previous summer was incensed by the opposition and complained that the clergy and the nobility were blocking the proposals and relying on the common people to shoulder the increased tax bill. He would have turned to his foreign secretary and one-time first minister Vergennes for a solution, but the trusty statesman had died as the Notables were gathering in Versailles. Instead, Calonne tried to outflank them, claiming that they were only interested in defending the edifice of corporate privilege. However, government ministers who were strongly suspected of 'despotic' ambitions could no longer expect to win the battle for the opinion of the educated, and with the king's support faltering as well he was dismissed and exiled to his estates

Resistance to the royal will

By April 1787, therefore, the ploy to substitute the sanction of an Assembly of Notables for that of the Parlement of Paris had succeeded only in increasing the number of voices calling for restraints to be placed on the powers of absolute monarchy. Loménie de Brienne, the prelate-administrator who replaced Calonne a month or so later, did try to find a middle way between proponents of the streamlined state and those who discerned in the Notables an opportunity to wreak an aristocratic revenge on the Bourbon monarchy for ever having pioneered the theory and practice of absolutism in the first place. But Brienne, the protégé Queen **Marie-Antoinette**, had no better idea than Calonne of how to overcome the fiscal deficiency in the short term. He did, however, have a medium-term strategy. The local government reform initiative would be used to draw regional elites into a new administrative partnership so as to widen the basis of consent to taxation (Miller, 2020). Chosen on the basis of a tax-paying franchise and unencumbered by distinctions of 'estate', these well-to-do landowners would occupy seats in a tiered structure of municipal, district and provincial assemblies. Over time – Brienne reckoned on five years – such a structure would give birth to a 'national' assembly of deputies recruited on the basis of their wealth and public spiritedness.

Such a vision belonged to the future, however; a future that even the small circle of enlightened advisors gathered around the chief minister could scarcely predict. Loménie de Brienne's most immediate problem remained the Assembly of Notables and, secondarily, the Parlement of Paris. Having succeeded only in embittering the political atmosphere, the Notables were sent home by the king towards the end of May. This turned the spotlight onto the Parlement and simplified the battle lines in the sense that a confrontation between the monarchy and the powerful body of Parisian magistrates could not now be averted. Ministers resolved on a softly-softly approach initially, although Chrétien François de Lamoignon, the newly appointed Keeper of the Seals and a firm adherent of absolute monarchy, expressed his misgivings. As a result, the Parlement was induced to accept the proposals regarding the grain trade and the *corvée*. More surprisingly, the magistrates also endorsed the local government reform. However, on the land tax and the stamp duty they were obdurate. Only an **Estates General** representative of the entire 'nation' could sanction new taxes, they declared, thereby echoing a call first uttered in the Assembly of Notables. Brienne thus had little choice but to proceed on 6 August 1787 to a *lit de justice* and enforced registration of the key financial reforms. When the magistrates persisted in their resistance to the royal will, the whole body was sent into internal exile.

Exile to some dismal provincial town (Troyes in this case) far removed from the pleasures of the capital was a method of cooling heads that the monarchy had employed before. Most dispassionate observers drew the conclusion that the advantage now lay with the government. The new provincial, district and municipal assemblies were coming into being amid widespread satisfaction, and the Parlements risked being left behind by events. Hailes, writing from the British embassy, thought them at their 'last gasp' (Browning ed., 1909: 232) unless the call for that long-forgotten institution – the Estates General – could somehow be rooted in the public's imagination. In a polemical foretaste of what was to come, the *abbé* Morellet, a reform-minded *philosophe*, informed Lord Lansdowne that the magistrates were defending nothing more than their privileges: 'You should know, milord, that there is not a single counsellor in the Parlements of the realm who pays his *vingtième* or *vingtièmes*, nor a tenant farmer of these messieurs who pays his *taille* on the same footing as his neighbours' (Fitzmaurice ed., 1898: 248).

What would change these perceptions of relative strength, however, was a foreign policy crisis in the Netherlands. For several years, the seven Dutch provinces had been moving in the direction of civil war as a 'patriot party' of lesser bourgeois and artisans exerted pressure on the chief magistrate (*Stadhoulder*) William V and the Orangeist oligarchy. The liberal outlook of the Patriots had been nurtured during the American War of Independence when the Dutch had lined up with France and Spain against Great Britain. Shortly after the resolution of this conflict, France had signed a defensive alliance with the Patriots. The ruling House of Orange, by contrast, maintained ties with both Britain and Prussia. These ties became stronger in 1786 when the brother of the Princess of Orange (the *Stadhoulder*'s consort) acceded to the throne of Prussia as **Frederick William II**. Having secured promises of assistance from Britain, Prussia decided to intervene decisively in the Dutch crisis and on 13 September 1787 sent troops over the border to aid the Orangeists. The Patriots now looked to France for military assistance, but the conclusion of a full-blown alliance between Britain and Prussia early in October forced ministers to face the fact that they were no longer in a position to back up their clients with force. Although there were divisions in the Royal Council, Brienne concluded with the support of Marie-Antoinette that another land war, which might well involve a confrontation with Britain on the high seas, was out of the question (Murphy, 1998: 80–87).

In any case the news had just come through of a fresh confrontation in the Levant. Turkey had declared war on Russia in August, which soon drew Russia's ally Austria into the conflict. The Turks looked to their 'old friend' France, but to no avail. The paralysis of French foreign policy that autumn and winter strengthened Frederick William's hand immeasurably and raised searching questions about the state of France. Pledges previously given to the Dutch Patriots were repudiated.

A more immediate and humiliating demonstration of the connection between taxation, diplomacy and the capacity to wage war could scarcely have been conceived. Therefore some form of accommodation with the Paris Parlement, even if only short-term, would have to be reached. In return for their recall, the magistrates agreed to endorse the continuation or reinstatement of the *vingtièmes* taxes for a further five years – this despite the fact that they had earlier declared themselves incompetent to approve any additional taxes whatsoever. But Brienne's needs were more pressing still, and this enabled the magistrates to wring from the government a major political concession. As the price of its endorsement of a 420 million *livres* loan spread over five years, the Parlement secured an undertaking from the monarchy to call an Estates General by 1792. Presumably, the Principal Minister reckoned that he would have his new system of consultative assemblies up and running by this time in any case. As for Lamoignon, the other strong figure in the government, he intervened to make sure that it was understood that a future Estates General would serve merely as an adjunct to the king's existing councils. It would not possess any legislative or executive authority. Disconcerted, the magistrates prepared to resist once more, whereupon the king forced through the registration of the loan by means of a *lit de justice* on 19 November 1787. When his cousin, the Duke of Orleans, protested, he was ordered to his estates and two outspoken magistrates were arrested.

The year ended in suspicion, recrimination and stalemate, then. The Parlement of Paris, together with its lesser brethren in the provinces, stood accused of wishing to turn the monarchy into an 'aristocracy of magistrates', probably unfairly, whereas ministers fumed at the waste of another year in procrastination and palliative measures that failed to address the key issues. Investors in government funds, meanwhile, had begun to weigh up the likelihood of a financial default. But at least there was no unrest in the country at large and the recent grain harvest had been plentiful.

The year 1788 would witness a deterioration on all these fronts, however. The denouement was put into effect by Lamoignon, the Keeper of the Seals, who has been described as 'the last true servant of the old monarchy' (Hardman, 1993: 136). In April it became known that the head of the judiciary was secretly planning to remove the constitutional powers of the Parlements once and for all, and to curtail severely their judicial competence. This was surely a gamble since measures of such gravity risked giving substance to the allegation of 'ministerial despotism' and provoking a general rallying of the discontented against the government. Daniel Hailes, the perspicacious diplomat in the British embassy, even alerted his superiors to the possibility that the populace might be swept into the conflict, resulting in 'the total subversion of the monarchy' (Browning ed., 1910: 33). For a comment made on 17 April, this was prophecy indeed. The blow fell in the shape of a *lit de justice* on 8 May, which compulsorily registered Lamoignon's Six Edicts dismantling the authority of the Parlements. The Venetian ambassador reported the event to his superiors as 'astonishing and almost unbelievable' (Fitzsimmons, 2015: 203). Henceforth, the formality of registering royal edicts would be transferred to a special 'plenary court' whose composition would be tailored to ensure that it remained a docile tool of government.

All thirteen of the Parlements reacted, often clothing their protests in the borrowed garb of contract government [**Doc. 3**]. By July 1788, nine had been sent into exile. That of Rouen railed against 'rash innovators [who] have dared to advance the fatal project of bringing everything into a system of *unity* ...' (Stone, 1994: 189). This is the familiar idiom of corporate, *ancien-régime* France. It suggests that, even at the moment of their greatest trial, many magistrates scarcely had the 'rights' of an undifferentiated 'nation' uppermost in their minds. But all would change with the news from Grenoble in the Dauphiné. On 7 June, as troops sought to enforce the banishment of the Parlement, they were assailed by riotous citizens who hurled tiles and bricks from the rooftops.

This 'Day of the Tiles', followed as it was by the meeting at Vizille a short distance from Grenoble (21–22 July), would transform the character of the parlementaire-led resistance movement. The magistrates and those of their supporters who re-assembled in the chateau of Vizille announced their intention to campaign not merely for the particular rights attaching to the inhabitants of the Dauphiné, but for those of 'all Frenchmen' (Jones, 1995: 152). Popular demonstrations against the king's representatives (the intendants and the military commanders) occurred in the towns of Pau and Rennes as well, but it was the Dauphiné example that became the pacemaker for constitutional change. Nevertheless, it should not be supposed that by the late spring of 1788 the whole of the country was up in arms. Provincial France, whilst mentally digesting the spectacle of judicial disobedience, remained calm for the most part.

Loménie de Brienne, if not his law enforcer Lamoignon, was not unduly alarmed by these developments. More than twenty of his provincial assemblies were now on an active footing, and the talk of a 'nation' embracing all Frenchmen was in some ways more of a help than a hindrance to his plans.

Figure 2.1 'The Day of the Tiles', Grenoble, 7 June 1788
© Wikimedia Commons, public domain

Detached observers agreed: 'This nation is rising from the dust' the American ambassador, Thomas Jefferson, reported to fellow diplomat William Stephens Smith. 'They have obtained, as you know, provincial assemblies in which there will be a more perfect representation of the people than in our state assemblies' (Boyd ed., 1956: 458). However, the model espoused in the Dauphiné envisaged that the 'nation' would come together within a framework of revived Provincial Estates rather than provincial assemblies. And there remained the ticklish question of the Estates General, of course. Loménie de Brienne's response was to lift what remained of the censorship and to invite suggestions as to how this rather anti- quated body might now be converted into 'a truly national assembly both in terms of its composition and its effects' (Brette, 1894–1915: vol. 1, 19–22).

So why did the ministry retreat, thereby negating the apparent gains of the spring? The plain answer is that the Bourbon monarchy was finally held to account for its debts. All governments relied on short-term credit in order to carry on day-to-day business – that is to say on the willingness of bankers to accept promissory notes drawn against future income in return for cash advances. That willingness ebbed away during the first week of August 1788 even though Brienne signalled that he was ready to abandon the idea of a 'plenary court' and to bring forward the calling of the Estates General to 1 May 1789. On 16 August, he was forced to announce a delay in payments to creditors and part reimbursement in Treasury bills rather than cash. As the Comte de Ferrand, a veteran campaigner in the Parlement of Paris immediately recognized, these measures amounted to 'bankruptcy in disguise' (Murphy, 1998: 35). Confidence collapsed.

While a few historians consider that the revolution truly began with the convening of an **Assembly of Notables** (Gruder, 2007: 4; Hardman, 2016: 270) most do not. The twenty-month period from February 1787 until September 1788 is often described as a phase of 'pre-revolution', but this term makes hindsight assumptions about the direction of events. As far as we can tell, the duel between ministers and the Parlements involved a large number of inactive spectators but not many active participants. Even the capital's intelligentsia, who were in the best position to judge what was going on, seem to have been caught unawares when absolute monarchy suddenly imploded in the summer of 1788.

The nation awakes

Loménie de Brienne left the ministry in a matter of days, notwithstanding efforts by the queen to protect her favourite. He was replaced by the Swiss banker and reputed miracle worker Jacques Necker, whom public opinion considered to be the only person capable of retrieving the situation. Since the king agreed with Necker that it would now be necessary to recall the Parlement of Paris (from a second episode of banishment), Lamoignon's days as Keeper of the Seals were numbered too. Sure enough, the embittered yet triumphant magistrates demanded a complete return to the old status quo. Consequently on 23 September 1788 a royal declaration rescinded the Six Edicts. Financial confidence was already returning when on the day following, the magistrates were escorted to their courthouse like conquering heroes by a jubilant Parisian crowd. After the excitement and tumult of the previous months, their pronouncement that the up-coming Estates General would be 'regularly convoked', i.e. summoned in accordance with the precedents established in 1614 (when it had last met), seemed like a detail [Doc. 5].

Signs that the ripples from this long-running and highly visible dispute between the government and the sovereign courts had spread beyond the confines of polite society were not wanting by the autumn of 1788. The departure of both Brienne and Lamoignon was accompanied by rioting in the central districts of Paris. Not unconnected was the fact that the price of bread rose sharply in the capital towards the end of the summer as it became apparent that the harvest would not be abundant. Anticipating trouble, Necker advised that the policy of unlimited trade in corn enacted only a year or so earlier should be suspended. By November, the first reports of food riots in the provinces started to come in. By November also, the implications of the Parlement's determination to follow the precedent and protocol of 1614 began to strike home. Since the Estates General would be a gathering of 'orders' or 'estates', it followed that each order would meet, deliberate and indeed vote separately. This meant that the commoner deputies of the Third Estate would be unable to make their numerical presence felt; in fact, they would find themselves in a permanent minority. One of Brienne's last acts before retiring had been to solicit opinion on the reformist path that the monarchy should follow in the months ahead; in effect, therefore, to remove the last remaining restraints on open political discussion. The sudden removal of royal censorship controls struck contemporaries forcibly inasmuch as it tacitly invited ordinary people to think for themselves.

The freedom of the press could now be directed with devastating effect against the Parlement of Paris and its provincial siblings. They were accused – rightly or wrongly – of having mounted a selfish defence of their own privileges under the pretence of the national interest from the very beginning. The proof, if proof were needed, could be found in the magistrates' efforts to stay in control of events by recommending that the procedures adopted on the occasion of the meeting of the Estates General of 1614 be adhered to.

Pamphlets, lampoons and even political satires had long been an accompaniment to the public life of the monarchy. Such squibs were easily produced on the small, hand-operated printing presses that could be found in virtually all provincial towns. Anonymity, if required, could be guaranteed and street vendors would see to the business of circulation. That autumn, the trickle of such material became a flood. In Paris, about 150 political pamphlets and manifestos were produced in the six weeks following the reinstatement of the Parlement. But by mid-November, they were appearing at a rate of three or four a day, and by mid-December ten to twelve a day (Garrett, 1959: 126). Between 12 and 27 December, over 200 pamphlets were offered for sale or posted on walls at street corners. At the turn of the year, moreover, *abbé* Sieyès's devastating critique of the 'privileged orders' entitled *What is the Third Estate?* [**Doc. 4**] came out. In a sharp escalation of the political temperature, he encouraged his readers to believe that they already possessed everything required for incipient nationhood.

If it is true that ordinary French men and women did not have much of a political vocabulary before 1789, the means of acquiring one now lay readily to hand. Book production alone had increased nearly six-fold between 1786 and 1789 (Burrows, 2015: 79) 'Precisely who read and what?' is not a question that can be easily answered, and no doubt the inhabitants of Paris and Versailles were ahead of the rest of the population. Nevertheless, outside observers were in agreement that an elemental shift in the focus of public opinion was under way. The Spanish ambassador reported on 10 November 1788 that 'The passion for the Parlements is diminishing. A third party is rising up with nothing but the word *liberty* on its lips, which it shouts out to the point of breathlessness' (Mousset, 1924: 41).

With all around in movement, it seems strange that Necker, the Director General of Finance, should confine himself to budgetary matters and decline to use his ministerial power to take the initiative. But all the government's reform agendas were now on hold until such time as the Estates General was able to take on the burden of advising the monarch. Louis, for his part, was not giving his full attention to the business of government and may not have grasped the direction in which events were heading. In fact, he may have been suffering from depression (Hardman, 2016: 270). The word 'revolution' had been uttered at intervals as we have seen, but chiefly in the now largely redundant context of the monarchy's conflict with the Parlements. Further ingredients would need to be added – fear, famine and the numbing cold of an exceptional winter – before 'revolution' could be construed to mean the possibility of a collapse of the state rather than simply an alteration to its fabric. Yet the notion that 'reform' could simply be placed on hold was pure fiction in practice. The ministry might have wished to wait upon the meeting of the Estates General but no one else saw any reason to do so, whether in Paris or in the provincial capitals of the kingdom. Pamphleteers filled the political void with an increasingly well-articulated agenda for change, which identified both short- and medium-term objectives.

The most pressing matter had to be a revision of the protocols governing the convocation of the Estates General. Time had moved on since 1614. The wealthy elite of the Third Estate were now more numerous and more socially adept and it made no sense to restrict the contribution they might make to the regeneration of the kingdom purely on the grounds of respect for precedent. The representation of the Third Estate should be doubled so that it at least matched that of the other two orders, and the deputies of all three orders or estates should be required to work together in a common assembly. However, this was alarming talk to the magistrates, much of the aristocracy and the upper clergy (also nobles by birth), and to anyone else who still considered the corporate heritage of the monarchy to be sacrosanct. More alarming still was the tendency of pamphlet writers to take their cue from the polemical clergyman Emmanuel Sieyès and argue as though the Third Estate alone constituted the source of the common good [**Doc. 4**].

Necker bestirred himself sufficiently to call into being a second Assembly of Notables on 6 November. Yet five out of its six working committees declared against the political ambitions of the Third Estate. He had brought forward the opening of the Estates General to January 1789, but this proved unrealistic and the event was rescheduled for April. Even this deadline would allow barely sufficient time to make the necessary preparations. There could be no avoiding executive action, though, and in December, after a marathon session of the royal council, the king took a weighty decision. He would grant the Third Estate the same number of representatives as the clergy and the nobility combined. Although greeted as a great victory for the nation-in-the-making when made public on 27 December 1788, the 'Result of the King's Council' said nothing about the issue of voting (by 'order' or by 'head'), however. On the other hand, Louis XVI did take the opportunity to declare his sincere wish to rule henceforward as a constitutional monarch.

Countdown to revolution

At this point the clock started to tick for some kind of 'revolution' – if only because the initiative began to pass from powerful men in Versailles and Paris to individuals unknown, or barely known, on the streets of the great cities and in the small towns and villages of the provinces. Three factors can be identified, all acting one upon the other. Rural France had been a silent spectator to the political manœuvring and jousting of the past two years, but this was now coming to an end. From November onwards agrarian distress caused by the harvest shortfall of 1788 was exacerbated by the severest winter conditions that anyone could remember. Country dwellers in eastern France led the way: on 5 January 1789 the local newspaper in the Franche-Comté acknowledged that 'agitation has spread from the towns to the countryside' (Jones, 1988: 61). At this stage the unrest was mostly confined to threats directed towards the owners of monastic storehouses and the collectors of feudal dues, but in February and March it spread to the rural populations of the Dauphiné and Provence and took on a more purposeful appearance. By April, the reports coming in were describing the mobilizations in the southeast of the country as both organized and explicitly anti-seigneurial in character.

The second factor in play can be described as the mobilization of minds consequent upon the publication, in late January, of detailed electoral regulations for the forthcoming Estates General. All three orders, that is to say the clergy, the nobles and the commoners, were to choose deputies and to draw up lists of grievances (*cahiers de doléances*) for eventual presentation to the monarch. Since the Third Estate of commoners alone amounted to a constituency of between 4 and 5 million adult males, this was a massive and complicated undertaking. In small towns and rural parishes there can be no doubt that the consultation process conjured up thoughts and hopes for the future that would have been literally unthinkable only a few months earlier [**Doc. 9**].

The third factor in the equation which looked as though it might trigger something more radical than an orderly rectification of fiscal abuses once the Estates General had settled down to business, was the ongoing pamphlet campaign. By comparison with 1787 the output of pamphlets had nearly quadrupled (Burrows, 2015: 79). As early as December, the **Princes of the Blood** took fright and signed an urgent appeal to the monarch warning that the state was in mortal danger – all of them, that is, save for the Duke of Orleans and the Comte de Provence [**Doc. 6**]. The Princes were concerned lest the debate over tax exemptions should become the pretext for a more general questioning of the legitimacy of a society based on rank or order. It is true that spokesmen for the Third Estate were starting to emerge and to toy with the possibility that the Estates General might acquire legislative powers, enabling it to enact a bill of rights and a modern constitution. The utility of social distinctions had even been raised for discussion, as had the feudal regime and the corporate status of the clergy.

The opinions of historians differ as to just how much was at stake when, after further delay, the Estates General opened in Versailles on 5 May 1789. Had a metropolitan caucus of liberal nobles persuaded their order to make timely and prudential sacrifices? It seems unlikely. The American ambassador Thomas Jefferson is our surest guide. On 13 March, he felt able to assert that 'equal taxation is agreed to by everybody' and went on to predict that the majority of noble deputies would accept voting by head. Two months later, however, on 9 May, he reported that 'the Noblesse on coming together shew that they are not as much reformed in their principles as we had hoped they would be. In fact there is a real danger of their totally refusing to vote by persons.' He went on to clarify the nature of the impediment in a subsequent despatch: 'The great mass of deputies of that order which come from the country shew that the habits of tyranny over the people are deeply rooted in them' (Boyd ed., 1958: vol. 14, 652; 1958: vol. 15, 110). In other words, the elections to the Estates General had exposed the fault-line between 'enlightened' opinion in the capital and the mood of the Second Estate in the kingdom at large [**Docs 7 and 8**].

In a sense, though, the divisions within the nobility (or, for that matter, within the clergy) were not the most telling factor. What soured the Estates General almost from the outset was the protracted political stalemate running from early May until the middle of June. The refusal of clerical and noble deputies to countenance common voting with the Third Estate prevented a meeting of minds from taking place, while the ministry itself proved to be internally divided and therefore incapable of responding to the gravity of the situation with clear advice for the king on how he should intervene.

With the benefit of hindsight, it is possible to identify three steps that, once taken, led in the direction of a full-scale revolution. On 17 June 1789, an impatient chamber of Third Estate deputies – or Commoners as they now chose to call themselves – decided to adopt the title 'National Assembly'. This amounted to an acceptance of Sieyès's logic that sovereignty resided in the majority of the nation. As a corollary, they then 'decreed' (as befitted a sovereign body) that the collection of existing taxes should be brought to a halt if, for any reason, they were dissolved. Thus, a group of deputies who had come to Versailles with no real intention of challenging the prerogatives of the Crown took their courage in their hands and claimed control of the most important sinew of government.

Louis XVI's response to this defiant and quite illegal act reflected both his vacillating character, episodic moroseness and the deep disharmony among ministers. It brought forward the second step in the direction of revolution. While not opposed to reform per se and having some sympathy for the Third, the king was assailed on all sides with conflicting advice and in the throes of mourning the death of the dauphin, his eldest son, which occurred on 4 June. Nonetheless, he agreed that firm action was required, but what kind of action? The Parlement of Paris urged that the upstart National Assembly be disbanded, by force if necessary, and a powerful faction of courtiers and ministers headed by the Comte d'Artois (youngest brother of the king) and Barentin (the Keeper of the Seals) appear to have shared this view. In fact, Louis adopted the less brusque middle course of calling all of the deputies together again and telling them what he would, and would not, accept.

In the Royal Session of 23 June 1789, the Bourbon monarchy stood at the crossroads. Had the king made the gentler, more accommodating statement proposed by the liberal-minded Necker, it is possible that the final crisis might have been averted. But this assumes that the Commoner deputies – notwith-standing the famous Tennis Court Oath sworn three days earlier – did not really possess the courage of their convictions. In the event, though, Louis delivered a judgement mainly scripted by the hardliners. Although some fiscal and budgetary concessions were offered, he declared that the 'decrees' issued by the National Assembly on 17 June were unacceptable to him and therefore null and void. As for the ancient distinctions between the orders, they were to remain. Since Versailles was packed with troops for the occasion, the 'body language' of the Royal Session was scarcely conciliatory either, and indeed Necker opted to absent himself. On being ordered to return to their separate chamber by the master of ceremonies, the Commoner deputies hesitated; but then their resolve was stiffened by an intervention from within their ranks by a *déclassé* nobleman, the **Comte de Mirabeau**. He retorted: 'We shall not leave; return to those who have sent you and tell them that we shall not stir from our places save at the point of the bayonet' (Goodwin, 1959: 70).

The third and final step towards revolution followed swiftly on the heels of this riposte. Louis's conservative advisors – and particularly his sibling, the Comte d'Artois – argued for the military solution, but Necker had agreed to remain a part of the ministry and the noisy demonstrations in his support urged caution. Moreover, the pressure (or menace) directed towards those who were now routinely dubbed 'the privileged classes' was beginning to have an effect. Already large numbers of deputies drawn from the lower clergy had defected to the National Assembly and the more progressive nobles were beginning to follow suit, encouraged by royal assurances that the distinction of orders was not in jeopardy. By 27 June, the intransigents among the clergy and the nobility had dwindled to 371, whereas the representatives of the so-called nation numbered some 830 individuals.

At this point, the king simply ordered the diehards to fuse with the Third Estate. The English agricultural commentator Arthur Young, who was in Paris when the news came through, recorded in his travel journal: 'The whole business now seems over, and the revolution complete' (Young, Betham-Edwards edn, 1794/1900: 182). Historians have found it difficult to interpret this decision on the part of the monarch. Most likely it was taken under duress – under the threat or rumour of an invasion of the Palace of Versailles by an expeditionary force of Parisians. But it was also a decision that bought time – time to bring up more troops and to position them in and around the capital. When Louis XVI was finally prevailed upon to dismiss Necker on 11 July, he must have had some inkling of what could happen. Hopefully, the troops would contain any violent reaction on the part of the populace. They did not, and the seizure of the Bastille was the outcome. The movement of troops was the step that acknowledged the failure of reform from above and pitched France into a revolution.

3 Renewal, 1789–91

The king had been out hunting as usual when the first reports of disturbances in Paris reached him. 'So, this is a revolt?' he is said to have remarked, only to be corrected: 'No Sire, this is a revolution' (Cobb and Jones, 1988: 61). There can be no doubt that the news that a lightly armed crowd of Parisians had managed to take control of the principal royal fortress in the capital produced an electrifying effect. The intention of the new ministry formed after the removal of Necker and headed by the ultra-conservative **Baron de Breteuil** had been to use the troops to secure Paris. There is little actual evidence that an offensive operation to dissolve the National Assembly sitting in Versailles had also been in preparation (Price, 1990: 318). However, this is not how matters appeared to the Parisians. In the aftermath of the uprising, the Comte d'Artois and a number of courtier families swiftly packed their bags and left Versailles.

Ordinary Parisians could scarcely comprehend their success. Even before accounts of the events of 14 July and days following had penetrated to the extremities of the kingdom, they were busily at work knocking down the Bastille. The building contractor **Pierre-François Palloy** took charge of the operation and hired hundreds of labourers, equipping them with picks and shovels. Twinned with this initiative was a masterly grasp of the marketing potential of the site. The lugubrious myth of the Bastille as a lock-up for state prisoners was embellished with the 'discovery' of dungeons and a skeleton. Visitors were escorted round and urged to make contributions to relieve the families of the 83 Parisians killed during the assault. Blocks toppled from the walls were transformed into effigies of the Bastille. In the months that followed they would be distributed throughout France by Palloy's team of 'apostles of liberty'. The city of Lyons received their batch of 'relics' in three large crates weighing 700 lbs (342 kgs). In addition to the miniature Bastille, the crates contained a floor slab from the dungeons, a cannon ball, a breastplate, and a selection of educational books and paintings (Babelon, 1965: 217–30).

Two mutually reinforcing impulses now began to drive events: a desire both to dismantle and to rebuild. This chapter will explore each in turn, and will emphasize the negotiated character of the regime that subsequently came into being. Amidst the euphoria of national unity rediscovered, it was only natural that French men and women should imagine that their collective energies would

DOI: 10.4324/9781003156185-5

Figure 3.1 Model of the Bastille made from stones of the Bastille
© Musee de la Ville de Paris, Musee Carnavalet, Paris, France/Bridgeman Images

wipe away the past and put something different and superior in its place virtually overnight. However, this was not to be. Even if France's newly installed legislators had possessed a blueprint for renewal, which seems very unlikely, the business of obliterating the *ancien régime*, converting Bourbon absolutism into constitutional monarchy and building consensus around a new set of institutions would prove harder than anyone imagined in the summer of 1789.

Ending the *ancien régime*

The uprising in Paris produced a ripple effect across Europe. In the Galton household at Great Barr near Birmingham, young Harry Priestley burst into the drawing room waving his hat and shouting 'Hurrah! Liberty, Reason, brotherly love forever! Down with kingcraft and priestcraft. The Majesty of the People for ever!' He had just received a message from his brother William who was in Paris (Hankin ed., 1858: vol. I, 216–17). A thousand miles to the east on the coast of the Baltic, Johanna Schopenhauer was at home nursing her new-born son. Waiting for the postman to deliver the papers from the city of Danzig, she saw instead her husband ride into the yard bearing tidings of 'the first triumph of freedom, the storming of the Bastille' (Schopenhauer, 1847: vol. I, 123).

Even in localities where there were few disturbances and little violence, servants of the monarchy (intendants, sub-delegates, military commanders, etc.) either abandoned their posts or remained studiously inactive and inconspicuous in an effort to determine which way the political wind was blowing. In many towns and rural areas, though, violence was a part of the reaction to the news.

The self-appointed oligarchies running the cities made haste to attach to themselves 'committees' consisting of individuals who enjoyed a greater measure of public confidence. Even so, it was not always possible to contain the anger. The English traveller Arthur Young arrived at the gates of Strasbourg on 20 July just as an insurrection looked about to start. The populace, he recorded, 'show signs of an intended revolt. They have broken the windows of some magistrates that are no favourites; and a great mob of them is at this moment assembled demanding clamorously to have meat at 5s[ous] a pound' (Young, Betham-Edwards edn, 1794/1900: 206). His remark reminds us that hunger consequent upon the harvest shortfall of 1788 reached a distressing climax in the northerly half of the kingdom during the second and third weeks of July. Indeed, he declared elsewhere in his journal that 'the *deficit* would not have produced the revolution but in concurrence with the price of bread' (Lough, 1987: 293). This is a debatable point, but it can be taken as certain that the scale and the scope of the rural uprisings did not stem solely from the reverberations of the taking of the Bastille.

Country dwellers were already on a mobile footing as we have noted. Refusals to pay taxes, attacks on grain convoys, episodes of price fixing by crowds in the market places (*taxation populaire*), food-rioting and even punitive expeditions to chateaux had all been widely reported throughout the spring. Once the news from Paris arrived, the maintenance of law and order broke down almost completely and whole new theatres of insurgency (Normandy, Alsace, the Maconnais) appeared. Moreover, the *jacqueries*, as they were known, became increasingly anti-seigneurial in character. Lay and ecclesiastical overlords who removed to their own barns a portion of the harvest by virtue of their right to feudal dues or the **tithe** were obvious targets during periods of seasonal scarcity. But reports, albeit garbled, of Necker's disgrace, of the Paris insurrection and of courtiers leaving the Palace of Versailles under cover of darkness triggered a sudden shift in popular perceptions of the aristocracy.

A surge of fear and anxiety coursed through the countryside, motivated, it appears, by the suspicion that departing aristocrats had recruited bands of 'brigands' to destroy the ripening crops in a spiteful act of class revenge. Marie-Victoire Monnard, the twelve-year-old daughter of a tenant farmer, remembered helping to block the bridge at Creil, a fortified town to the north of Paris, with farm wagons before she and other children were told to go home and hide in the barn (Boutanquoi, 1928: 28). Few, if any, such bands were ever positively identified, but the merging of at least five regionally distinct 'fears' into a single overarching Great Fear (20 July–6 August 1789) had huge repercussions on events. Pre-existing theatres of insurrectionary activity acquired fresh energy, whilst in others, such as the Dauphiné, the insurgency of the winter flared up anew.

The biggest impact was in Paris, or rather in Versailles twelve miles distant from the capital, however. To the deputies of the Estates General, the dramatic and bloody scenes that had punctuated the week of Necker's dismissal came as a sudden and not entirely welcome surprise. They had been settling down in a fairly unhurried fashion to debate the future of the country, and to that end had resolved on 9 July to rename themselves the 'National Constituent Assembly'. Nobody at that time supposed that the drawing up of a constitution would take more than a few weeks, and no one – again at that time – had a clear set of ideas as to what other changes it would be necessary to make, save perhaps in the fiscal domain. This was the context in which the first reports of agrarian uprisings began to filter through to the deputies, mainly by way of letters from constituents. As the volume of such correspondence grew so did the level of alarm in the Assembly, with the result that the need to pacify the countryside rose swiftly to the top of the agenda. The outcome was the evening session of 4 August during which the new National Constituent Assembly voted to dismantle the *ancien régime*. In the small hours of the next morning, deputies from the province of Anjou sat down to draft an account of the session from which they had just emerged. They related how a liberal nobleman from Nemours, **Louis-Marie de Noailles**, had argued that the only sure means of restoring law and order was to offer country dwellers concrete reforms. He had then put the motion that all feudal rights and obligations be abolished without further ado. Once this had been accepted, a spate of other, more or less disinterested, motions had been put, resulting in a massive and collective act of repudiation of the past.

Whatever the mix of motivations in the minds of the deputies, there can be no doubt that the 'night of 4 August' tore the old order to shreds. Sacrificed on the altar to national renewal were all forms of provincial and municipal privilege, all remaining traces of serfdom, all feudal jurisdictions and courts, all harvest dues and quit rents, exclusive hunting reserves, the sale of public offices, ecclesiastical pluralism, the tithe, and much else besides. On the days following, the deputies contemplated what they had done with 'stupefaction' and not a little 'consternation and regret' according to the Spanish ambassador (Mousset, 1924: 67). More prosaically, Jefferson reported to John Jay that 'They last night mowed down a whole legion of abuses', adding, 'this will stop the burning of chateaux and tranquilize the country more than all the addresses they could send them' (Boyd ed., 1958: vol. 15; 334). Although there was some backsliding subsequently (notably on the subject of feudal dues and the tithe), the deputies were prepared to live with what they had done and the bonfire of privilege lit that night did achieve the desired effect in the sense that lawlessness in the countryside gradually subsided. It also gave them the courage and the confidence to hack away at those other pillars of the corporate state: the Parlements, the Provincial Estates and the Gallican Church. On 3 November, the Parlement of Paris and its twelve siblings were 'buried alive' – to use the Comte de Mirabeau's striking phrase. That is to say, they were put on permanent summer vacation until such time as a new system of courts could be brought into being.

Not surprisingly, the Parlements were deeply offended at their sudden ejection from political life and imminent extinction. Several questioned publicly the authority of 'the deputies of the *bailliages*' as the Parlement of Toulouse rashly referred to the National Assembly. During the Terror they would pay with their lives for that remark; but by that time about 40 per cent of magistrates (*parlementaires*) had chosen the path of emigration (Stone, 1986: 252). The other big institutional losers as the new regime began to take shape were the Provincial Estates. Their claim in 1787 and 1788 that they constituted a bulwark against the tendency to despotism of absolute monarchy had mostly been exposed as a sham. In Brittany, Burgundy and even Languedoc, the defence of provincial 'liberties' had amounted in practice to the defence of the privileges of the nobility, the Church and venal office holders. Provincial Estates, the deputies decided, belonged to the old order of things and could not be fitted into the new. The same applied to the tax and audit courts (*cours des aides, chambres des comptes*), which also claimed 'sovereign' status on a par with the Parlements. Despite much grumbling and even obstructionism – the Chambre des Comptes of Lorraine is a case in point – they were disbanded. With the nation now claiming sovereignty, there could be no role for such 'intermediate' bodies.

The decision on 5 November 1789 to get rid of the distinction of 'orders' or 'estates' flowed naturally from this conception, of course. But opinions were divided as to whether a regenerated nation could allow a category of 'citizens' in possession of the honorific title of 'noble' to subsist in its midst. Whatever constitutional theory now implied, the 1,315 deputies comprising the National Assembly could not but think of themselves as commoners or nobles (or clerics), as we shall see. Nevertheless, on 19 June 1790, they voted to do away with honorific privilege in a decree abolishing hereditable nobility, together with all the titles and symbols attaching to it. **Pierre-François Lepoutre,** one of the few Third Estate deputies from a farming background, described the decree with relish in a letter to his wife as 'the final humiliating blow to the nobility' (Jessenne and Le May eds, 1998: 278). Charles-Elie de Ferrières, the erstwhile noble deputy representing the *sénéchaussée* of Saumur in Anjou, was more matter-of-fact: he counselled his wife to stop writing to him as 'Monsieur le Marquis', and to have the family coat of arms obliterated with whitewash (Carré ed., 1932: 212). Whitewash could always be removed at a later date if necessary.

It is true that the definition of the citizen and more especially of the 'good' or 'useful' citizen had been subject to debate for several decades before the revolutionaries began to grapple with the question. *Ancien-régime* citizenship was essentially a legal category attaching to specific groups in the absence of a national community. However, the Enlightenment had launched the notion of 'universal' citizenship and it is clear that from around the time of the Seven Years War a slippage was under way as the concept shifted from the judicial to the political sphere. The events of 1787–89 accelerated this process, prompting some historians to identify a 'citizenship revolution' (Sahlins, 2004: 12) in the making. It would eventually give birth to the concept of national citizenship – one of the founding categories of modern democratic politics. Eventually, because the word 'nationality' was not coined until after the revolution and, in any case, France's new revolutionaries would find it difficult to reconcile the aspiration towards universalism with the day-to-day requirements of political decision-taking. While groups such as nobles were offered admission to the new polity, others would soon find themselves treated as aliens. In the colonies, for example, there existed intermediate groups whose ethnicity was considered a barrier to inclusion. Eurasians (**topas**) in France's Indian Ocean territory of Pondichéry (Puducherry) (see Map 0.5) demanded citizenship and so did male members of the indigenous Tamil community who were of catholic ancestry (Gobalakichenane, 1996–97: 38, 47).

Building the nation and the citizen

The work involved in clearing away the rubble of the *ancien régime* and building afresh were overlapping tasks. Although the majority of the deputies shared certain fixed ideas (devolution of power, employment on merit alone, public accountability, equal distribution of fiscal burdens, etc.) they did not plan what they were going to do between 1789 and 1791. After all, none of them arrived in Versailles with a mission to legislate, and no one expected to be in office for more than a few months at the most. After July 1789, most historians would agree, they fell under the influence of events like any other group of politicians. And it was the largely unscheduled events of the night of 4 August that propelled them into a frenzy of renewal. Yet even the dawning realization that the kingdom would now require a complete institutional overhaul could not be translated neatly into a plan of action. For all its anomalies, the *ancien régime* had worked. Until 1787 ordinary people paid their taxes more or less on time, had little difficulty in securing basic judicial redress and made few complaints about the quality of the spiritual care available to them. Simply to destroy without a thought for the continuities of daily life was not an option, no matter how appealing such an approach seemed in abstract, ideological terms. For two years, therefore, France would resemble a vast building site with old structures left temporarily in place even as the foundations of new ones were being dug alongside them. Tax revenue was still needed by the revolutionary state, and people still needed to have access to courts. Not until 1791 did it prove feasible to replace the old system of direct taxes; and seigneurial courts – nominally abolished on 4 August 1789 – would continue to operate until the end of 1790.

Renewal was taking place simultaneously with demolition and on a broad front, then. But for the sake of clarity it is worth separating the legislative achievements of these years and looking at each in turn. Fiscal reform preoccupied the deputies right through the decade. Indeed, it was not until 1807 and the Imperial government's decision to initiate a new, thorough and comprehensive land-holding survey that some of the most objectionable features of the *ancien-régime* tax system would start to be tackled. The financial situation of the monarchy towards the end of the summer of 1789 was every bit as precarious as it had been when Brienne left office a year earlier, if not more so. Jacques Necker, who had been recalled after the crisis of July, estimated that 170 million *livres* would be needed just to survive until the end of the year. Shocked by his report, the deputies resolved, on 2 November, to place the property of the Catholic Church 'at the disposal of the nation' – a delicate way of declaring that it would be itemized for sale and knocked down to the highest bidders. In return, the state would assume responsibility for the clerical debt, the funding of public worship (essentially, the salaries of the clergy) and for poor relief. Since the selling off of landed property and buildings owned by the Church would take a little while to organize, the National Assembly created a paper currency known as the ***assignats***. These notes were not paper money in the first instance; rather they were financial instruments intended for circulation among capitalists like bills of exchange. They would be withdrawn progressively as the cash proceeds of the sales were booked by the Treasury. They would, therefore, have no inflationary impact on the economy. At least this was the theory and for a time the expedient of the *assignats* did create a financial breathing space, enabling both commitments to creditors and the costs incurred in rebuilding the country to be managed. However, by the end of 1791 smaller denomination *assignats* were being issued for more general circulation and within a few years they had become the main if not the only medium of payment in day-to-day transactions. As a result, their value in the hands of consumers diminished. By the end of 1795, in fact, the *assignats* had become almost worthless, and the prospect of state bankruptcy was looming once more.

As a buttress to the confiscation of the possessions of the Church the deputies took two further steps of a financial nature: they introduced a special one-off income tax, known evocatively as the **contribution patriotique** and payable over three years, and they satisfied the heartfelt wish of the nation that everybody should now pay tax on the same footing with a backdated levy on the 'privileged' (i.e. those hitherto largely exempt from paying direct tax) to cover the last six months of 1789. The question of indirect taxes was more difficult to resolve for the reason that the monarchy had come to rely heavily on them, and yet they were abolishing themselves willy-nilly. Some of the toll-houses erected around Paris had been destroyed by fire in the disturbances leading up to the taking of the Bastille. As for the *gabelle* or salt tax, its inequity has already been mentioned, but the deputies were initially reluctant to forgo this source of revenue notwithstanding violence against customs offers and widespread smuggling. Only the realization that resistance to collection would continue indefinitely prompted abolition in March 1790.

It was the same story with the drinks taxes (***aides***) and municipal tolls (***octrois***). Both were only finally dispensed with in the spring of 1791, by which time the new universal land tax (***contribution foncière***) had replaced the *taille* and the *vingtièmes*. Edmond Géraud, a young student from Bordeaux, watched national guardsmen demolish the toll-gate at Chaillot on the western outskirts of Paris on the first day of May. All the roads leading into the capital, he reported, were soon jammed with heavy wagons carrying wine, cider, sugar and foodstuffs (Maugras, 1910: 113–14). In so far as tax is concerned, one of the central aims of the reformers ever since the 1760s had therefore been realized by the summer of 1791: everyone now contributed to the running costs of the state. But it was a rather hollow satisfaction for individual commoners who had assumed that they would be paying less because the 'ex-privileged' were now paying more. The long-standing problem of regional differences in tax 'load' had still to be sorted out as well.

The urgency of a territorial and administrative reorganization of the kingdom could have escaped no one after 4 August. The privileges enjoyed by individual provinces had been repudiated, the municipal government of towns and cities was in turmoil and Brienne's ambitions for tiered regional assemblies were in a state of suspended animation. Until the new regime had some solid local government institutions of its own, the chances of restoring law and order must have seemed remote. On 7 September, Sieyès suggested the setting up of a Constitution Committee, and in November it duly proposed that the kingdom be divided into about 80 roughly equal subdivisions to be known as 'departments' (see Map 0.2). In view of the hesitation in some parts of the country to espouse the new gospel of national 'togetherness', it was thought best to avoid the *ancien-régime* administrative vocabulary of 'provinces', 'estates' and 'assemblies'. And besides, power devolution rather than Bourbon centralism was the new watchword. The historic provinces were dismembered, therefore: Brittany was split into five departments, Normandy into six, Languedoc into seven, and so on. Each department was subdivided, in turn, into districts, cantons and a parish or village unit that would become known as the 'commune'. By mid-January 1790, a definitive list of 83 departments was ready to receive the Royal Assent – just as soon as names could be found for them. In addition, the new post-1789 administrative map would mark out 547 'districts', 4,872 'cantons' as well as around 44,000 communes (Margadant, 1992: 359; 361 note 91).

The second phase of this remarkable local government operation overlapped the first and consisted of attaching executive organs to the newly created territorial entities. Everyone agreed that it was necessary to begin at the base, partly because the lower units of jurisdiction would play a role in generating recruits for the higher echelons, and partly for the reason that the regime urgently needed a buttress of law and order that only local institutions created by consent could offer. In December, the deputies resolved that each 'town, *bourg*, parish or community' (Jones, 1995: 195) would henceforth enjoy the right to manage its own affairs through the institution of a municipality whose members would be elected. The elective principle enshrined the early revolutionaries' commitment to merit, transparency and accountability. It would be applied across the board and resulted in the creation of something like 1.2 million public offices (Edelstein, 2014: 1). Once the municipalities were securely in place, in February and March 1790, the voters would be called upon to choose the personnel forming the administrative bodies of the districts and the departments (the cantons had no elective councils attached to them). By the end of the year, they had been called out on numerous occasions, in fact, and a *de facto* primary electorate comprising around 4.4 million adult males had come into being. Voting fatigue would be one of the first signs that this rather unwieldy local government structure owed more to idealism than a firm grasp of administrative realities. Nevertheless, there can be no doubting the enthusiasm with which the local government reforms were received – initially. By the end of the first full year of revolution, scarcely any reminders of the rather patch-work civil administration of absolute monarchy remained. By the standards of *ancien-régime* Europe, change was happening at a break-neck speed. The fixed points in the lives of many generations of French men and women were being over-turned or uprooted – literally, in some cases. On 10 July 1790, the newly elected council of the Yonne department authorized a contractor to dig up and dispose of the wooden post that since time immemorial had marked the border between the provinces of Burgundy and the Ile-de-France.

While the inspiration behind some of the features of the local government reorganization can be traced back to Calonne and Brienne's assemblies' initia-tives of 1787–88, the judicial reforms of the National Assembly unquestionably marked a sharp break with the past. They were constructed around three principles: the notion that justice was a public rather than a private expression of authority with the nation as its source; the notion that judicial redress should be cost-free to consumers; and the notion of public accountability enshrined in the decision to subject judges and their assistants to a process of election. At the base an entirely new institution – the Justice of the Peace – would take over the role performed by seigneurial courts. These unpaid magistrates provided official documents without charge, a conciliation service for complainants and, where that failed, adjudicated on low value pleas.

In the Charente-Inférieure department, to take an example, roughly 500 seigneurial jurisdictions were replaced with 53 elected Justices of the Peace once the system was fully up and running towards the end of 1790 (Crubaugh, 2001: 7; 139). Whereas the judicial services provided by lords tended to be slow, expensive and incurred suspicions of partiality, the Justice of the Peace and his assistants judged speedily and with minimal formality. The institution was one of the great success stories of the revolution and despite an attempt by Napoleon Bonaparte to curtail it, Justices of the Peace survived until modern times. First-instance justice was dispensed at the level of the canton, a subdivision which otherwise played only a small part in the new administrative landscape, it should be said. More serious cases were sent before higher courts where, again, the legislators built on the foundation of their newly created units of civil administration. Each 'district' subdivision became the site of a civil court, and each 'department' a criminal court. Needless to say, there was no room for the Parlements in this new scheme of things and little room either for the multitude of more specialized courts and jurisdictions that had textured the *ancien régime*. Appeals would be heard by a single high court (*tribunal de cassation*), but its elected judges did not take office until 1791.

At least a reform of the judiciary had been prefigured in the *cahiers de doléances*. Yet no one could have foretold the fate in store for the Gallican Church on the basis of opinions circulating in the early months of 1789. A wider measure of religious toleration was on the table for discussion to be sure, for in 1788 the monarchy had already taken a big step in this direction in respect of Calvinists. But the restructuring of the Catholic Church began almost incidentally as a by-product of resolutions passed on the night of 4 August and subsequent days. However, once the 'in principle' decision had been taken to treat the Church as a bloated corporation whose wealth did not qualify for the protection normally afforded to individual private property, the deputies set to work with a will. Enlightenment convictions, and prejudices, which had been reined in by a spirit of pragmatism, now began to come out into the open. Having created a common template for civil and judicial administration, the National Assembly could see no reason why the spiritual infrastructure of the emerging nation should not be pulled into line as well. Bishoprics were reduced in number from 136 to 83 (one per department) and plans were made to streamline the parish structure – a contentious move that would provoke opposition in the years to come. In keeping with the utilitarian spirit of the age, monastic orders and cathedral chapters were abolished outright, forcing a flood of ordained men and religious women to go in search of more productive occupations. Those clergy who retained their posts found themselves salaried employees of the state and, as such, liable to much tighter discipline. Pluralism and non-residency had been outlawed and parish priests now had secular responsibilities thrust upon them. For example, a decree of 23 February 1790 required them to read out the laws from the pulpit on Sundays and explain their meaning to worshippers.

The representatives of the lower, parish-based clergy had been among the first to break the deadlock in the Estates General of course, but even they were starting to grow nervous as the scope of the National Assembly's reforming ambition for the Church became apparent. The move to dismantle the corporate structure of the Gallican Church was understandable, even laudable, to many, but where would the reform impulse of legislators lead next? Towards a *de facto* situation in which adherents of all religions, and indeed those adhering to none, were accepted on an equal footing? The pointed refusal of the National Assembly, in April 1790, to endorse a motion calling for Roman Catholicism to be declared the sole religion of state was none too reassuring in this respect.

Nor was the determination of the majority of deputies to apply the electoral principle to the priesthood as though ecclesiastical appointments were no different from any other type of office-holding. Priests, whether bishops or mere country parsons, would be chosen by voters – just like mayors, municipal officers and judges. The spiritual confirmation and canonical institution of bishops – powers vested in the popes as heirs of Saint-Peter – were repudiated in common with all other manifestations of jurisdictional supremacy asserted by the Holy See. Having been elected by their fellow citizens, bishops would be consecrated by their metropolitans. As for monks and nuns, they were to leave their cloistered houses. In the case of the latter, the abolition of solemn vows (poverty, chastity, obedience) had the unanticipated consequence of restoring their civil rights. Ex-nuns could now own and inherit property. They could swear oaths and even marry (Gressang, 2020: 334–47).

All these far-reaching changes were packaged together in a legislative text known as the Civil Constitution of the Clergy [**Doc. 12**]. The National Assembly approved the draft on 12 July 1790 and it was sanctioned by the king, despite grave misgivings, a few days later. Such was the brimming confidence of the deputies that no one imagined that the clergy might demur, or the pope prove reluctant and withhold his endorsement. The Civil Constitution only regulated the Catholic clergy and laity. Protestants and Jews had first to validate their civil status within the new polity; only then could a framework of constitutional law be applied to their respective communities. Protestants (Calvinists and Lutherans) were admitted to the same rights as Catholics quite swiftly. Their rehabilitation was even extended to descendants of the Huguenots. In Paris a Calvinist community of about 7,000 individuals regrouped around pastor Paul-Henri Marron whose ancestors had fled France after 1685. They rented a disused catholic church and decorated the interior with inscriptions taken from the Declaration of the Rights of Man which were clearly chosen to underline their claim to citizenship (Maugras, 1910: 231–32). But the situation of Jews in France was altogether more complex. There were only about 40 to 50,000 of them and they were considered to be foreigners in both a civil and a religious sense. In pure theory, all Jews were liable to expulsion from France at a moment's notice, although some had purchased a 'privilege', if not a right of residence. As we have seen, *ancien-régime* monarchs and their ministers did not pay much attention to the letter of the law when opportunities for revenue-raising or making an investment in wealthy and entrepreneurial foreigners arose. Even so, the Ashkenazim Jews of eastern France whose capacity for assimilation was a matter for some doubt would not secure full citizenship rights until the constitution was completed in September 1791.

Expanding horizons

With the anniversary of the fall of the Bastille approaching, town and country dwellers alike prepared to celebrate a festival of thanksgiving for the achievements of the past year. Observers commented on the mood of pride and optimism that had taken hold among Parisians. On a stroll through the Champ de Mars, deputy Pierre-François Lepoutre noticed smartly attired women as well as men pushing wheelbarrows of earth in an effort to get the public space ready in time for the Festival of Federation.

There can be no doubt that at this juncture – 14 July 1790 – men and women of virtually all backgrounds were willing the revolution to succeed. In the tiny hamlet of Rennemoulin on the outskirts of Versailles, the entire population assembled at the appointed hour, but only the men stepped forward to swear the oath of allegiance as custom and practice demanded. However, the women of the village then insisted that the whole ceremony be staged afresh eleven days later so that they, too, could affirm in a public way their commitment to the new regime [Doc. 11]. The king showed less grace, by contrast. In the vast and rain-soaked arena of the Champ de Mars, he lounged in his elbow chair throughout the lengthy ceremony and close observers noticed some hesitancy when his turn came to swear.

Figure 3.2 The Festival of Federation, 14 July 1790, as recorded on a 5 *sol* token
© The Birmingham Assay Office

Hundreds of miles to the southeast the people of the hill village of Allan had also been willing on the revolution. But as in many small localities far removed from the new sources of political power, the speed and the magnitude of the changes taking place since the summer of 1789 required a real mental effort to keep up. For centuries the villagers had formed part of the 'nation' of Provence and, consequently, had looked to Aix, the provincial capital, for political leadership. Now the momentum for constitutional change was coming from a different direction. Yet it was not until the late autumn that it finally dawned on the elders of the village that they were caught up in a truly fundamental process of regeneration, which was likely to bypass time honoured pleas for the reinstatement of the Provincial Estates of Provence (suspended since 1639). The turning point came in December when they were invited to send a delegation of national guardsmen to an encampment, or federation, at Montélimar. In a collective act of solidarity intended to transcend all sectional allegiances, they swore an oath of fidelity to the law and to a nation of undifferentiated French men and women. Within a matter of months, their mental adjustment had been accomplished. In March 1790 the village council waved goodbye to provincial privilege forever and voted to join a new territorial entity 'known by the name of the department of the Drôme' (Jones, 2003: 106).

There would be no turning back for rural, provincial France. It was perhaps an awareness of the past being sacrificed to an uncertain future that explains the energy the inhabitants of Allan brought to the celebration of year one of revolution. Dawn on 14 July 1790 broke to the drumbeat of their tiny **national**

guard. After Mass and with flags deployed, the population marched in procession to the seigneurial rabbit warren. With the village clock striking noon, the administering of the oath began. The choice of the warren for the climax to the day's events was no accident: during the Great Fear, Allan had re-enacted the taking of the Bastille with an invasion of its own feudal chateau. To the backdrop of the news of events in Paris, the villagers ceased bringing their dough to the seigneurial bread oven and put the payment of harvest dues and the tithe on hold. Then, in September 1790, with an almost palpable sense of satisfaction, the village council acknowledged the legislation being issued by the National Assembly which made clear that it alone was vested with the power of police, not their seigneur.

Anti-seigneurialism would prove to be a powerful political glue. During the phase of renewal it helped to cement loyalty to the new regime and provided the incentive country dwellers needed to stay involved in the work of reconstruction. When it was discovered that the promises made by the deputies on the night of 4 August were not likely to be honoured in full, ordinary men and women likewise discovered that they had within their grasp a hitherto undreamt-of capacity to resist and exert pressure. Elected municipalities possessed a range of powers to hold the agents of seigneurs to account, national-guard detachments could be mobilized to ensure compliance, or to intimidate; and, if all else failed, there always remained the option of insurrection. In fact, localized peasant uprisings did punctuate the early years of the revolution. Often enough they were driven by the realization that many feudal obligations would continue in force, until they were extinguished by payment of compensation. Not until the summer of 1792 would the legislature acknowledge the futility of expecting peasants to buy their way out of the seigneurial regime. In the meantime, the issue helped to maintain an impressive degree of support for the revolution in the countryside – even if that support was often manifested in turbulent and disquieting ways. In June 1790, Pierre-François Lepoutre urged his wife to have a private word with the seigneur's agent so that the gibbet could be taken down 'in order to avoid the possibility that the populace would come and demolish it' (Jessenne and Le May eds, 1998: 278).

Towards a political settlement

Even though French men and women wanted desperately to associate Louis XVI with their reforming efforts, his goodwill towards the revolution could not be taken for granted. Louis's visit to his capital three days after the assault on the Bastille was received by Parisians in stony silence; and in the aftermath of the **October Days**, they would insist that he, the royal family and the National Assembly take up residence in Paris rather than Versailles. Louis and his queen came to regard this enforced residence in the capital as tantamount to imprisonment, and for good reason. Yet the king's speech before the Assembly on 4 February 1790 in which he promised his full co-operation in the task of renewal, had the deputies in semi-religious transports of delight and devotion.

Lepoutre hailed the experience as 'one of the finest days of my life' (Jessenne and Le May eds, 1998: 187), and sent a copy of the speech to his wife so that it could be read aloud to the farm servants.

The actual distribution of political power within the regime that was now taking shape represented something of a problem, though. Patriarchal leadership by a good king who had forsworn the practice of absolutism implied a subordinate role for the Assembly; on the other hand, a monarch whose goodwill remained open to question and who appeared beholden still to the Court suggested the need for a strong and vigilant parliamentary body. This is what the debates of September 1789 on the subject of a veto and a two-chamber legislature were all about. In the aftermath of the blood spilt on 14 July and subsequent days, a group of deputies who came to be known as the *Monarchiens* had learned to fear popular violence more than they feared the prospect of a counter-attack launched by the aristocracy or from the Court. However, they were opposed by tougher-minded individuals whose political outlook was most effectively expressed by the barrister-deputy from Grenoble, **Antoine Barnave**. These deputies continued to distrust the monarch and when it came to a vote, the majority in the Assembly backed their judgement. The proposal to build into the constitution a power of absolute veto that would have enabled Louis to block reformist legislation indefinitely was lost, as was the proposal to establish a hereditary second chamber which would have exerted a moderating influence on the model of the English House of Lords.

It is true that appalling acts of violence, including public beheadings, impalings and butchery, had soiled the 1789 uprising against absolute monarchy, prompting some historians to consider that 'terror' was intrinsic to the revolutionary experience from the very start (see Part III). It is also true that the political education of the masses was proceeding at a pace that many of those who had been involved in the long guerrilla struggle against absolute monarchy found deeply disturbing. The American businessman Gouverneur Morris would capture in his diary the fumbling progress of ordinary folk as they grappled with totally new ideas and the language in which they were being expressed. Whilst walking the streets of Paris on 5 October, he overheard a street-corner orator declaiming against bread shortages with the words: 'The king has only had this suspensive veto for three days and already aristocrats have bought up the suspensions and sent corn out of the kingdom' (Morris, 1939: vol. 1; 244). Informal bodies such as the 'electors' of Paris and the militias (national guardsmen) that had sprung up all over the kingdom in response to the law and order emergency of July and August were also starting to show signs of becoming a source of unrest and agitation.

In the meantime, however, the deputies' own legislative pronouncements were beginning to mark out the social frontiers of the revolution that was now getting under way. Their principle of accountability raised an obvious question: 'Accountable to whom?' Having completed the move from Versailles to Paris, the National Assembly began to debate such matters towards the end of October. In an all-male legislature, almost no one considered seriously the right of women to the vote. At this juncture, the most that women could hope for was some easing of paternal authority within the family (see Part III). Rather, the issue became one of determining a framework for 'citizenship'. According to the Declaration of Rights approved on 27 August 1789 as a preliminary statement of the constitution to come: 'Men are born, and always continue, free, and equal in respect of their rights' [**Doc. 10**]. But this ambitiously egalitarian doctrine proved something of an embarrassment when the time came to construct viable institutions of government. Instead, the deputies devised a gradated form of 'political' citizenship, based on the size of individual tax contributions. Those in the lowest tier (described as 'passive citizens') would not be allowed to vote at all, whereas those in the upper tier ('active citizens') were entitled to participate in electoral assemblies and, provided they paid enough tax, to stand as candidates as well. Between 37 and 40 per cent of adult males over the age of 25 were denied the suffrage as a result (Edelstein, 2014: 70). The 'sovereign' nation of political rhetoric was already starting to look somewhat reduced by the end of the first full year of revolution, then. However, it is worth remembering that barely 17 per cent of Englishmen possessed the vote at this time and even fewer Americans.

The rather artificial distinction drawn between 'political rights' and 'civil rights' attracted much criticism at street-level. This was unsurprising, since freedom of expression had enabled an explosive growth to occur in the publishing industry. The number of print shops operating in Paris would more than quadruple (from 47 to 223) during the revolutionary decade, and it is probable that in excess of 600 newspaper titles started up in the provinces over the same period of time (Hesse, 1991: 167). Paris alone provided a market for about 300,000 newspaper copies a day in 1790 (Burrows, 2015: 79). Many of these publications were short-lived, of

Figure 3.3 Detail of a newspaper vendor from Philibert-Louis Debucourt, 'Eventaire de presse. Détail de l'Almanach National pour 1791'
© Photo Josse/Bridgeman Images

course, but there can be no doubting the overall size of the reading public, or that it was increasing by leaps and bounds. Organs such as Camille Desmoulins's *Révolutions de France et de Brabant* or Marat's *L'Ami du Peuple*, among many others, maintained a constant and critical commentary on the doings of the deputies.

The desire to participate also found expression in the creation of political clubs. Initially, these meeting places were confined to parliamentarians and the bourgeois elite of the great cities, but they, too, quickly expanded down the social scale and outwards into the smaller centres of population. The Cordeliers Club began life as an assembly of electors in the Cordeliers district of Paris, and it would become a nursery for many future radicals (Danton, Desmoulins, **Santerre, Chaumette**, etc.). By 1791 it was allowing 'passive citizens' and even women into its meetings [**Doc. 14**]. However, the most successful forum for the new political sociability of the revolution was the Society of the Friends of the Constitution, otherwise known as the Jacobin Club. The origins of this body can be found in the informal gatherings of commoner deputies hailing from Brittany during the opening weeks of the Estates General. It would be dominated by deputy-members and nearly always reflected official, patriotic opinion in the successive revolutionary legislatures. Unlike the other Paris clubs, though, the Jacobins managed to replicate themselves across the length and breadth of the country. By 1794, the Jacobin network would embrace around 5,500 clubs, all working in close collaboration with the local authorities (Boutier, Boutry and Bonin eds, 1992: 6).

Historians tend to refer to those deputies undeterred in their determination to renovate the country by the spasms of violent and vengeful activity in July and October as the 'patriot party'. But the label does not fit very well because the revolution never at any point generated parties in the modern sense. In any case, the political dynamics of the National Assembly remained fluid for many months. In all likelihood many, perhaps the majority, of deputies continued to think of themselves in *ancien-régime* terms – as former members of 'estates'. That being said, though, observers who were actually present at the sessions, such as Lepoutre, recognized the existence of political affiliations or groupings linked, usually, to prominent personalities (**Lafayette** and Barnave for example); and they increasingly referred to a contingent of irreconcilables known as the 'blacks' ('*les noirs*'). In fact, it was the continuing strength of conservative opinion, even after the debates on the veto and the second chamber in September 1789, that prompted the 'patriot' opposition to organize more effectively. The Jacobin Club, properly speaking, came into being in January 1790 and over the next twelve months or so the 'patriots' not only became more coherent as a body of deputies seeking to control the business of the Assembly, they began to subdivide into moderate and radical 'patriots' as well. If ever there was a specific moment that revealed the spectrum of opinion, it was the vote to abolish noble status and titles on 19 June. After this unexpected event nobles all over the country took stock, pondering, perhaps for the first time, whether they had a part to play in the new regime.

Yet all but the extreme right-wingers (the 'blacks') and the trickle of ex-Second Estate deputies who were starting to absent themselves from the

Assembly, remained committed to reaching a political settlement that would endow France with a constitution. Crowd violence in Paris had subsided; assisted no doubt by the much-delayed arrival of the new harvest, and by the deterrent of the **Martial Law** decree (21 October 1789). Nagging fears about the goodwill of the monarch persisted, however. Louis retained control of his ministers and, of course, he could delay the implementation of many laws by invoking his suspensive veto right. Yet matters were not quite so straightforward in practice. Ministers tended to defer to the superior authority of the committees of the Assembly; as for the veto, it had limited value if its use risked inciting a popular disturbance. Of all the legislation that Louis XVI was persuaded to sanction during the first year of revolution, it is likely that the Civil Constitution of the Clergy gave him greatest pause for thought. When, on 27 November 1790, the National Assembly resolved to enforce clerical compliance by means of an oath which all serving priests would be expected to swear (see Chapter 4), Louis was distraught. A pious man left rudderless by the failure of the Holy See to make known its verdict on the revamping of the Gallican Church, he sanctioned the measure (on 26 December) only to regret his action for the rest of his life. The decision to try to extricate the royal family from the revolution may have been taken at about this time. However, the gap that was now starting to open in the project to give France a written constitution only became fully and painfully apparent in April of the following year.

At the start of Holy Week 1791, Louis ordered his carriage to be brought to the Tuileries so that he could go to Saint-Cloud – a royal palace just outside Paris – and receive the sacraments from a clergyman who had not sworn the oath of allegiance to the as yet unfinished constitution. An unruly crowd prevented him from leaving, although Lafayette as the commander of the Paris National Guard offered to force a passage. Apart from revealing the equivocal character of the monarch for all to see, the Saint-Cloud affair served notice on Barnave and other senior 'patriot' deputies that the settlement towards which they had been working might very well collapse under its own weight. A constitution without a monarch as its chief fixture and ornament was not to be contemplated. Yet some sections of radical opinion in the capital appeared to be pushing in exactly this direction. Moreover, they could expect support from the intransigent deputies of the extreme right who scarcely bothered to conceal their hope that the experiment in constitutional monarchy would prove unsuccessful.

By the spring of 1791, the political horizon no longer seemed quite as trouble-free as it had appeared twelve months earlier, therefore. Speculation against the new paper currency (the *assignats*) was driving coin underground and hindering the street-level retail trade. Parisians no longer worshipped the very ground on which Lafayette stood, for a national guard made up mainly of 'active citizens' was losing the close link with ordinary people that had attended its creation. In the country at large, meanwhile, the clerical oath legislation was driving a wedge into the very heart of the nation; indeed the word 'counter-revolution' had begun to be heard. Barnave and his political allies took note and redoubled their efforts to finish the constitution.

4   The failure of consensus, 1791–92

After two years of continuous effort, the deputies had become weary and were anxious to go home. Pierre-François Lepoutre had not once been back to his farm near Lille since arriving in Versailles to attend the Estates General in the spring of 1789. Its management was entirely in the hands of his wife whom he had only seen twice during that period, although they exchanged letters every five or six days. Like everyone else, he wanted to bring the revolution to a satisfactory conclusion and then retire gracefully. Why, then, does the story not end on 14 September 1791 when Louis XVI, King of the French, swore an oath to uphold the constitution? On receiving the news of the king's acceptance Madame Lepoutre wept tears of joy and relief, describing the event as 'a knock-out blow for aristocrats' (Jessenne and Le May eds, 1998: 523). Festivities were organized in the village in common with localities all over France.

The revolution did not end in September 1791 for the simple reason that the consensus embedded in the constitution so laboriously negotiated by the National Assembly was more apparent than real. As we shall see, a significant number of those enjoying privileges under the *ancien régime* had opted out by this date, the revolutionaries themselves had fallen into disarray, and the king's own approval of the transition from absolute to constitutional monarchy was patently insincere.

The flight and its aftermath

The departure of the royal family from the Palace of the Tuileries in the centre of Paris during the night of 20–21 June 1791 caught everyone unawares except for those closely involved in the preparations. This is surprising in view of the many months of planning that had taken place, the logistics of the operation and the fact that the king kept changing his mind at the last moment. Louis left behind a *Déclaration* or statement, written in his own hand, which recorded his objections to the revolution as it had unfolded since June 1789. While not a plea for a complete return to the *ancien régime*, it reads nonetheless as a pretty uncompromising document [Doc. 13]. It is uncertain whether the royal travelling party intended actually to cross the frontier into the Austrian Netherlands because they were recognized and stopped in the little town of Varennes

DOI: 10.4324/9781003156185-6

(department of the Meuse), some 35 miles short of the border. The king would subsequently claim that he was heading towards the citadel of Montmédy.

For the leading 'patriot' deputies in the National Assembly, who were close to putting the finishing touches to the constitution, the flight was extremely bad news. However, their nerve held: the legislature took over the executive functions of government, placed the nation in a state of defensive readiness and circulated the message that the king had been 'kidnapped'. This fiction would prove very convenient when the king and the queen were found and brought back to Paris some four days later. Pierre-François Lepoutre was among the crowds of Parisians who watched their coach approach. Not a word was uttered, nor a hat removed, although soldiers rattled their bayonets against the carriage as it passed by. On his return, Louis was suspended from office rather than dethroned without further ado – a clear indication that a group of deputies under the leadership of Barnave had already started work on a negotiated solution to the crisis provoked by the flight. Yet the calm deliberation of the Assembly contrasted starkly with the turmoil and apprehension in the clubs and the radical press. Many aristocratic army officers serving on the frontiers had chosen this as the moment to emigrate, as had the Comte de Provence, the king's younger brother and the future **Louis XVIII**. Over 2,000 officers of the line army left France that autumn in fact (Forrest, 2015: 391). Many were anticipating a war of intervention with Leopold II of Austria – the brother of Marie-Antoinette – at its head.

In fact a war was very unlikely at this stage, although few in France could have known this. Leopold was a reformer not a crusader, and took the view that his brother-in-law should strike the best deal he could secure in the circumstances. This was also the view of Barnave, Adrien Duport and Alexandre de Lameth (the so-called Triumvirate) and their allies; on 15 July they induced the Assembly to exonerate Louis and to blame unidentified others for his 'abduction'. Desperate to achieve a political settlement, they had been exploring options secretly with the queen and had offered to revise the constitution in a sense more favourable to the monarch if she, in turn, would prevail on her brother the Emperor to obtain international recognition of France's transformation since 1789. Barnave put the issue neatly in a rhetorical question to his fellow deputies: 'Are we going to finish the revolution, or are we going to begin it afresh?' (Jessenne and Le May eds, 1998: 491).

The issue was not as clear-cut at street level, or in the villages, however. For all his equivocations, the monarch was seen as the cornerstone of the new regime and confidence in him plunged leaving public opinion rudderless. In Paris radical journalists responded with a campaign against the pragmatic solution of reinstating Louis following his acceptance of the constitution, although they scarcely had a better alternative to offer. In Caen a statue of the monarch was overturned by angry citizens, but elsewhere in the departments it appears that public opinion was willing to go along with the kidnap explanation. This was the political line that René Hyacinthe Thibaudeau *père* fed to the local authorities in Poitiers (Carré and Boissonnade eds, 1898: 145).

The attempted exodus of the king had plainly aggravated tensions within the patriot camp that had been growing since the start of the year. However, the situation was by no means irretrievable: even in the cockpit of the revolution – Paris – the views of ordinary people were not yet sharply polarized (Andress, 2000: 137, 166, 223). What started to change the face of politics as far as firm supporters of the revolution were concerned was the so-called massacre perpetrated in the Champ de Mars on 17 July 1791. A noisy, if unfocused, barracking of the deputies had been in progress since the start of the month, but it gained in intensity as the news came through that the Assembly was preparing to reinstate Louis as though his dereliction of duty had been a mere peccadillo. Hostile petitions and demonstrations were organized in which the Cordeliers Club played a major role; however, the protestors displayed little unity of purpose. Should the king's fate be determined by a popular referendum? Should a regency be declared under the Duke of Orleans – a republic even? In the event, it was the petition-signing ceremony organized by the Cordeliers for 17 July that caused the reinstatement crisis to detonate a far greater explosion. Bloodshed that morning (the lynching and beheading of two men found hiding beneath the platform) provided the authorities with the pretext to intervene and the municipality ordered the proclamation of Martial Law. Under Lafayette's command and in the presence of the mayor of Paris, Jean-Sylvain Bailly, the national guard fired volleys of shots into the crowd of petitioners when they failed to disperse. Perhaps as many as 50 were killed.

If the spilling of blood in the Champ de Mars had not been premeditated, there can be little doubt that the majority of the deputies had willed the confrontation. A trial of strength was felt to be necessary in order to clear the political air and prepare the way for an eleventh-hour revision of the constitution. In the aftermath of the 'massacre', the infrastructure of a street-level republicanism that dared not speak its name was dismantled. Danton fled to England, Desmoulins, Santerre and other leading lights of the Cordeliers were arrested, and Marat temporarily disappeared following the seizure of the presses on which *L'Ami du peuple* was printed. Even the survival of the Jacobin Club was placed in jeopardy as a large number of its more moderate members – including Barnave – withdrew to a different meeting place (the former monastery of the Feuillants).

Yet the crisis had weakened the staunchest parliamentary friends of the revolution as well, for the blood shed by the national guard, supposedly a pillar of the new order, now became a festering source of division [**Doc. 14**]. On the other hand, the possibility of a pre-emptive strike against the revolution by the Great Powers had been averted, and conditions now existed for an orderly revision of the constitution. However, a war in the summer of 1791 had never been a serious prospect and the rebalancing of the constitution would never take place. The **Feuillant**, or more moderate wing of the 'patriots' could not win a cross-party vote to achieve anything substantial. For this they would have needed the support of the alienated block of strongly royalist deputies who no longer bothered even to participate in the life of the Assembly. Indeed, the intransigents among them could see no advantage at all in helping to turn the country into a conservative constitutional monarchy. What about Louis himself? In theory, he could have rejected the constitution when it was finally submitted to him on 13 September but had he done so, the only alternative would have been abdication.

Managing the new regime

With the acceptance by Louis XVI of the constitution, the deputies' task came to an end. They spent the last few days of September settling outstanding business, which included a generous recompense to the owner of the covered tennis court in Versailles that had sheltered the Third Estate in its hour of need on 20 June 1789. They also passed an amnesty law applicable to all men and women who had been accused of riot since May 1788. Then, on 30 September 1791, the president pronounced the words: 'The National Constituent Assembly declares that its mission is fulfilled and its sessions are over' (Jones, 1995: 237). The transition to constitutional monarchy was now complete, on paper at least. Since the deputies had voted through a 'self-denying' decree, making it unlawful to prolong themselves in office, the new men who gathered for the opening session of the successor Legislative Assembly on 1 October were just that. Moreover, their powers would be circumscribed by a constitutional text that they were not allowed to alter.

The revolution had gone on longer than anyone had expected, but it was now officially over. All that remained was the routine business of legislation: the managing of the new regime. Of course, this neat distribution of powers and responsibilities rested on a fallacy as all French men and women with a modicum of political awareness must have understood. The constitution had *not* been achieved consensually, and a great deal of unfinished business was waiting in the wings. Far from being 'over', the revolution was only just beginning or, as one of the king's advisors put it, 'the storms in store for us will be far greater than those we have experienced' (Bacourt ed., 1851: vol. 3; 194).

The individuals elected to seats in the Legislative Assembly may have been new to the hot-house world of Paris, but they were not political novices. Many had served an apprenticeship in local government, which was usually how they had come to the notice of voters in the first place. The deputy Pierre Dubreuil-Chambardel, for example, served as clerk to the municipality of his parish in 1788, before being chosen to convey his constituents' *cahier de doléances* to the **bailliage** assembly in 1789. The following year he joined the administration of the department of the Deux-Sèvres (Llorca ed., 1994: 13–29).

Not surprisingly, most of these men were drawn from the ranks of the old Third Estate. Only about 12 per cent hailed from the former privileged orders (compared with 54 per cent in the National Assembly). By profession the majority were small-town attorneys or barristers, although a sprinkling of bourgeois land owners (like Pierre Dubreuil-Chambardel), bankers, merchants and military men had been chosen as well. In effect, they constituted the upper and most visible stratum of a 'revolutionary class-in-the-making' (Edelstein, 2014: 135–65) which had its roots in the well-to-do peasants and tenant farmers of country parishes, and in the notaries, ex-seigneurial officials and small-time professionals (doctors, barber-surgeons, land surveyors, teachers, millers, etc.) who could be found in every market town. They were politically opaque on arrival in Paris and most were keen to remain so. Whereas 169 of the new deputies joined the re-opened Feuillant Club (to which Barnave and the Triumvirate, as out-of-office politicians, had retreated) and 51 the Jacobins, the majority (547) tried to steer clear of the re-alignments spawned by the Flight and the Champ de Mars affair. Courtiers such as the Comte de La Marck heaped scorn upon these hand-me-down revolutionaries: 'Nineteen-twentieths of the members of this legislature', he commented to the Austrian ambassador, 'are equipped with nothing but clogs and umbrellas' (Bacourt ed., 1851: vol. 3, 246).

The desire to make a name for themselves and the lack of seasoned leadership may help to explain why the deputies of the Legislative Assembly were so ready to throw caution to the winds. They showed little appetite for the managerial role outlined for them by the king, which presupposed a focus on mundane economic and judicial questions. Instead, in three main policy areas they sailed cheerfully into the eye of the storm, losing the 1791 Constitution on the way and jeopardizing the very survival of the revolution. The split in the constitutional Church that the oath legislation of November 1790 had provoked would have required real statesmanship to mend, it is true. There had been signs in the spring that the Triumvirate had recognized the need for a more conciliatory approach to 'non-jurors' – that is to say clergymen who were refusing to swear the oath. However, the newly elected deputies were vulnerable to pressures exerted by their former colleagues in the Department and District administrations. The warning they received from them was blunt and to the point. Only if the activities of the non-jurors were curbed could the Civil Constitution of the Clergy be made to work. Accordingly, a law of 29 November imposed a fresh (albeit purely political) oath with sanctions for those who failed to comply. Non-jurors lost the right to hold autonomous services in church buildings and their pension entitlements. They were also subjected to municipal surveillance, a form of scrutiny that could result in expulsion from their homes in extreme cases of religious in-fighting. Granted the Assembly stopped short of ordering the imprisonment of non-jurors. Nevertheless, the king still made use of his suspensive veto to block the measure.

The mounting hostility towards the intractable or refractory clergy as they were known was undoubtedly linked to the fear that such priests might become aiders and abettors of counter-revolution. In October and November, the new deputies worked themselves into a fury on the subject of those French men and women who had fled France and the revolution. The news of the king's formal acceptance of the constitution had triggered a fresh wave of departures which probably involved hundreds of families, it is true. The Duchess (now Madame) d'Elbeuf locked up her hotel near the Tuileries and left for the Austrian Netherlands on 20 September. But she returned six months later having run short of ready cash (Rougé, 1910: 339; 342). It required a fertile imagination to suppose that all those leaving were counter-revolutionaries, and that *émigré* 'armies' represented a serious threat (Jones, 2013: 286–89). Without Great Power support the militant *émigrés* were powerless. Neither **Leopold II** of Austria nor Frederick William II of Prussia was at this stage prepared to commit troops to an intervention in France, notwithstanding their joint **Declaration of Pillnitz** (27 August 1791). Still, the rhetoric of national solidarity in response to a perceived threat of invasion had a good deal of populist appeal and on 31 October the Assembly warned the Comte de Provence that he would lose his right of succession to the throne if he did not return to France within three months. A few days later, all *émigrés* were put on notice that they risked confiscation of their property and denunciation as conspirators if they remained outside the country beyond the end of the year. Even firm patriots such as Nicolas Ruault, bookseller and now editor of *Le Moniteur* newspaper, thought these measures rather draconian and, in any case, they were vetoed by the monarch who was receiving advice from Barnave and other ex-deputies.

The third and most glaring sphere in which the deputies of the Legislative Assembly gambled with the nation's fortunes was that of foreign policy. While the split in the Church and the posturings of a few *émigrés* were irritants, there was nothing inevitable about the recourse to armed conflict. Great Britain remained firmly neutral if suspicious of the revolution, and the continental Powers were far more preoccupied with events in eastern Europe (the fates of the Turkish Empire and of Poland) than with the embarrassments of the King of France. As for the revolutionaries, they had in May 1790 proclaimed their pacific intentions and renounced the use of force for the purposes of territorial conquest. The diplomacy of self-determination (the notion that the rights of peoples override those of states) was still in its infancy. It would be invoked in September 1791 as a partial justification for French annexation of the two papal enclaves of Avignon and the Comtat Venaissin, but that is all. The strident and bellicose ideology of nationalism and 'national' citizenship lay in the future.

What changed, then, during the winter of 1791–92? Most accounts emphasize the central role played by the deputies themselves in the decision-making process that led to a war, and in this regard it is helpful to recall the circumstances that had brought the Legislative Assembly into being. Because of the 'self-denying' decree, there could be no carrying over of accumulated parliamentary wisdom from one legislature to the next. All the deputies who had become household names as the new France was being forged were now out of office. The caucus built up by Barnave (latterly known as the Feuillants) were on the sidelines and scarcely able to control events; likewise were Lafayette and his allies who are usually depicted as unwilling to collaborate with the Feuillants. Even the so-called democrats were in tactical disarray. The best-known parliamentary radicals – **Maximilien Robespierre** and **Jérôme Pétion** – had been lauded by the Paris crowd as they exited the National Assembly. Yet, after 30 September, they too were confined to journalism and the oratorical platform provided by the Jacobin Club. They were replaced on the parliamentary rostrum by new men such as

Jacques Pierre Brissot, François Chabot and Pierre Vergniaud who dangled the prospect of demagogic leadership and forthright policies that would offer the Assembly the means of escaping from the shadow of its illustrious predecessor.

According to Brissot and his allies (who would be known as the **Girondins** in the next legislature), a policy of squaring up to the Habsburg Emperor, albeit in the knowledge that it would probably unleash hostilities, offered the prospect of settling the *émigré* issue once and for all. More important, though, were three concrete advantages that such a policy might also deliver. First and foremost, the king would be forced to opt for one side or the other, thereby resolving the ambiguity at the heart of the constitution. Second, a war of 'liberation' would release the supposedly oppressed peoples of Europe from the twin yokes of feudalism and monarchical absolutism. Third, a war would reinvigorate an economy ailing as a result of economic dislocation, unemployment and the effects of overreliance on the *assignats*. All of these supposed advantages were predicated, of course, on the conviction that war could be fought on foreign territory and would result in a victory for the armies of revolutionary France.

Others begged to differ. Feuillants both inside and outside the Assembly saw clearly that any descent into hostilities would destroy the constitution they had laboured long and hard to bring into being. Though he had little confidence in the leading men of 1789 (Barnave, the Lameth brothers, Lafayette, etc.), Robespierre came to agree with them. In a series of speeches between mid-December and the end of January, he subjected Brissot's blithe foreign policy assurances to relentless scrutiny. A war might very well resolve the king's divided loyalties, but who was to say that the revolution would be the gainer thereby? An imperfect constitution was better than no constitution at all. A war, he continued, would create opportunities for powerful generals to intervene (an oblique reference to Lafayette who had resigned as commander of the Paris National Guard and taken up a military post on the eastern border). Finally, and in a memorable phrase, he pointed out that no one likes 'armed missionaries' (Hampson, 1974: 100) – a retort to Brissot's prediction that French troops would be welcomed with open arms once they had crossed the Rhine. Reasonable and prophetic though these arguments were, Robespierre found himself in a minority even in the Jacobin Club. As for the bulk of the deputies, they quickly rallied to a policy that provided an opportunity to leave their mark on history.

The harvest of 1791 had been poor unlike that of 1790, and in Paris basic food prices started to rise again from the month of November. However, it was the interruption in the supply of semi-luxuries (coffee, sugar) that triggered the first urban crowd disturbances. Ever since the summer the plantations on the French Caribbean island of Saint-Domingue had been convulsed by a slave revolt. The consequence was a sharp increase in prices and, by mid-January 1791, repeated invasions of grocers' shops in order to commandeer the commodities in question and sell them off at a 'fair' price (*taxation populaire*). Urban rioting broke out again in February and observers noted particularly the leading role played by women drawn from the *faubourgs* of Saint-Antoine and Saint-Marcel to the east and southeast of the city. The disturbances served notice on the deputies that after an interval of fourteen months the Paris 'crowd' was on an active footing once more and could easily be politicized by problems related to provisioning and food supply. In fact, ordinary Parisians by no means confined their activism to matters of daily subsistence. In March, Pauline Léon, the daughter of an artisan chocolate maker and a regular at the Cordeliers Club, read out a petition before the Assembly calling for the right of women to organize their own national guard units.

The situation was becoming just as precarious in the countryside around the capital, and also in the south of the country. Large-scale peasant disturbances broke out in the Beauce that same month, resulting in the death of the mayor of Etampes at the hands of a riotous crowd when he refused to put controls on bread prices. In the southwest, the prime source of frustration was the failure to legislate a clean break with the seigneurial regime as we have seen. Attacks on chateaux resumed, prompting Georges Couthon – a radical invalid lawyer elected in September – to warn his fellow deputies that the revolution was running the risk of forfeiting the support of the rural masses.

But all eyes in the capital were fixed on the prospect of war. Even the disturbances occasioned by shortages and the faltering value of the *assignats* died down as the event approached. For Robespierre and his small band of suspicious democrats (**Couthon, Danton, Desmoulins, Billaud-Varenne**, etc.) the dangers inherent in Brissot's reckless sabre-rattling were demonstrated by the fact that the king's ministers, and also the Court, had swung round in favour of war. The Comte de Narbonne, a distinguished career soldier who had been appointed Minister of War in December 1791, was probably hoping that a military promenade in the Rhineland would bring the generals to the fore. They could then use their military muscle to enforce an alteration to the trajectory of the revolution in a manner more favourable to the monarch. The Court, by contrast, was desperate for a military intervention on almost any terms, even one led by *émigrés*. Louis wrote personally to Frederick William II of Prussia to seek help and Marie-Antoinette asked her brother to come to her aid. Evidence of rudimentary counter-revolutionary plotting inside the country was also coming to light, with the southern uplands of the Massif Central and the West the main theatres of unrest at this juncture. The deputies, who were starting to develop a conspiratorial cast of mind, riposted. On 9 February they made the first move towards a seizure of *émigré* property in France.

The sudden and unexpected death of the Habsburg Emperor on 1 March removed one of last remaining barriers to the outbreak of hostilities, particularly when the king dismissed his Feuillant ministers and replaced them with a cabinet of allies of the Brissotins (**Dumouriez**, Clavière, Roland, Servan, etc.) instead. The new Minister of Foreign Affairs, Dumouriez, was a professional soldier with a taste for politics – exactly the breed Robespierre and his band of democrats so distrusted. On 20 April 1792, the Assembly voted overwhelmingly, and in the presence of Louis XVI, to declare war on the new Emperor Francis II. Since Prussia was now in alliance with Austria, Frederick William II riposted with a declaration of his own a month or so later.

The fall of the monarchy

As Louis Becquey – one of the few deputies to vote against the motion for war – predicted would happen, the constitutional settlement reached only seven months earlier now began to unravel at alarming speed. Although Britain, Holland and Spain would not join in the conflict until the following year, France found herself diplomatically isolated. Prussia was now firmly attached to Austria and Marie-Antoinette had taken steps to ensure that Dumouriez's plans for a thrust into the Belgian provinces were known in Vienna. Moreover, as Robespierre had anticipated, France's state of military preparedness left much to be desired and the country appeared to have been thrown on the mercy of ambitious generals.

What no one anticipated, however, was the extent to which war would alter the implicit social contract on which the revolution had rested until this point. If the regenerated nation was about to ask ordinary French men to make a blood sacrifice, something would have to be offered in return. From the spring of 1792, therefore, fictions such as the active/passive citizenship distinction that were designed to keep the 'people' at arm's length began to look out of place. So, too, did an approach to government that concentrated on matters of 'high politics' to the exclusion of day-to-day concerns such as food shortages and hoarding, inflation, taxation and land hunger. Ordinary Parisians were already infiltrating and democratizing the bottom tiers of local law enforcement (the **Sections**; the national guard), and the crisis of the summer would show that they alone had the energy required to move the revolution forward. The task facing the new Brissotin ministry was how to adjust to these developments while keeping in step with events on the frontiers.

To judge from the letters of the printer-publisher Nicolas Ruault to his brother, the first reports of military reverses around Lille and Valenciennes started to reach the capital in the early days of May. Rosalie Jullien, who seems to have been a semi-permanent fixture in the spectator gallery of the Assembly, confirmed as much. In a regular correspondence with her husband and son she linked the bad news from the front to the activities of an 'Austrian committee' at Court (Lockroy, 1881: 96–101). As one of the institutions most closely associated with the *ancien régime*, the army had found it particularly difficult to adjust to the values of the revolution. There had been violent mutinies in several parts of the kingdom and by the start of 1792 about a third of the officer corps had resigned their commissions. Many were nobles of course who had not merely quit, but emigrated. Ruault's missives would pass on two more scraps of information: the Flemings had not risen, as expected, to welcome French forces, and Lafayette's army encamped at Metz had neither advanced nor retreated. Despite the critical voices being raised against this general, he felt it necessary to add: 'I am far from believing [him] a traitor' (Ruault, 1976: 284). Nevertheless, the spectacle of aristocratic officers defecting in some numbers, and the realization that French troop movements had been betrayed, caused accusations of treachery to fly in all directions. While calling for volunteers to be rushed to the front, the deputies lashed out with punitive measures against the non-oath-swearing priests and the royal bodyguard. In addition, they summoned 20,000 provincial national guardsmen – known as *fédérés* – to Paris in order to protect the Assembly, whether from the threat of a military *coup* or an armed intervention of the Paris Sections.

The 48 Sections were the municipal subdivisions of the capital. They had replaced the 60 electoral districts whose existence had been formally recognized in 1790. Each possessed a deliberative body and organs of control and repression, and although the political complexion of the Sections tended to vary, some were becoming vehicles for popular militancy. Ruault had observed in February that the well-to-do were withdrawing from the assemblies of the Sections, leaving the field of action open to shopkeepers, artisans and workmen. As a result, the socio-economic agenda underpinning popular militancy began to come to the surface. There were calls for corn prices to be fixed (the **Maximum**) in both Paris and Lyons; and in May **Jacques Roux**, a future spokesman for the *enragés*, demanded that hoarding be made punishable by death. Dr Guillotin's new beheading machine had been brought into service the previous month, it is true. Although the apparatus was impressive to look at, Pierre-François Palloy reported that Parisians found its action rather too swift compared with hanging by the neck.

With help apparently close at hand, the king took the risk of withholding his consent to the deportation legislation directed against non-jurors and to the proposal for a *fédéré* encampment. In fact, he dismissed most of his Brissotin ministers on 13 June – a move that finally persuaded Ruault to abandon all illusions and to conclude that a mixed constitution was unattainable. Lafayette's violent letter of denunciation aimed at the Jacobin Club shattered another illusion: Rosalie Jullien described it as 'having the smell of a despot' (Lockroy, 1881: 131). The scene was now set for a confrontation with the monarch – unless of course the Austrians and the Prussians reached Paris first. A massive, broad-based demonstration organized by the militants of the eastern Sections on 20 June, and no doubt aided by the Brissotins who wanted to get themselves back into office, failed to sway Louis. He agreed to don the red bonnet of liberty that had become the fashion throughout the capital, but refused to withdraw his veto. Eventually Pétion, the mayor, came to the rescue and ordered that the demonstrators be cleared from the Tuileries Palace.

The clock of insurrection was now ticking, though, and everyone looked to the deputies of the Legislative Assembly for a lead. Yet the deputies were paralyzed by constitutional scruples and turned a deaf ear to the calls for the king to abdicate. With the Court on one side and the Sections on the other, they had very little room for manœuvre to be sure. Exasperated, General Lafayette came back to Paris in the hope of galvanizing the Assembly into taking action against the Jacobin Club and the street-level militants who had organized the *journée* of 20 June. But if many of the deputies and a large swathe of the national guard were alarmed by the tide of events, they were even more alarmed by the prospect of military dictatorship. Lafayette returned empty-handed to his army and, a week after the fall of the house of Bourbon, defected to the Austrians.

The insurrection that finally produced the dethronement of Louis XVI could have happened at any point from late July onwards. The distinction between 'active' and 'passive' citizenship was collapsing, the *fédérés* were arriving in droves irrespective of the royal veto, and individuals who are hard to identify were making contingency plans for an uprising which would take the form of an outright attack on the royal palace. The only uncertainties lay at the higher organizational level: what roles, if any, would the Brissotin deputies play, or radical figureheads such as Robespierre, **Marat** and Pétion? By the end of that month, nearly all of the Sections had expressed an opinion in favour of abdication, whether obtained by legislative action or physical force. An abortive call to arms occurred on the night of 26–27 July and there was another false start on the night of 4–5 August. Threats issued by the commander-in-chief of the advancing Austro-Prussian forces (the so-called **Brunswick Manifesto**) served only to make matters more tense and, on 6 August, a meeting of *fédéré* and Sectional chiefs warned the Assembly of what lay in store if it did not act immediately. Rosalie Jullien, who had switched attendance from the Assembly to the Jacobin Club, advised her son that violence was unavoidable and imminent – 'it is going to rain blood, I am not exaggerating' (Lockroy, 1881: 213).

The deputies' reluctance even to start proceedings against Lafayette was the last straw. During the night of 9–10 August, bells sounded the tocsin all over Paris and delegates from the Sections converged on the Hôtel de Ville where they ousted the legally constituted municipality [**Doc. 15**]. Mayor Pétion was confined to his room. This insurrectionary General Staff then directed battalions of national guardsmen towards the Tuileries Palace, which was defended by Swiss guardsmen, an assortment of nobles and a body of national-guard volunteers drawn from the more affluent Sections of western Paris. The king and the queen found safety in the chamber of the Legislative Assembly before the fighting started. By 11.30 on the morning of 10 August, it was all over. Several hundred assailants and defenders were killed in the exchanges of gunfire, and perhaps as many as 600 Swiss guardsmen were massacred subsequently.

The *journée* of 10 August 1792 amounted to a fresh start as was widely recognized at the time. James Price, an American merchant who witnessed the event, noted in his travel journal that the men and women of Paris had 'begun a Second revolution' (Chew, 2012: 98). The uprising marked the end of the experiment with constitutional monarchy; it marked the beginnings of partnership government between the bourgeois elite of the old Third Estate who had inherited power in 1789 and the people; and, in the view of some historians, it signalled the onset of the Terror. For the next six weeks or so, France scarcely had a properly constituted government. Politically bankrupt, the Legislative Assembly gave up any pretence of independence and awaited its replacement. Two days after his second departure from the Tuileries Palace, Louis was placed in detention, together with his queen and their two surviving children. That ever-obliging handyman of the revolution, Pierre-François Palloy, was called in – first to put out the fires still raging at the scene of the fighting, and then to fit up makeshift central heating in the gloomy

La Jolie sans Culotte armée en Guerre.

Figure 4.1 A female sans-culotte
© Photo 12/Alamy Stock Photo CW8X4M

Temple prison so as to provide the royal family with a modicum of physical comfort. Louis's next move would be to the scaffold. In the capital, meanwhile, nearly everyone accepted the inevitability of the abolition of the monarchy and the proclamation of a republic, but Ruault spoke for many when he asked himself: 'Are we fit, are we worthy enough to be republicans?' (Ruault, 1976: 303). For many educated French men and women, the idea of a republic could scarcely be grasped outside the pages of classical authors.

Partnership with the people took two forms: the presence of the people's spokesmen in government and the issuing of overdue legislation that finally addressed the hopes and fears of ordinary town and country dwellers. In the aftermath of the uprising, the Insurrectionary Commune (as the municipal body representing the Sections became known) could see no reason why it should play second fiddle to a discredited Assembly which had been elected indirectly and by 'active' citizens alone. For six long weeks, therefore, it held power alongside an interim executive body in which Georges Danton, playing the role of Minister of Justice, was the moving force. Only when new deputies had been chosen on the basis of universal manhood suffrage would the municipal authorities of Paris return, reluctantly, to their normal sphere of activity. Chastened by the experience of 10 August, the deputies dutifully passed ameliorative legislation under the watchful gaze of the Insurrectionary Commune. Virtually all outstanding feudal dues were now abolished without compensation and orders were given for the partition of common land and the sale of *émigré* property in small and more easily affordable parcels. The responsibility for the registration of births, marriages and deaths passed from the clergy to the municipalities and, on 20 September, a law was passed to enable divorce by mutual consent (Phillips, 1981: 11–12). There was also some easing of policy on the contentious question of the food supply and price controls, although even the most radical deputies and their allies in the Commune and the clubs were not prepared at this stage to compromise the principle of freedom in the economic sphere.

In his letter of 28 August 1792, Ruault pondered the implications of the fact that the first guillotinings on a charge of 'royalism' pure and simple had just taken place. There can be little dispute that the revolution crossed a civil rights frontier during that summer. Words like 'suspect' and 'aristocrat', or indeed 'royalist', had acquired connotations of subversion that would have made very little sense back in 1789 or 1790. Guilt by association, or by social category, was starting to become acceptable. Hundreds of Swiss defenders of the palace had been killed *after* the fighting on 10 August – that is to say, in acts of reprisal and exemplary public 'justice'. The same would happen again in Paris (and several provincial towns) early in September as murderous squads went around the prisons and systematically emptied them of their 'political' prisoners (nobles, non-oath-swearing priests, alleged counter-revolutionaries, etc.), not to mention a number of common criminals. European governments were appalled by these massacres; even more so than by the dethronement of King Louis XVI. As for Ruault, on 8 September he told his brother that he had stepped in puddles of human blood in the courtyard of the former abbey and now prison of Saint-Germain.

Citizenship and the colonies

Bourbon France had colonies in both the Caribbean and the Indian Ocean. They were exploited using slave labour on plantation estates which produced tropical foodstuffs (sugar, coffee, spices) for European consumers, and supplies for passing vessels. In the case of the Caribbean possessions (principally Saint-Domingue, Guadeloupe, Martinique and French Guiana), the bulk of the workforce consisted of enslaved blacks shipped from ports on the west coast of Africa, along with their descendants. Saint-Domingue (the western third of the island of Hispaniola) had been ceded to France by Spain in 1697 and was a precious colonial asset as we have noted. In the second half of the eighteenth century, it was the source of half of the sugar and coffee traded in Europe and has been described as the western world's most lucrative piece of real estate. Although they were less valuable possessions, France would maintain her grip on Guadeloupe and Martinique as well. In fact, she would give up the whole of the Canadian province of Quebec at the conclusion of the Seven Years War in 1763 in order to retrieve them from British occupation.

As for France's colonies beyond the Cape of Good Hope, that is, to the east of the southern tip of Africa, they consisted of two islands (Ile Bourbon and Ile-de-France) and a number of territorial enclaves in the Indian subcontinent: Chandernagore, Pondichéry, Karikal, Yanam and Mahé (see Map 0.5). Like the Caribbean possessions, they tended to change hands quite frequently in accordance with the ebb and flow of Franco-British rivalry on land and on sea. Whilst slavery and plantation agriculture were issues here, too, France's policy objectives in the Indian Ocean were mainly strategic. The wealth extracted from her Indian islands and **'factories'** on the Indian mainland was modest compared with the contribution of the Greater Antilles. At the end of the *ancien régime*, Ile Bourbon (Réunion) had an enslaved population drawn mainly from Madagascar and East Africa that was four times larger than its resident white population, and on Ile-de-France (Mauritius) the disparity was greater still. However, the plantation economies of both islands came to rely increasingly on indentured labour from the subcontinent. As for the French 'factories', their population was quite mixed, but included far fewer slaves. In 1777 the territory of Pondichéry, for example, contained about 1,100 white Europeans, nearly a thousand mixed race *topas* and around 27,000 inhabitants of south Indian ethnicity.

Since Saint-Domingue would emerge from the revolutionary cycle as the independent black republic of Haiti whereas the Indian Ocean colonies mostly succumbed to British imperialism, it is to here that we should go first (see Map 0.4). This extraordinary development came to pass in 1804 and has been described as one of the events that helped to define the modern world (Popkin, 2007: 1). By 1789, the fertile coastal plain and lower mountain slopes of Saint-Domingue had been covered with plantations which necessitated the importation of around 30,000 slaves each year in order to maintain and expand production. The total population of the colony by this date probably amounted to a little over half a million (523,000), of whom 89 per cent were slaves, about 6 per cent whites and 5 per cent of mixed race (**gens de couleur**). The latter were an intermediate population between the free whites and the enslaved majority. Although of African descent for the most part, they were legally free, often educated and fluent in French. In fact, many had become land owners, and some even owned slaves. Yet they suffered disabilities *vis-à-vis* the whites and were discriminated against even before revolution broke out in the metropole.

Guadeloupe and Martinique were much smaller, but, with tiny white populations, their racial make-up was not dissimilar to that of Saint-Domingue, or for
that matter the Indian Ocean islands. French Guiana, by contrast, was very
thinly inhabited, yet still about 86 per cent enslaved (Régent, 2015).

Contrary to what we might suppose, Enlightenment authors did not pay
much attention to the issue of colonial slavery. This, despite the fact they
acknowledged the iniquities of serfdom as a form of human bondage in the old
world and called for the recognition of civil rights throughout Europe. Hence
the paradox: the institution of slavery and the slave-driven economic system
being developed in the Caribbean and the Indian Ocean were consolidated at a
time when 'freedom' had become the watchword not only of *philosophes*, but
of reform-minded government ministers as well. This paradox was not unique
to France, of course. Britain, Spain and Portugal also possessed colonial empires
which were substantially reliant on slave labour. However, in Britain domestic
public opinion had been sensitized to the issue of slavery in the late 1770s and
within a few years campaigns to boycott the consumption of sugar were afoot.
We find nothing of the sort in *ancien-régime* France. In fact, the Société des
Amis des Noirs, founded in Paris by the future revolutionary politician Jacques
Pierre Brissot, did not come into being until the start of 1788 and was chiefly
inspired by the activities of the British abolitionists, not least the Quakers.

In any case, Brissot's Society of Friends of the Blacks focused primarily on
the need to recognize the claims of *gens de couleur* to rights; the emancipation
of enslaved blacks was a very distant campaign objective and one, moreover,
which produced virtually no echo when the *cahiers de doléances* were being
drawn up. Enslavement of fellow human beings was understood primarily in
moral terms: it had yet to acquire an explicitly racial logic. Nevertheless, the
notion of 'whiteness' as a qualifying attribute of citizenship did make some
headway in the Caribbean in the aftermath of the Seven Years War (Burnard
and Garrigus, 2016: 3). In Saint-Domingue, planters pushed through measures
that attached greater weight to race than to wealth or socio-legal status. In
India, by contrast, the colonial elite seem to have been more relaxed about race.
When the revolution broke, they showed greater flexibility in dealing with the
hopes and ambitions of ethnically diverse native populations. The *topas* of
Pondichéry, for example, were not automatically excluded from the franchise
(Carton, 2008: 597).

The debate about slavery in France only really started with the meeting of the
Estates General, then. Yet it would raise important questions about the meaning of citizenship under the new order. Reports of what was happening in the
metropole reached the Caribbean with a delay of up to three months and the
first issue to arise was that of representation. Should the colonies be represented
by deputies of their own and, if so, who exactly was entitled to a political
presence in Versailles (or Paris) – resident whites only, or the scarcely less
numerous *gens de couleur* as well? That said, however, rumours had begun to
circulate on the island of Martinique that the outright abolition of slavery had
been proclaimed by the king in the Estates General. This was not true; nor had

the deputies who made up the National Constituent Assembly any intention of taking this step. A proposal put forward on the night of 4 August to abolish slavery had been ignored, while the Declaration of the Rights of Man and the Citizen promulgated several weeks later was never envisaged as applying to the colonies. Yet a consensus of opinion that seemed relatively secure in Versailles and Paris looked anything but that on the spot. The tiny white minorities subdivided into supporters and opponents of the changes being ushered in, whilst mixed race inhabitants spotted an opportunity to exploit the rhetoric of revolution in order to obtain citizenship for themselves, if not for the enslaved majority.

After all, the rhetoric of revolution applied universally did it not? What did 'Men are born, and always continue, free, and equal in respect of their rights' [Doc. 10] mean otherwise? Subaltern groups in France's colonies were not alone in supposing that laws and manifestos should be taken at face value, it should be said. After 4 August 1789 French peasants drew the conclusion that the feudal regime had been entirely abolished for identical reasons. The deputies of the National Assembly might have been certain in their own minds about the limits attaching to their policies, but these limits still had to be understood and explained by officials on the ground. When the tricolour cockade reached Guadeloupe in September 1789, it was adopted with enthusiasm by younger creoles. After some misgivings on the part of the colonial administration, mixed race inhabitants were *not* prevented from wearing this emblem of liberty either. However, the governor warned of severe penalties should the slave population choose to do the same. It is fair to say that in Paris the important role which free people of colour played in the colonies was not well understood and, of course, the planters' representatives had little interest in clarifying it. Those white planters who were prepared to acknowledge the metropole's revolution nonetheless argued that its legislation had no jurisdiction over internal arrangements in the colonies that had grown up over many years in response to highly specific conditions. As for the Indian Ocean territories the news from the metropole took much longer to penetrate – up to six months. Pondichéry learned of the events surrounding the taking of the Bastille in late January 1790 when a vessel put into port and the crew distributed national cockades.

The confusion and heat generated whenever the Assemblies proceeded to debate colonial issues are scarcely to be wondered at, therefore. Throughout 1790, the campaign by *gens de couleur* to enlarge the definition of citizenship produced contradictory results in Paris. It was followed by a brief uprising in Saint-Domingue at the end of that year. Then, in May 1791, a partial concession of civil and political rights to free blacks passed through the National Assembly [Doc. 21], albeit in the teeth of opposition from white colonists and their supporters. However, this rather mealy-mouthed acknowledgement that race was not, after all, a fundamental impediment to French citizenship did not hold for long. The Saint-Domingue planter lobby managed to obtain the repeal of the law in the dying days of the legislature (24 September 1791). Only in April of the following year was this internecine struggle between the 'free' finally resolved with the granting of full rights to all men of mixed race.

By this stage, though, the context had completely changed because an insurrection of the enslaved majority was under way in Saint-Domingue and the white planters responded by calling on the British for assistance. This massive slave revolt, which began in August 1791, was known about in the metropole by the start of November and was causing shortages in the grocery shops of Paris by early the following year as we have seen. Even though the insurgents were not initially fired with a vision of liberation, it was this long struggle in Saint-Domingue which finally prompted the Convention on 4 February 1794 to emancipate the majority black population with immediate and unconditional effect. A product of the struggle with Britain and with royalism in the Caribbean, the decree owed more to *realpolitik* than to the undiluted application of Enlightenment benevolence.

In constitutional matters the Indian Ocean colonies were content to let the well-resourced planters of Saint-Domingue make the running in the metropole. Enslavement was much less of an issue in the Indian enclaves and with pressure being exerted by the British in Bengal, colonial elites were willing to go through the motions of banning the transportation of Indian child slaves. This affected Pondichéry much less than the 'factory' of Mahé on the Malabar coast which had a good harbour. The slave-based plantation economy was the very life blood of Ile Bourbon (Réunion) and Ile-de-France (Mauritius), on the other hand. Between 1791 and 1793 captains of slave ships brought in another 5,000 and, by one route or another, the servile population continued to increase throughout the revolutionary decade. On the eve of the islands' occupation by Britain in 1810 the combined slave population totalled almost 133,000 (Allen, 2015: 14). As for the planters, they had made it abundantly clear to Paris in 1790 that they would not countenance any move towards abolition. They were therefore appalled to receive the emancipation decree in August 1794, packaged with an inflammatory address calling on the islands' Jacobin militants to treat wealthy landowners as public enemies [**Doc. 22**]. The colonial authorities simply refused to implement the decree and when enforcement commissioners were sent out a couple of years later, they were beaten back by a riot. Privateers, meanwhile, continued to bring in slaves disguised as general cargo.

Perhaps we should not be too surprised by this outcome, for the notion of citizenship would evolve in the metropole as well. Following the removal of the *ancien-régime* disabilities attaching to 'foreigner' status, anyone choosing to reside in France was automatically considered to be a naturalized citizen. This much extended and largely voluntarist conception of citizenship was underlined in the Constitution of 1791 which abolished the requirement for passports. The ultimate expression of revolutionary cosmopolitanism can be found in the 'philosophical' naturalizations of August 1792 which bestowed citizenship on a number of worthy Europeans who had 'developed human reason and prepared the path of liberty' (Perović, 2012: 97), even though *non*-resident. The Prussian Anacharsis Cloots and several eminent Englishmen (Tom Paine, Joseph Priestley and Jeremy Bentham) counted among them. But by this date the legislation targeting *émigrés* and the pressures of war were already beginning to chip away at the inclusive vision of citizenship. Quakers whose commitment to brotherly love appeared to make them ideal citizens had discovered that their refusal to accept marks of distinction, to swear oaths or to bear arms excluded them from citizenship. Their spokesman Jean de Marsillac was arrested in 1792 when walking the streets of Paris without a cockade (Banks, 2017: 375). In any case passport controls were soon reintroduced on the grounds of public security and, as the war turned into a struggle for survival, the rhetoric of the nation-in-arms and suspicion of the foreigner tested to destruction the idea of a dawning age of universal brotherhood. By the time of Napoleon, the revolutionary concept of citizenship was slipping into oblivion. The Convention's decree granting slaves their freedom was reversed in 1802 amid a scientific propaganda campaign intended to underline the 'natural' inferiority of the black race (Chappey, 2015: 562).

5 War and terror, 1792–94

The deputies of the Legislative Assembly concluded their business on 20 September 1792, all too aware that they had failed to steer the revolution into calmer waters. Indeed, many abandoned their posts before that date. Having held power – ingloriously – for barely twelve months, most of them would be relegated to the footnotes of history. The revolution was heading into uncharted waters on which few vessels of state had sailed before.

At least there no longer existed any constitutional obstacle to prevent the most experienced and talented legislators and former legislators from assembling on the bridge. The National Convention, as the new legislature was called, would contain a large contingent of representatives (269) who had sat before, whether in the first or the second Assembly. Thus, Robespierre, Pétion, Sieyès, **Buzot, Merlin de Douai** and **Reubell**, to name only those already launched on significant careers, returned to office, while the mandates of Brissot, Vergniaud and Couthon were renewed without interruption. On the benches of the old royal riding school which had served as the debating chamber since November 1789, they were joined by men who had yet to become national and international figures: the young **Saint-Just**; Danton, who had resigned as a minister; Desmoulins and Marat, the fiery street-level journalists; Fabre d'Eglantine and **Collot d'Herbois**, both dramatists; and **Billaud-Varenne**. But would these individuals be able to work together? Many of those named had been chosen by the electorate of Paris, and their past went ahead of them so to speak. Some were Cordeliers militants who had graduated to the Jacobin Club; a few were suspected of involvement in the prison massacres which had taken place earlier in the month. How would they respond to the pressures for partnership in government? The democratization of public life that was now under way implied a radical revision of policy objectives. After all, about a million formerly 'passive' citizens now had the vote. Then there was the question of 'terror': should it be employed solely as a means of preserving the nation from its lengthening list of enemies, or as a tool with which to forge a new and purer society?

A Jacobin republic

The decision to turn France into a republic was taken in about a quarter of an hour at the inaugural session of the National Convention while most of the

DOI: 10.4324/9781003156185-7

deputies were still making their way to the capital. We can assume that the Paris electoral delegation – stalwart Jacobins almost to a man – played the major role, although there is no reason to suppose that Brissot and his allies were opposed to the move. All the contenders for power were members of the Jacobin Club at this stage in any case, and it would be several months before definable political groupings emerged in the new legislature.

The threat of an invasion was still real as the new deputies hastened to Paris. The Austrians had almost cut off Lille and everyone was anticipating a long-drawn-out siege. Reinforcements were called up and patriotism surged throughout the departments of the north. When Charlotte Biggs paid a call on her milliner in Amiens, she found her rehearsing the words of the new battle anthem of the revolution – the **Marseillaise** – while she worked (Biggs, 1797: vol. 1, 131). But relief came unexpectedly in late September when the balance of military operations suddenly shifted in favour of France and the Brissotin war party. Generals Kellermann and Dumouriez halted the advance of Prussian forces at Valmy, a village a few miles to the west of Sainte-Menehould. Since the enemy chose to withdraw after the action, the French went onto the offensive and, by the end of October, Dumouriez was able to cross over the border and into the Austrian Netherlands, while General Custine in the east proceeded to occupy the German Rhineland. At Jemappes on 6 November an infinitely greater battle was fought – and won – that threw open Belgium and even the Netherlands to the advancing French forces. Meanwhile, another army under General Montesquieu occupied Savoy and Nice. After the setbacks and disappointments of the previous spring, the liberationist rhetoric spouted by Brissot seemed to be taking on substance at last and his popularity soared.

Yet even the encouraging news from the frontiers could not disguise the fact that the people's representatives were far from united. Many of the newly arrived deputies found the radical atmosphere of Paris to be deeply troubling and they were particularly incensed by the 'insolence' of the Sections, whose experience of power-broking during the summer had whetted political appetites. Ruault remarked upon the intimidating climate in his own Section where militants were insisting on 'out loud' voting. In the Convention, Buzot attributed the effervescence to the deputies of the Paris delegation and even went so far as to suggest that the legislature would be unable to deliberate freely if it remained in Paris. This was the germ of a subversive idea, for it expressed a widespread feeling in the country that the Parisian populace were taking over the revolution – heedless of the fact that they only constituted a tiny fraction of the 'sovereign' nation. A game of blame for the September Massacres increased the strain, as did the question of the fate of the king. These tensions would be instrumental in the gradual 'separating out' of the Convention into two mutually antagonistic wings (known as the Girondins and the **Montagnards**), plus a large body of uncommitted deputies (known as the Plain). According to the well-connected Rosalie Jullien, Girondins and Montagnards were united in their attachment to the republic, but differed over the degree to which it should be focused on the needs of the poor and dispossessed (Lockroy, 1881: 303).

In prison and dethroned, Louis's person appeared to be inviolable unless it could be demonstrated that he had broken his oath to the Constitution. However, the Constitution of 1791 no longer existed in practice. Moreover, compromising evidence had come to light of potentially treasonous correspondence between Louis (and Marie-Antoinette) and foreign Powers. A trial appeared to be the proper solution, although many questioned whether such a straightforward procedure might not become a dangerous hostage to political fortune. What court of law could be considered competent to judge a king, albeit an ex-king, in whose name the law itself had been administered until 10 August? What fate lay in store for those who had overthrown the monarchy if Louis were found to be innocent of the charges laid against him? And what if he were found guilty? The penalty prescribed for treason was death. The deputy Saint-Just, in his maiden speech, argued that the office of kingship was inherently culpable, and Robespierre agreed that the only question requiring deliberation was not the verdict but the sentence. In the light of the September prison massacres, Louis himself had no illusions as to his fate and expected death to come by one route or another. Nevertheless, the majority of the deputies concluded that a trial *was* necessary and that only the legislative body was competent to serve as the court. The trial of Louis Capet, formerly King of the French, began on 10 December and he was found guilty of treason. After procedural manœuvres, first to refer sentencing to the electorate (the *appel au peuple*) and then to suspend the death penalty, had failed, Louis was decapitated on 21 January 1793. The patriot Palloy celebrated the event that same evening by consuming a meal of stuffed pig's head with his family.

The behaviour of Brissot, Buzot, Vergniaud, Roland and company during the ballots on sentencing raised a suspicion that they had wanted to save Louis. Only one of the future Girondin leaders (Barbaroux) voted for death without a reprieve. As a result, the trial greatly exacerbated the factionalism afflicting the Convention. On 6 February 1793 Nicolas Ruault reported to his brother: 'We now have two sorts of Jacobins or patriots who hate each other as desperately as the original Jacobins and royalists used to hate each other. The latest kind of Jacobins refer to themselves as Girondins, or Brissotins or Rolandists' (Ruault, 1976: 324). In fact, there is not much reason to suppose that the latter were camouflaged moderates on this or any other issue. For as long as the war effort continued to go forward smoothly, the Gironde could expect to remain in the ascendant in the Convention. As yet, none of the newly assembled deputies was showing much interest in the street-level political agenda which was largely economic in content. In September, it is true they had momentarily flinched in their ideological commitment to economic freedom, but once the armies of the republic had moved on to foreign soil the argument for some kind of centralized control of prices and provisioning lost all purchase.

Thus, when a fresh round of attacks on Paris grocery stores materialized in February 1793 Robespierre and Marat – supposedly the deputies closest to the common people – dismissed the calls for a price 'ceiling', or Maximum, to be applied to commodities of everyday consumption in the same vein as everyone else. This was a thoughtless response, for it implied that the overwhelmingly

bourgeois deputies had not yet grasped the implications of the 'second revolution' of 10 August if they supposed that a popular front could be maintained on
a diet of military expansionism and repressive legislation against priests and
émigrés alone. If no one was willing to speak on their behalf in the Convention,
the Sections were quite capable of finding leaders of their own. These *enragés*
(Roux, Varlet, Leclerc, etc.), as their opponents dubbed them, were no respec-
ters of persons or reputations and as tension increased between the Gironde and
the Mountain, it became apparent that they could not be ignored indefinitely.

Reactions in the departments

The shocks administered to provincial public opinion since the events of the
summer of 1792 should not be underestimated. Although peasant unrest subsided
nearly everywhere once the feudal regime had finally been laid to rest, small-town
Jacobins found themselves embarked on a steep learning curve. They were
expected to swallow, in rapid succession, the abolition of the monarchy, the
proclamation of the republic, and then the trial and execution of Louis XVI. The
correspondence of Louis Louchet, a little-known deputy sent to sit in the Convention by the voters of the department of the Aveyron (see Map 0.2),
allows us to plumb the political fissure which was now opening up between
Paris and the provinces. The persistent silence of the local authorities of
Rodez spoke volumes and in October, Louchet pleaded with them to issue
an 'energetic and laconic' address congratulating the Convention on its
decision to proclaim a republic (Louchet, 1792–94). More coaxing letters
were required to induce the Rodez Jacobin Club to accept the authority of
the supreme legislative body in the matter of the trial of the ex-monarch; to
allay its fears that even oath-swearing clergy were now under threat; and in
due course to persuade club members that the Parisian insurrection of 31
May–2 June 1793 had been carried out in the public interest.

The pace of events was also testing loyalties in the great cities, particularly in
centres such as Lyons, Marseilles and Bordeaux where the regeneration of
France as a single, undifferentiated nation had severely dented regional pride.
Bordeaux had not done well out of the administrative reforms of 1789–90. The
legal bourgeoisie considered the city's role as the administrative seat of the new
department of the Gironde to be poor compensation for the loss of their ancient
Parlement, while the merchant community reacted with understandable alarm
when, in February and March, the Convention added to the list of enemies with
declarations of war against both Britain and Spain.

March was a critical month on several fronts in fact. The momentum of
French military success in the Low Countries was finally halted when the Austrians counter-attacked and forced the evacuation of Aix-la-Chapelle.
Dumouriez, the general whose victories had earned the Brissotins huge political
capital, was badly beaten at Neerwinden on 18 March. His desertion to the
enemy a few days later, having failed to persuade his army to march on Paris
and restore the monarchy, did immense damage to all those who had harnessed

their political fortunes to Brissot's policy of military adventurism over the previous year or so. The populations of the northeastern departments, Louchet noted with relief and satisfaction, remained utterly unmoved in the face of Dumouriez's blandishments. In the west, however, the news was less reassuring, for the activities of recruitment officers seeking to bolster the strength of the army had provoked a rash of riotous incidents.

The deputies were too preoccupied to pay much attention to these outbreaks at first. However, by April it was becoming apparent that a rural counter-revolution centred on the department of the *Vendée* (see Map 0.2) was in the making. It was in this context of crisis at home and abroad that much of the institutional fabric of the Terror came to be put in place. On 9 March, the Convention voted to send out around 80 deputies as ***représentants en mission*** to 'revolutionize' the departments – in other words, to enforce the vision of the revolution as perceived in Paris. The following day a special court (the Revolutionary Tribunal) was set up to try conspirators. On 21 March, police committees (*comités de surveillance*) with powers of summary arrest were enacted; on 26 March, the disarmament of so-called 'suspects'. Then, on 6 April, a powerful new body which blurred legislative and executive responsibilities – the Committee of Public Safety – was brought into being.

In sullen or disaffected departments, the arrival of *représentants en mission* often proved to be the last straw. François Chabot and Jean-Baptiste Bo, two colleagues of Louchet who were sent out to the Aveyron and the Tarn departments strutted around like pro-consuls, commandeering whatever they needed, arresting and imprisoning individuals on the slightest pretext. The legally constituted authorities were powerless to intervene, for an emergency concept of law-and-order that was rooted in considerations of 'public safety' was starting to take over, and it had no time for procedural niceties. Indeed, the highly decentralized local government system that committees of the National Assembly had devised in 1789–90 now appeared to be a luxury that the revolution could barely afford. In a sense, therefore, the provincial reaction to any further browbeating of deputies by the militants of the Paris Sections would not have been too difficult to predict. In his letters of April and May, Louchet mingled indignation at the military reverses, reassurances as to the freedom of action of the Convention, and veiled comments that certain deputies appeared to lack the stamina for the stern measures that the political situation now demanded.

In fact, it is unlikely that the tacticians of the Mountain had any more desire than the Gironde to enlist the populace of Paris in their feud. Yet they were in a parliamentary minority as Louchet acknowledged on 6 May in a letter to the Jacobins of Rodez – not least because the bulk of the roving *représentants en mission* had been selected from among their ranks. In the end, it was Robespierre and his closest associates who took the gamble and accepted, with misgivings, the help of the Sections to engineer a parliamentary coup that could not be achieved by any other means. After an abortive mobilization on 31 May, the armed squadrons of the Sections returned to the task two days later. Compliantly, Couthon drew up a list of deputies who were to be placed under house detention, although few of the individuals named were actually present in the Convention at the time.

The news that on 2 June 1793 the Convention had been forcibly purged of 29 Girondin deputies caused consternation. The 'anarchists' of Paris had got their way again! In what has become known as the Federalist Revolt, perhaps half of the departments in the country expressed varying degrees of annoyance and outrage at the turn of events. Only a handful of local authorities took steps to organize a more concrete and menacing response, though. In Bordeaux, there was a feeble attempt to march an expeditionary force against Paris in a reaction to the outlawing of several of the city's deputies. It proceeded barely 50 kilometres before disbanding. Marseilles, too, despatched an armed force which advanced up the Rhône valley as far as the town of Orange. Potentially more serious was the regrouping of fleeing Girondin deputies in the Norman capital of Caen much closer to Paris, which included François Buzot among others. But troops loyal to the Montagnard Convention removed the threat in mid-July. For all their hostility to the Paris Sections, the great majority of the Federalists had no desire to see the republic overturned, whatever Montagnard propaganda might have asserted to the contrary. Historians discern instead a revolt in defence of local autonomy, exacerbated in departments such as the Aisne by urban rivalries and grievances over the distribution of the benefits of the revolution (Brassart, 2013: 196–231). This stance hampered their effectiveness. Only occasionally – as in the case of Lyons – did Federalists make common cause with counter-revolutionaries. However, such distinctions became almost meaningless once the Terror was up and running.

The proscription of legally elected representatives of the people who had been entitled to parliamentary immunity from prosecution was a grim first for the revolution. However, it is likely that neither side actually willed the lethal outcome of the expulsions. During the *journées* of 31 May–2 June the deputies of the Mountain also felt themselves to be under threat. They showed little desire to pursue their opponents initially, and the situation only seems to have become irretrievable towards the end of June (Whaley, 2000: 155–63). The arrest warrant against Brissot was not issued until three weeks after the intervention of the Sections – by which time most of the proscribed deputies had left Paris. However, the news that some of them were inciting resistance in the departments caused a distinct hardening of opinion in the Convention. The shock of Marat's death on 13 July at the hands of a lone female assassin who, if not a Federalist, came from the Federalist outpost of Normandy, completed this process of embitterment. It was widely assumed that the perpetrator, Charlotte Corday, was the instrument of a counter-revolutionary plot.

Terror and cultural revolution

The abiding image of the Terror is the guillotine. This beheading machine was proposed initially as a humane replacement for hanging, though as we have noted, spectators complained that it delivered death too quickly and failed to ensure that victims suffered. Punishment, suffering and delusional fear were integral to the period of the Terror, the beginnings of which can be traced back to the war emergency and September Massacres in Paris and Versailles (see Part III). But if arbitrary arrest, imprisonment and summary justice were hallmarks of the Terror, it would be wrong to suggest that the whole country succumbed to these phenomena as early as September 1792. The great mass of French men and women did not come into contact with the repressive politics of Terror until the late summer and autumn of 1793, and the abandonment of Terror as a policy of central government can be fairly precisely linked to the aftermath of the upheaval of 9–10 **Thermidor** II (27–28 July 1794) which removed Robespierre and his supporters from the Convention. Although violent repression at the hands of local authorities and *représentants en mission* continued in several regions after this date, in most of the country the liquidation of Robespierre and his faction brought about a relaxation of tension.

What we have termed the 'politics' of the Terror developed informally and without much direction from the centre between August and December 1793. In the Aisne department, for instance, emergency measures were first taken by local administrators on 8 August, a matter of days after the surrender of the fortified town of Valenciennes to the Austrians. They were taken, that is to say, in the absence of a sufficient response from Paris. Terror as a deliberate weapon of government, on the other hand, was chiefly a feature of the late winter, spring and early summer months of 1794. For the so-called Federalists and the many other categories of political 'suspect' that the revolution had left in its wake by this time, the difference was mainly one of emphasis, however. Autumn victims of the Terror were rounded up locally and dealt with locally, but once the institutions of Revolutionary Government had been put in place [**Doc. 18**] victims were more likely to be judged centrally – albeit no less ruthlessly – and within a framework of legal, or quasi-legal, procedure. Perhaps half a million men and women saw the inside of a prison cell during the period of the Terror, and around 16,000 mounted the steps to the guillotine. However, many thousands more were killed during spectacular acts of collective repression, in Lyons, in Toulon and in the villages of western France. The civil war fought in the Vendée has been estimated to have cost between 400,000 and 500,000 lives alone (Linton, 2015: 471) [**Doc. 20**].

Historians have concluded that no one set out consciously to create a regime of Terror. The notion that it was formally declared by the Convention – although widely believed at the time – does not withstand scrutiny (Martin, 2006: 186–93). We are bound, therefore, to ask where this punitive mentality came from and how it came to be incorporated into the apparatus of local and central government. Just as foreign invasion, fear of the 'enemy within', and a general sense of embattlement helped to trigger spasms of killing in September 1792, it can be argued that the threats facing the republic during the summer of 1793 gestated the Terror. Even those historians who believe that extremism and the rejection of compromise were embedded in the revolution from the very start (see Part III) would accept this argument of 'circumstance' to some degree.

There can be no doubting that the situation facing the purged Convention immediately after the near insurrection mounted by the Paris Sections on 31

May–2 June was extremely serious. Throughout June and July, the news reaching the capital was uniformly bad: half of the departments were complaining loudly about the expulsion of the Girondin deputies; the Austrians were preparing to invade from the northeast; the Prussians through Alsace; Vendean rebels were probing the defences of the republic along the river Loire; and British fleets were prowling in the Caribbean and also in the Mediterranean. In Lyons, Marseilles and Toulon, hostility to Jacobinism was positively visceral and, by the late summer, visibly contaminated with counter-revolutionary sentiment. Marseilles would make its peace with the Convention at the eleventh hour, but both Lyons and Toulon broke away from the republic and would only be returned to the fold by force of arms.

Grim tidings on this scale were enough on their own to engage the repressive reflex of the Committee of Public Safety – the nerve centre of government for the next twelve months. But the punitive mentality was also fuelled at street level and the combination of studied savagery from above and impulsive brutality from below created a tension in the Terror that was never entirely resolved. Many years later Marie-Victoire Monnard could still recall her fear and horror on seeing three *sans-culottes* kill a wealthy man in a Paris street. They took his watch and stripped him of his clothes, after which a band of women delighted in taking turns to stamp on the corpse of an 'aristocrat' (Boutanquoi, 1928: 43).

Having enabled the Mountain to take power on 2 June, the militants in the Paris Sections, or *sans-culottes* as they had taken to calling themselves [**Doc. 16**], expected to receive something in return. Indeed, they were prepared to barrack the deputies and even to threaten them with another revolutionary *journée* until they obtained satisfaction. The popular 'programme' had come a long way since the sugar riots of 1792 and now consisted of a relatively sophisticated mix of political and economic demands that depended on public vigilance and inflexible 'justice' – not to say terror – for its enforcement [**Doc. 17**]. The *sans-culottes* clamoured for the expulsion of all the deputies who had voted for the *appel au peuple* after the trial of Louis XVI, the speedy transfer of captured Girondins before the Revolutionary Tribunal, and the arrest of anyone who had signed a motion in support of them. They demanded that the offices of government be purged of former nobles and anyone else who manifestly did not need, or deserve, to be supported by the republic. They wanted the prices of all foodstuffs and articles of everyday use to be fixed invariably. As a deterrent to hoarding, they insisted that the deputies enact a law making the practice punishable by death, and they called for the creation of effective institutions of repression (a blanket 'suspects' law, civilian militias, etc.) that could be mobilized against the economic as well as the political enemies of the people.

Faced with a huge array of responsibilities, not the least of which was the need to keep 750,000 fighting men supplied and in battle order on the frontiers, the Committee of Public Safety preferred to avoid actions that would cause disruption and quite likely increase the number of the nation's adversaries. Yet the Sections were formidably organized by the late summer of 1793 and in no mood to give ground. The news of Toulon's 'great betrayal' (the surrender of this port town to the British Admiral Hood's Mediterranean squadron), which arrived in Paris on 2 September, proved to be the final straw. Three days later, a noisy demonstration that could easily have turned into an insurrection browbeat the Convention into semi-submission. In the days and weeks that followed, most of the demands enshrined in the plan of action that the *enragés* had been the first to formulate and which **Hébert** and his clique had taken over in the late summer, were turned into law.

To all intents and purposes, the Committee of Public Safety was now the executive arm of the revolution, and destined to remain so until such time as peace was restored and conditions made possible the implementation of the new Constitution that had briefly seen the light of day in June 1793. The crisis of early September had taught it a valuable lesson in the art of partnership government. Robespierre replaced Danton as the dominant personality in late July and in September Billaud-Varenne and Collot d'Herbois, two deputies who had spoken in favour of the Terror agenda of the Section militants, were taken on board. It seemed safer to have such men inside the government than on the outside. Thereafter, the composition of the body that controlled the destiny of France for the next eleven months scarcely altered.

That autumn was the heyday of *sans-culotte* power in Paris. An orator speaking on behalf of the Paris Commune called for 'terror' to be made the 'order of the day' and the Sections positively pulsated with militancy and activism. The Convention allowed itself to be swept along on a tide of lethal rhetoric. With Marie-Antoinette, the Duke of Orleans, the Girondins, the Feuillants and the flower of the *ancien-régime* aristocracy queueing at the foot of the scaffold, it would have been quite dangerous for the deputies to have reacted differently. As the Committee of Public Safety had anticipated, acceptance of the popular demands resulted in a substantial loss of control over the nature and direction of the Terror. Only with the enactment of the law of 14 Frimaire (4 December) did it become possible to redress the balance somewhat [**Doc. 18**]. Even so, reasserting control over the Terror as it had evolved in the departments proved to be a protracted and delicate business. The autumn wave of *représentants en mission* and those to whom they had delegated their powers had to be called to order; the excesses of police committees, military commissions and sundry militias curbed; and the chain of command linking the institutions of central and local government reconfigured.

Repression

One of the most grotesque episodes of this 'anarchical' Terror was the **dechristianization** campaign which resulted in the closure of churches in much of the country from November onwards. The trend towards secularization is not difficult to understand, nor is the revolutionaries' impatience with the Catholic Church. By the summer of 1793, even law-abiding, oath-swearing clergy found themselves relegated to the margins of public life, and in October the Christian calendar was replaced with a secular version in which the years were counted from the date of the proclamation of the republic (22 September 1792). But the closing down of churches, the forcible defrocking of priests, forcing ex-nuns to marry and heavy-handed attempts to deny Christian revelation in favour of a state policy of atheism (the worship of 'reason') belonged more to the politics of the Terror and attempts at 'cultural revolution' than to anything that had gone before [**Doc. 19**].

Left to their own devices, the Committee of Public Safety would probably not have countenanced such a policy, and it is significant that the first steps towards the deliberate 'dechristianization' of the republic were taken by deputies 'on mission' in the departments. **Joseph Fouché** began the purge in the department of the Nièvre early in October, ordering local officials to secure the termination of Christian worship in parish churches and to put up notices outside cemeteries proclaiming 'Death is the sleep of eternity'. Other *représentants en mission* followed suit. At the instigation of Chaumette and Hébert, militants in the Sections then jumped onto the bandwagon. Pierre Gaspard 'Anaxagoras' Chaumette was a visceral anti-clerical who had previously used his position in the Commune to prevent the capital's churches from holding a midnight Christmas Mass. The *sans-culotte* Jesus detested priests, he declared. The Sections forced Jean-Baptiste Gobel, the constitutional archbishop of Paris, to resign, and on 10 November the cathedral of Notre-Dame was 're-consecrated' a Temple of Reason in the midst of a festival of liberty. In the weeks that followed, all the Paris churches were shut down.

Even if 'dechristianization' was popular in Paris, it seems unlikely that the policy attracted much bedrock support in the departments. In the corridors of government opinion was divided. The offices of the Police Ministry (known as the Committee of General Security) contained enthusiastic anti-clericals, but the senior Committee of Public Safety, whose responsibilities were more wide-ranging, adopted a reserved attitude. Robespierre, like most educated men of his generation, held broadly Rousseauist beliefs in matters to do with religion and regarded atheism as a vice of the aristocracy. In any case, he was suspicious of the individuals who had instigated the frenzy of church closures. The randomized and gratuitous Terror favoured by the Commune and the Sections, he felt, was more likely to weaken than to strengthen the republic.

In any case the need for Terror and systematic repression was open to question as the autumn of 1793 turned into winter. Following successes against an Anglo-Dutch force outside Dunkirk and against the Austrians at Wattignies, the military situation on the northeastern border had eased. True, the Army of the Rhine was still badly demoralized having nearly lost control of Strasbourg, but Saint-Just and Philippe Lebas were restoring discipline and by the end of the year enemy forces would be cleared almost totally from Alsace. The Convention was also regaining the initiative in the struggle against its internal opponents. **Federalism** had been quelled everywhere by October, and rebellious Lyons was finally overrun on the 9th of that month. In the counter-revolutionary Vendée, however, the fortunes of war see-sawed alarmingly throughout September and October. A victory at Cholet on 17–18 October gave the advantage to the forces of the republic, but the Vendeans were not crushed beyond all hope of recovery until 23 December (battle of Savenay). Almost simultaneously, the news came through that the forts overlooking the harbour of Toulon had been recaptured and that the British were now evacuating the port.

Pressure for a moderation – or perhaps we should say a de-escalation – of the Terror has been attributed to Robespierre, to Danton and to Camille Desmoulins, the talented journalist and Cordeliers militant turned Montagnard deputy. The involvement of the latter in the campaign for 'indulgence' is not in doubt, whereas the motives and behaviour of the others are harder to work out. Robespierre who had not hitherto shown much interest in the rhetoric of Terror wanted to bring the 'dechristianizers' to heel. As for Danton he may only have been trying to protect a number of politically vulnerable friends. Be that as it may, disagreements over the Terror and the rationale for repression once the immediate danger to the republic had passed would end up destroying an emergency government that had no opponents except those of its own making, whether in the Convention or in the country at large.

What disturbed deputies and dispassionate observers such as Nicolas Ruault was the way in which the bloodshed continued unabated, notwithstanding the easing of the military situation. In the aftermath of the fall of Lyons, *représentant* Couthon oversaw a moderate repression which resulted in the judicial execution of around 200 individuals. But Couthon was recalled and replaced in late October by Fouché and Collot d'Herbois, who proceeded to organize mass shootings and guillotinings that took a further 1,667 lives. It was the same story in the Vendée. Although the rebels no longer posed a threat, General **Turreau** laid waste the countryside from January onwards, while *représentant en mission* **Carrier** ordered, or connived at, the mass drownings and shootings of Vendeans, refractory priests and common criminals who had been incarcerated in the prisons of Nantes.

The diary of another detached observer of public events, Célestin Guittard de Floriban, offers us a glimpse of the extent to which the repressive reflex became normalized in the spring and summer of 1794. From early April until late July, he noted down the executions carried out in Paris, pausing to reflect on what was happening only when the tumbrels contained a number of women victims. As the Terror entered its final paroxysm in mid-June, he stopped systematically recording the names and contented himself with a recital of numbers instead (Figure 5.1). On 31 July, as the score-settling of Thermidor reached its term, he awoke from this blood-soaked stupor and noted with surprise, 'there have been no executions today' (Aubert ed., 1974: 441).

In conditions such as these it is scarcely to be wondered at that the widened definition of citizenship pioneered since the start of the revolution disappeared almost without trace. Anacharsis Cloots and Tom Paine, who had accepted election to the Convention after the grant of honorary citizenship in 1792, were expelled from the legislature as suspect foreigners after a year or so. Cloots was subsequently guillotined and Paine would be lucky to keep his head on his

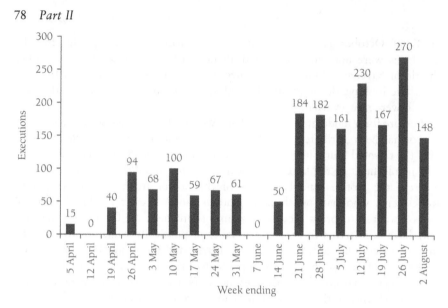

Figure 5.1 Weekly executions in Paris, April–August 1794
Source: Aubert, R. (ed.) (1974) *Journal de Célestin Guittard de Floriban, bourgeois de Paris sous la Révolution*, published by Editions France-Empire, pp. 333–441.

shoulders. All British subjects residing in France had been rounded up by this time in a reprisal measure implemented after the admission of Admiral Hood's fleet to the harbour of Toulon. From the end of May 1794, moreover, British and Hanoverian prisoners-of-war became liable to immediate execution. The only glimmer of light in this dark tunnel of escalating paranoia was the slave emancipation decree. On 16 Pluviôse II (4 February 1794) the Convention ratified the decision taken by its agents in Saint-Domingue the previous summer, referring the question of implementation to the Committee of Public Safety. A couple of weeks later a celebratory festival took place in the Temple of Reason (ex-cathedral of Notre-Dame) during which Chaumette and **Jean-Baptiste Belley**, the first black person to sit in the Convention, gave speeches, and a mixed-race woman named Lucidor F. Corbin intoned an anthem to freedom [**Doc. 21**].

The difficulty Camille Desmoulins faced when criticizing, in veiled terms, the excesses of that autumn and winter in the columns of his *Le Vieux Cordelier* newspaper was that the mind-set of Terror made bedfellows of 'moderation' and 'counter-revolution'. Moreover, anyone who had carried out brutal deeds at a time when no questions were being asked had an obvious personal investment in the continuation of a policy of stern measures. When Collot d'Herbois received reports that the Convention and even the Jacobin Club were talking about releasing suspects and relaxing the Terror, he rushed back to Paris in order to justify himself and, by extension, all the other *représentants en mission*, Section, club and local authority militants whose activities rendered them vulnerable to criticism. How far the Committee of Public Safety as a whole was prepared to countenance a retreat from the Terror is difficult to determine, though. After all, it knew all about the activities of Turreau's 'infernal columns' in the Vendée [**Doc. 20**]. If we may judge from the law that spelled out the workings of Revolutionary Government (14 Frimaire II/4 December 1793), the Committee was aiming to centralize and concentrate the punitive will of the nation, not to weaken it.

These divergent visions of the direction in which the revolution should proceed, together with the gradual breakdown of personal relations and trust between individual members of the two Committees, help us to understand why a government constructed in adversity could not long survive in the less testing conditions of the late spring and summer. Having witnessed the furious reaction of 'ultras' (Collot d'Herbois, Fouché, Hébert, Carrier and others) to the calls for clemency expressed in the pages of *Le Vieux Cordelier*, Robespierre grasped that the future of the Montagnard government was itself at stake. The balance between the contending groups had been lost, however. Amid fears that supporters of Hébert in the Cordeliers Club and their allies in the Sections might exploit a recrudescence of food shortages and launch an insurrection, the Committee of Public Safety carried out a pre-emptive strike against them in March [**Doc. 23**]. Hébert, Ronsin, Vincent, Momoro and fourteen lesser-known figures from the Sections were accused of involvement in a 'foreign faction' and executed on 24 March 1794.

However, this alerted and probably antagonized their allies in the two Committees. The move made it difficult to resist demands for equivalent action against more highly placed 'plotters' – notably a group of deputies linked closely to Danton who were suspected of financial misdemeanours. Some of these *pourris* were already in detention, but the remainder were arrested on the night of 29–30 March. Because the deputies who had been calling for some relaxation of the Terror (Desmoulins, Delacroix, Philippeaux and Danton) could not be easily, or safely, separated from them, they were arrested, too. As the printer of the *Moniteur* newspaper, Nicolas Ruault was able to watch what was going on from close quarters, and on 1 April he reported to his brother that the 'patriots' were now waging a fierce struggle among themselves. After a show trial, the embezzlers and the so-called **indulgents** were jointly sentenced to death. They mounted the steps of the scaffold together four days later.

In the cart on the way to the guillotine, Danton expressed frustration that he was going to die six weeks before Robespierre (Ruault, 1976: 350) – a reminder to us that the revolution was now heading in the direction of so many emergency dictatorships. In fact, the rule of the Committee of Public Safety lasted another sixteen weeks before it, too, fell prey to a lethal bout of in-fighting which destroyed the authority of the Committee of General Security as well. Robespierre did indeed aspire to some form of dictatorship in the weeks that followed the extermination of the factions. The so-called Great Terror, as chronicled by Guittard de Floriban, became almost entirely disconnected from political necessity. The Paris Sections, whose vitality had been ebbing ever since the start of the year, were now largely excluded from the decision-making

Figure 5.2 Danton led to the guillotine
© Musee de la Ville de Paris, Musee Carnavalet, Paris, France/Bridgeman Images

machinery of government; activism waned and citizens were encouraged to turn away from participatory politics and find fulfilment instead in passive worship of the Supreme Being. The regenerationist rhetoric of the early revolution was directed instead to the task of founding a 'republic of virtue'. Ordinary people would, it was supposed, derive their sustenance from a cultural revolution rooted in an unceasing round of civic festivals and a calendar that abolished the past and aligned the revolution with nature. As for female Jacobinism, it had been on the back foot ever since the autumn of 1793 when the Société des Républicaines Révolutionnaires had disbanded in the face of criticism both from deputies and from working women of the central markets. The right of women to bear arms was also curtailed when the War Ministry reissued an instruction that female soldiers were not acceptable at the front.

The final episode of blood-letting on 9–10 Thermidor II (27–28 July 1794) seems to have been triggered by the entirely human reflex of fear rather than major differences of policy, or ideology, or social background. Having withdrawn from the day-to-day business of managing Revolutionary Government several weeks earlier, Robespierre threatened to denounce his unnamed opponents inside and outside the two Committees. This caused the survivors of the opposing factions – 'ultras' and moderates – to band together and organize a pre-emptive strike. Contrary to received wisdom, large numbers of Parisians also mobilized, but chiefly in defence of the Convention which proceeded to outlaw anyone supporting Robespierre and his cronies. On 10 Thermidor and days following, it was therefore the turn of Robespierre, Couthon, Saint-Just, Lebas and 100 others to be loaded aboard the executioners' carts. Few of the deputies who engineered this *coup* sought explicitly to end the Terror, but unaligned members of the legislature moved quickly to exploit the power vacuum which resulted and a progressive dismantling of the central institutions of repression was the outcome.

6 The search for stability, 1795–99

The Jacobin levelling experiment of 1793–94 left in its wake an embittered society. As a reaction to the events of Thermidor gathered pace, the country seemed to divide into those who had been involved in the politics or the bureaucracy of Terror and those who counted themselves among its victims. The readmission to the Convention of the surviving Girondins, together with those other deputies who had protested against the 31 May–2 June purge carried out by the Montagnards and their street supporters, only exacerbated the tension. Before long, the stern figures in the two Committees who had helped to dislodge Robespierre (Billaud-Varenne, Collot d'Herbois, **Vadier, Amar,** etc.) would be called to account as 'terrorists' in their turn. The task facing France's legislators from the autumn of 1794 was an exceptionally difficult one, therefore. They had to find a means of repairing the damage done by the Terror to the social fabric of the nation, whilst at the same time devising a system of government that would enshrine both freedom of parliamentary expression and solid guarantees against any move towards dictatorship by the executive arm. Their failure to resolve the bitter legacy of the Terror is one reason why historians tend to pass over these years as though nothing durable or constructive took place between 1795 and 1799. Better, therefore, either to 'end' the revolution with the fall of Robespierre, or to treat the regime brought into being by the new Constitution of 1795 as an extended chronological prelude to the arrival in power of Napoleon Bonaparte.

It is true that the cast list of the period did not change much. On taking office in October 1795 the Executive Directory would find itself confronted by intransigent royalists, *émigrés*, non-oath-swearing priests and latter-day Jacobins who regretted the passing of the Terror. In this regard little of substance had altered since the events of Thermidor in the Convention. France's foreign adversaries had not greatly changed either, nor had the arguments for and against war. Was the Directory therefore little more than a chaotic transitional regime located between two periods of robust and single-minded government? Recent research suggests that this view needs to be modified. The Directory was the first regime actually to build on the electoral achievements of 1790–91 and, for a time, to make democratically sanctioned institutions work. Thanks to a still broad franchise, a vibrant press and frequent voter consultation, Frenchmen served an extended apprenticeship in the values of representative government during these four years

DOI: 10.4324/9781003156185-8

[Doc. 24]. The regime also gestated institutions of financial administration, tax raising and local government which anticipated innovations more commonly associated with the rule of Napoleon Bonaparte. Indeed, those researchers who have paused to consider the Directory in its own right go further and propose a periodization that blurs somewhat the traditional focus on Bonaparte's anti-parliamentary coup of 18–19 **Brumaire** VIII (9–10 November 1799) as the single most important event of these years. It is true that contemporaries were not as impressed by the significance of Brumaire as generations of historians have been subsequently. They were probably well aware that the transition from a politics rooted in debate and the free exchange of ideas to one predicated on a reflex of authority was under way even before a victorious general decided to try his hand at civil government.

A Thermidorian republic

The best way to make sense of the complex events of these years is to divide the period into two. From the summer of 1794 until the summer of 1797, objectives that were closely entwined preoccupied the men of the revolution: how to dismantle the repressive apparatus of a Jacobin dictatorship without at the same time clearing the way for a revival of royalism that might serve as the curtain-raiser to a Bourbon restoration. But from the autumn of 1797 until the summer of 1802 when Bonaparte, as First Consul, was continued in office for life (see Chapter 7), the emphasis increasingly shifted from constitutionalism to authoritarianism. Thanks to the *coup* of 18 Fructidor V (4 September 1797), carried out with the assistance of the army, the political threat posed by resurgent royalism declined. Instead, Directorial republicans and their successors in the councils of the Consulate grew to fear that *neo*-Jacobins – the men who had last held power during the Terror – would take over the regime from within. In order to stop them, they resorted to blatantly unconstitutional actions of which General Bonaparte's intervention was merely the most arresting and shocking example.

The Executive Directory should therefore be visualized as a see-saw regime which was periodically assailed by individuals representing the extreme ends of the political spectrum brought into being since 1789. To be sure, its principal upholders were firm republicans, but they were also committed to a philosophy of political liberalism. The challenge they set themselves was to detach the idea of the republic from its embattled and blood-soaked origins and to harness it instead to the principles of the early revolution. Their ultimate failure to achieve this synthesis was not a failure of political will so much as a reflection that the nation – post-Thermidor – appeared irretrievably divided.

The speed of the reaction against Jacobinism and all it stood for in the Convention once the powers of the Committee of Public Safety had been cut back surprised everyone. The Paris Sections were prevented from holding meetings and legislation banned collective petitioning by clubs or any other corporate bodies. Public brawling between moderates and militants was used as a pretext to shut down the mother Jacobin Club altogether, in fact. All the irksome policies that the deputies of the Plain had agreed to under duress were now put into reverse. The savage law of 22 Prairial II (10 June 1794) which pushed the conviction rate in the Revolutionary Tribunal to 80 per cent had already been rescinded, and during the autumn all the restraints that had been placed on the market economy under pressure from the Sections were removed. Price control was abandoned, the stock exchange reopened, and merchants and contractors recovered the freedom to go about their business unhindered.

The consequences were immediate and predictable inasmuch as the quantity of paper money in circulation very nearly tripled between Thermidor and the start-date of the new regime. Galloping inflation diminished the purchasing power of the *assignats* and the cost of living spiralled. By January 1795, real prices for day-to-day commodities were almost six times higher than they had been five years earlier. The cold winter of 1794–95 only made matters worse. Distress rose to levels without parallel in the cities. In Paris crowds forced their way into the Convention in April to demand bread. A young American named Thomas Parkin was visiting the capital at the time and recorded the activism of womenfolk in particular: 'I saw a woman who kept a coffee-house tear the national colours down from her door, stamp and spit on them and execrate the Republic and the Convention because bread was scarce' (Chew, 1912: 365). Suicide was one solution: in Rouen the death rate doubled in the year after Thermidor. Famine, even starvation, accompanied the retreat from the Terror, then, and it fuelled political resentments. That spring, the deputies started to receive reports from the south and southeast of the country recounting the activities of extra-legal punishment squads (the so-called 'White' Terror). These gangs were systematically targeting for violence and intimidation anyone who had held office during the period of Revolutionary Government.

The dilemma that would run like a thread through these years was already apparent by the summer of 1795, therefore. Each act of relaxation and apparent reconciliation appeared simply to reinforce the extremes. Although the deputies in the post-Thermidor Convention had moved quite quickly to dismantle Terror as a body of law, it is less clear that the characteristic mind-set faded quite so swiftly. When the English detainee Charlotte Biggs emerged from house arrest in October 1794, she noticed that the 'fashionable dialect' of the Terror was still in widespread use among the general population (Biggs, 1797: vol. 2, 203). The habits and practices of political repression were not immediately discontinued either. For instance, the routine of the administrative purge persisted; indeed, it was intensified by a fresh wave of *représentants en mission* who revived the dechristianization impulse in some departments as well. And there was certainly no discernible retreat from 'cultural' aspects of the Terror such as the rigorous enforcement of *décadi* rest days (in place of the Sabbath), and civic festivals. Quite the contrary, the drive to mould citizens by means of festive educational initiatives was reaffirmed.

As for the *émigrés*, there was to be no retreating on this front either. Three or four months after Thermidor the Convention voted through a comprehensive decree which consolidated the repressive legislation relating to those who had

Figure 6.1 The planting of a liberty tree
© Granger Historical Picture Archive/Alamy Stock Photo FF8BKX

stayed outside France after May 1792. By now they numbered almost 130,000 (Carpenter, 2015: 330). On the other hand, the deputies did try to reach out to their armed opponents in the west (known as *chouans*) with an amnesty that included the freedom to worship as they pleased. In fact, a general law of religious pacification was eventually introduced which for a time restored to both juring and non-juring priests the use of churches. However, the loosening grip of the Convention only encouraged the western rebels to renew their struggle against the republic. The late king's one surviving son had died in captivity and his uncle, the Comte de Provence, now claimed the succession. Styling himself Louis XVIII, Provence issued a grudging Declaration from Verona which made it plain that whilst 'constitutional' royalists might be trying to secure control of France by parliamentary means, the 'pure' royalists remained committed to counter-revolution via the armed struggle. The failure of the Quiberon Bay expedition in June 1795, when British warships landed a large force of *émigrés* on the south coast of Brittany, would demonstrate the futility of this approach. Indeed, the deputies were more alarmed by the stealthy spread of royalism as priests returned from exile and churches cautiously reopened in various parts of the country. With a new constitution in the making and elections impending, the royalists saw the chance to weave together the many different strands of discontent.

The Convention also spotted the danger, though. On 5–13 Fructidor III (22–30 August 1795) it responded with decrees designed to ensure that two-thirds of the deputies remained in post into the next legislature, thus placing a considerable restraint on the freedom of the electorate. Was this a prudent move to maintain continuity in a context of accelerating political reaction, or a cynical manœuvre to save their necks? Both, probably, but the measure was greeted with an indignant crypto-royalist uprising on the streets of Paris and with extreme distaste in the country at large.

France finally emerged from the limbo of Revolutionary Government and returned to constitution-based legality on 28 October 1795 in the shape of a regime known as the Directory (*Directoire*). During the preceding months, a new constitution (the Constitution of 1795 or the Year Three) had been voted and ratified which preserved a broad franchise based on a threshold tax qualification. If not exactly universal manhood suffrage, around 69 per cent of adult males (5.5 million out of some 8 million) were entitled to participate in primary electoral assemblies. Significantly, it was accompanied by a re-issued Declaration of the Rights and the Duties of Man which referred not to *natural* rights (as in 1789 and 1793), but to rights acquired in *society*. In other words, the architects of the new regime were now stepping back from the universalistic claims which had served as the launch pad for revolution. The emphasis on equality and on sovereignty as an attribute of the people was watered down, too. In fact, the clause 'Men are born, and always continue, free, and equal in respect of their rights' (1789, art. 1) was quietly dropped, as was the clause in the 1793 text which proclaimed the 'sacred' right of insurrection (1793, art. 35).

These changes had the virtue of aligning constitutional theory with hard-won experience and some historians therefore detect in the transition of 1795 a fundamental shift in the political culture of the revolution (Jainchill, 2008: 30). Deputies on the Left, it is true, were in no doubt that a retreat had been sounded from the values that had sustained the revolution up to this point. The label citizen, for instance, was increasingly restricted to those in possession of voting rights. This would be to pre-judge the new regime and to deny it any capacity to evolve, however. Whatever the Thermidorian architects of the Directory may have had in mind, it would not lack for democratic credentials.

As always, though, the declared aim was to begin afresh. Two days prior to its dissolution the Convention voted to rename the Place de la Révolution where the guillotine had once stood, the Place de la Concorde. Moreover, in a more tangible attempt at reconciliation, a final decree granted an amnesty to those who had been charged with political crimes in the aftermath of the Terror. If only in terms of structure, the Directory would be a very different form of government from those that had preceded it. Such was the fear of would-be dictators and autocratic committees that the Constitution was built around the principle of a rigorous separation of powers. In order to curb the domineering tendency of the legislative arm of government, provision was made for two chambers on a model first proposed by the *Monarchiens* back in the summer of 1789. The authority to initiate and to examine legislation was entrusted to a Council of Five Hundred, whereas parliamentary approval of bills was lodged with a senate of more senior deputies known as the Council of Elders. The executive arm comprised five individuals put forward by the Council of Five Hundred and selected by the Council of Elders. They were known as Directors. While the Directors appointed the Ministers and the Commissioners – that is to say, the agents of the government in the departments – they had no authority to make or shape legislation. On the other hand, the power to conduct diplomacy, to supervise the armies and to handle appointments gave them very considerable scope to influence the formulation of policy. In the event of a stalemate or paralysis in the mechanisms of government, a procedure for constitutional revision could be invoked; however, a minimum delay of nine years was laid down before any changes could take effect. True, the Directors were subject to annual renewal, but one by one and by random ballot. Constitutional revision was all but impossible, therefore, which helps to explain why the Directory both resorted to illegal acts and fell prey to the illegal acts of others.

As we have seen, the democratic credentials of the Directorial regime rested on quite a broad franchise. It is true, however, that voting remained indirect. Also electors had to satisfy fiscal conditions that were much stiffer than they had been in 1790 and 1791, and a provision was made for a literacy test. But the opportunities to vote at the primary level were now more numerous since the Constitution required that ballots be held every year in the month of March. After the studied conformism of Revolutionary Government, some vigour and vitality returned to national political life in consequence. However, the Councils proceeded to cut off one of the sources of revolutionary energy in an attempt to discourage the more disruptive aspects of mass political mobilization. Elective village councils were abolished and replaced by canton-level municipalities instead.

Despite hunger, economic dislocation, fiscal collapse and the fragility of law and order in the south and the west, the early Directory years did prove conducive to the growth of a practice of participation. It was rooted in electoral assemblies, newspaper readership and, for city dwellers, reopened clubs. Some historians have even discerned signs of the development of embryonic political parties in this period. However, the combination of frequent elections and a vigorous marketplace for oppositional ideas also provided a platform for those on the margins of the political landscape – the more so as the Directory was not yet willing to use force against its parliamentary opponents. The '*républicains fermes*', as the Directory's latter-day Jacobins were called, had benefited from the amnesty law and, although the royalists proved to be the chief gainers from the elections to fill the places of the outgoing 'third', these neo-Jacobins posed the more immediate threat. Their clubs were infiltrated and their newspapers harassed; in fact, the Pantheon Club in Paris, which regularly attracted many hundreds of nostalgic supporters of the politics of the Terror, was closed down by the government in February 1796. This action would provoke a more sinister development. Led by 'Gracchus' Babeuf, editor of *Le Tribune du Peuple* and a man who had dabbled in democratic politics since the start of the revolution, a small group of partisans of the advanced social and democratic agenda outlined in the Constitution of 1793 began to plot an insurrection – or more properly, a *coup* – against the regime. Babeuf's 'Conspiracy of the Equals' was betrayed within a matter of months and it never amounted to much in any case.

Nevertheless, the Directory made the most of the 'threat', put the plotters in the dock and dressed up the case as a trial of Jacobinism as a whole. Babeuf and a fellow conspirator were guillotined in May 1797.

Despite the precautionary legislation introduced by the Convention during its final weeks, the main beneficiaries of regime change turned out to be the royalists. The elections that launched the Directory in October 1795 returned over 100 to parliament although they were by no means all 'purs' (i.e. counter-revolutionaries). On the contrary, many would have been content with a return to constitutional monarchy on the 1791 pattern, or something similar. But at least the citadel of government was held firmly by moderate republicans: the deputies who had been prolonged in office by virtue of the two-thirds decrees took care to ensure that the executive was filled by men of their own stamp. All five of the Directors had voted for the death sentence meted out to Louis XVI in 1793. Still, the royalists had achieved an important bridgehead and would draw strength from the fact that the rampart constructed around the republic by the outgoing Convention could only erode in the years to come. When the next electoral renewal fell in March 1797, the royalist leaders made a supreme effort of organization and propaganda, and they swept the board. Only eleven of the 216 retiring deputies were re-elected and, in total, about 180 of 260 seats being contested were taken by royalist candidates of one persuasion or another. This diluted considerably the political complexion of the Councils, with the regicides among the deputies now numbering barely one in five. As a consequence, the regime entered a phase of protracted crisis.

'*Une grande nation*'

From the late spring of 1794 the logistical efforts of the Committee of Public Safety, which had enabled the armies to expand to 750,000 men, began to bear fruit. Victory against the Austrians and the Dutch at Fleurus reopened the road into Belgium in June and before the year was out, Austrian forces had been pushed back across the Rhine as well. By the time the Directory took power, the territory of the republic was not even remotely under threat from foreign enemies. On the contrary, the 'natural' frontiers of France (the Rhine, the Pyrenees) had been secured and her armies were encamped on German, Spanish and Italian soil. Moreover, the Ottoman Empire, Europe's principal neutral monarchy, had been induced to recognize the legitimacy of the republic (Firges, 2017: 80).

How much this fortunate state of affairs owed to enhanced combat effectiveness deriving from the coupling of military service and citizenship is a matter for debate among historians. Yet the structural weaknesses which had bedevilled French military performance in 1792 and 1793 had certainly been remedied by 1794. If the troops were not always the missionaries of liberty of Brissotin rhetoric, a truly national, omni-competent and redoubtable fighting force had come into being. As an English observer put it in a letter to the prime-minister William Pitt: 'We are fighting with a Set of People enthusiastically bent on being Free' (Evans, 1990: 138).

The ideology of freedom permeated the navy as well. When, in the summer of 1794, the Russell sisters of Birmingham were captured in the Channel by a French frigate as they were heading for a new life in America, they were struck by the calm efficiency of the crew and the camaraderie between officers and sailors. Most of all, however, they were impressed by how they all sang the 'Marseillaise Hymn' morning, noon and night (Jeyes, 1911: 66–7).

Between 1795 and 1802, France proceeded to annex Belgium, the Rhineland and Piedmont, thereby enlarging the republic by a fifth (see Map 0.6). It was difficult to confine these expansionist thrusts to the realms of foreign policy, however. As in 1792–93, the successes (and failures) of the armies had a direct impact on political debate in the domestic arena. Many deputies were fearful that the acquisition of territory by conquest would fatally undermine the nascent republic and open the way to empire and despotism. While liberty could probably survive the securing of the 'natural' frontiers, any further aggrandizement might place it in serious jeopardy.

Why, then, did the Directory proceed to set up eight 'sister republics' in these years? Until the summer of 1796, the armies were kept on a fairly tight rein, the Directory believing that their successes should be employed chiefly to bring France's remaining adversaries (primarily Austria) to the conference table. After all, a weakened Sardinian monarchy on France's southeastern border might make better sense than a democratic republic of Piedmont. However, the thinking in Paris shifted radically the following year – in response no doubt to General Bonaparte's stunning successes in northern Italy. The concept of the sister republic seemed to offer an alternative to outright annexation which was still in keeping with a posture of defence. No less important, it enabled the regime's architects to persuade themselves that they were not, after all, embarking on the acquisition of a land-based empire. Moreover, the Directory could thereby accommodate politically native republican movements that were particularly vigorous in Italy. Yet we should be under no illusion as to the nature of the relationship between parent (France) and offspring (the sister republics). It was entirely one-sided – not a partnership [Doc. 26]

An entity calling itself an enlarged or '*grande nation*' was coming into being willy-nilly, then, and almost inexorably France's foreign policy was becoming offensive and even global in outlook. For all the effectiveness of 'cannon' diplomacy, though, the combination of victory *and* peace continued to elude the Directors. Whilst Prussia, Holland and Spain were all brought to terms in the course of 1795, Britain and Austria fought on. Indeed, Russia was induced to join the anti-French coalition once a third partition of Poland had been concluded. Not until October 1797 would the Habsburgs agree terms for peace (Treaty of Campo Formio), thereby securing for France recognition of her annexation two years earlier of the Austrian Netherlands. Despite war weariness and the loss of her bridgeheads in Europe, Britain remained resolute, however, and the conflict with the republic continued until March 1802 (the Peace of Amiens).

France owed her military achievements during these years to a number of fac-tors in addition to sheer fighting ability. Wherever French generals and civil commissioners went, they introduced reforms that tended to boost their own self-belief and sap that of the army commanders arrayed against them. Liberationist rhetoric could be an immensely powerful weapon of war on land and at sea as we have noted. However, it was probably sheer experience that turned them into such redoubtable foes. The novice volunteer recruits of 1791 and 1792 had become battle-hardened and systems had been put in place to blend old troops with new, and also to ensure that only the most capable individuals were selected for command positions. In the process, the old royal army with its aristocratic officer elite was almost entirely submerged. By 1798, only a tiny fraction of sol-diers had service records dating back to the *ancien régime*. France also possessed a considerable reservoir of manpower which could be tapped in a relatively straightforward manner, thanks to the administrative reforms of the revolution. Informal conscription had been introduced with the *levée en masse* decree passed on 23 August 1793, and from 1798 it became routine and bureaucratic in the sense that all single males aged between 20 and 25 were automatically registered as liable for military service. This Jourdan Law encountered opposition and its enforcement in the west was delayed for a time. Nonetheless, systematic and open-ended conscription ensured that a further 280,000 men could be enrolled in the armies of the republic by the summer of 1800.

Of course, the growing professionalization of military life meant that the close bonding with the Jacobin 'nation-in-arms' of 1793–94 tended to weaken as well. Soldiers with long years of service, both behind and ahead of them, increasingly identified with the unit or the army corps to which they belonged. Thus, the Army of the Rhine and the Moselle commanded by **Pichegru** and then by **Moreau** acquired a reputation for crypto-royalist sympathies, whilst in Italy the troops under Bernadotte clashed with Masséna's ostentatiously republican division. The Army of Italy under General Bonaparte's command, by contrast, was distinguishable by virtue of its Jacobin sympathies.

Bonaparte had already made himself useful to politicians on several occasions when they were struggling to overcome the domestic royalist threat, and in March 1796 he was sent to Italy to take over from Schérer. In the absence of a decisive breakthrough on the Rhine front, the exploits of this modest-sized army, commanded brilliantly by its 27-year-old general, rapidly attracted the attention of the Directory back in Paris. In a whirlwind campaign Bonaparte split the Austrian and Piedmontese forces, causing Victor Amadeus III to relin-quish control over Nice and Savoy. He then headed into the Po valley in pursuit of the Austrians who were badly mauled at Lodi. On 15 May 1796, the French entered Milan and subjected the city to a huge ransom. Bonaparte paid his troops in cash, an unheard-of gesture, before advancing with what amounted to a private army towards Modena, Tuscany and the most northerly Papal States. A long siege of the fortress of Mantua followed, during which Bonaparte inflicted further defeats on the Austrians (Arcola, Rivoli). Mantua fell early in 1797, enabling the Army of Italy to continue its rampage. The Austrians were pushed back to Leoben, where an armistice was signed (18 April), whereupon the French proceeded to occupy Venetia.

By this date, the Directory was beginning to lose the ability to control its generals. Bonaparte, in particular, realized that he could act pretty much as he pleased provided that the flow of money and cultural resources being sent back to Paris was maintained [**Doc. 25**]. Parleying with the Austrians at Leoben, just 100 miles short of Vienna, had been his own idea and the terms of the armistice were presented to the Directors as a *fait accompli*. No doubt there was considerable relief in the corridors of political power when, the following year, this immensely popular general with apparently impeccable republican – if no longer Jacobin – credentials decided to take an army to Egypt. Britain's naval superiority in the Channel had forestalled the plan to launch an invasion against France's one remaining adversary. The decision was therefore taken to move on to the offensive elsewhere and cut her trading routes to India.

The invasion of Egypt and Syria was not a great success. It incensed the Ottomans who ruled in the Near East: almost alone among the Powers they had taken a relaxed attitude to the threat of the French Revolution as we have seen. At the international level a hostile diplomatic chain reaction occurred which resulted in the resumption of hostilities on the Continent (War of the Second Coalition, 1798–1802). Trapped by the destruction of their fleet in Aboukir Bay in August 1798, French forces would behave more like colonialists than liberators. Bonaparte left the theatre of war as soon as he could – after fourteen months.

Rule by *coup*

By the spring of 1797, the political problem that had perplexed all previous revolutionary regimes – namely the striking of a balance between the executive and the legislative arms of government – was beginning to reassert itself. The solution (tried originally in the Convention) appeared to be to engineer a balance by means of *coups* and purges. But the removal of 'disloyal' deputies (and Directors) simply risked weakening the loyalty of everyone to the political compromise worked out in 1795. Since the allocation of powers within government could scarcely be altered by constitutional means, the whole regime was brought into disrepute. Bonaparte's final *coup* pushed at an open door, therefore. It seems unlikely that it would have succeeded if those with executive authority had chosen to resist.

The landslide victory of the royalists in the March–April elections of 1797 set the scene, if only because the sheer number and temper of the new royalist deputies (who included men with links to the Pretender such as Charles Pichegru and Jacques Imbert-Colomès) galvanized the moderates into action. With Pichegru at the helm of the Council of Five Hundred and a pliant tool (Barthélemy) elected to the Directory in the place of the outgoing Le Tourneur, the royalists secured the lifting of the disabilities imposed on the relatives of *émigrés* and a substantial repeal of the persecutory legislation that still affected non-oath-swearing clergymen. They also manœuvred to deny the Directors control over expenditure – a crucial issue at a moment when the government was in the throes of withdrawing the paper currency and relying on remittances from Italy to stave off bankruptcy. On 4 September, in consequence, Parisians awoke to find troops loyal to one of Bonaparte's most trusted commanders encamped in the capital. François-Marie Barthélemy and 53 deputies were expelled (and condemned to the 'dry guillotine' of deportation), while the election results achieved earlier that year in 49 departments were overturned.

The use of the army to resolve a parliamentary crisis set a worrying example. However, it was not without precedent and was not inconsistent with the creeping militarization of public life that was taking place during the Directory years. In the late winter of 1795, the Thermidorians had broken the taboo and called out troops to put down disturbances outside bakers' shops. In May of that year during a final hunger-driven uprising of the Sections, the deputies had responded by sending soldiers and cavalry into the *faubourg* Saint-Antoine to enforce compliance with the will of government. Those involved in this Prairial insurrection (20–23 May), together with six ex-Montagnard deputies who had compromised themselves, were then sentenced using the expedient of a military commission. Just before the dissolution of the Convention, troops had again been called out – this time to quell a mobilization in Paris of crypto-royalists and others protesting against the two-thirds legislation. In principle, however, the architects of the regime deplored military intervention in domestic politics. General Augereau would twice offer himself as a candidate Director and would be turned down twice. By 1797, though, the army was no longer a pliant tool. The generals had largely emancipated themselves from civilian control when on campaign, and the politicians knew that they were playing with fire when seeking their help to overturn the wishes of the voters.

The *coup* of 18 Fructidor V (4 September 1797) would prove to be a defeat for royalists of all persuasions, and one from which they would never recover. But it was unquestionably a defeat for the Directory as well since it demonstrated that the adherents of the regime lacked the courage of their liberal convictions. Setting aside the legally expressed wishes of the electorate was no way for an apprentice parliamentary democracy to behave. All over the republic, priests and *émigrés* who had slipped back into the country in the hope of better times repacked their bags. In nearly half of the departments, large numbers of elected and non-elected officials were summarily dismissed in a purge reminiscent of the days of the Terror. Journalists who had helped to mobilize royalist opinion were arrested and 42 Parisian and provincial newspapers forced to close down. But if the triumvirate of Directors who had been chiefly responsible for the *coup* (**La Révellière-Lépeaux, Barras** and Reubell) supposed that it would enable the political 'centre' to regain the initiative, they were mistaken. The main beneficiaries in the country at large were the 'firm republicans' (that is to say, the neo-Jacobins) and, as a fresh round of legislative elections approached, it began to look as though they would come to pose the next challenge.

By any standards, the elections of March 1798 represented a huge gamble for a regime that had yet to fully embrace the logic of political pluralism. Not only had the final 'third' of outgoing deputies from the Convention to be replaced, but all the seats left vacant by deaths, resignations and purges had to be filled as well. In short, a contest involving 437 candidates was looming. With feelings running high against royalism, the neo-Jacobins naturally thought that their moment had come. Political clubs reopened and stern measures against priests, *émigrés* and ex-nobles were demanded. There was even an attempt to rehabilitate some of those who had been caught in the repression of Babeuf's quasi-communist conspiracy the year before. However, the government remained obsessed with the royalist menace. Only belatedly did it recognize that reliance on the neo-Jacobins in order to defeat the royalists might place the regime at risk from forces located at either end of the political spectrum. A law permitting the Councils to scrutinize the validity of the electoral results was introduced and, a month before the poll, the Directors alerted the electorate to the danger of 'royalism in a red bonnet' and started to close down neo-Jacobin press organs and clubs.

Notwithstanding the exhortations of the government, the voters turned out in smaller numbers than the year before: cynicism was beginning to take its toll. Yet those who responded gave strong support to the candidates with left-of-centre credentials. All in all, some 162 individuals who had sat in the Convention were returned, 71 of whom were on the record as having voted for the death of Louis XVI. Whilst scarcely overwhelming in numbers, the neo-Jacobins now constituted sizeable minorities in each of the two Councils. However, the government showed its mettle in its treatment of the results of disputed ballots, of which there were no fewer than 178. The elections of candidates who were thought to be hostile were systematically invalidated. And when this laborious process began to run out of parliamentary time, the Directors intervened (on 11 May 1798) and simply annulled results en masse. Around 127 deputies were denied the right to take up their seats in consequence, of whom roughly 60 per cent would have counted as neo-Jacobins.

The Fructidor *coup* had been carried out against a well-substantiated royalist threat. But no one pretended that the neo-Jacobins were bent on overthrowing the regime. The intervention of 22 Floréal VI (11 May 1798) would appear to demonstrate, therefore, that the Directory could not even reconcile itself to the existence of a constitutional opposition. The government did its best to manage the elections of the following year (March 1799) as well. Far better to secure the election of its own candidates than to resort *post facto* to yet another damaging administrative intervention. Clearly, it suited the Directory to depict the neo-Jacobin challengers as nostalgic throwbacks to the Year Two (1793–94) whose unsavoury links to the Paris *sans-culottes* had not yet been severed. Whether this picture is entirely accurate is a matter for debate. Some historians argue that neo-Jacobinism should be recognized as a maturing political force (if not yet a developed party), which would have come to occupy a niche within the Directorial system of representative government had the events of 1799 not determined otherwise (Gainot, 2001: 1–25).

At least the army had not been involved in the efforts to set aside the more inconvenient results of the 1798 elections. Still, the electorate drew its own conclusions: in March 1799 turnout dropped to the lowest level of the decade. By this time a crisis of the regime was fast approaching, and one which would be terminal. With their most talented general cut off in Egypt, the Directory suffered reverses in Italy that brought Austria into the fray once more. By June 1799, nearly all of Bonaparte's achievements in the peninsula had been wiped out; moreover, defeat in southern Germany had forced General Jourdan's army to retreat back across the upper reaches of the Rhine and into Switzerland. Emboldened by the re-election of some of the deputies who had been removed only the year before, the Council of Five Hundred attacked the Directors for their mishandling of the war effort and succeeded in carrying out their own purge. The one-time priest Sieyès had already been elected in the place of Reubell who had drawn the unlucky ball in the annual renewal ballot, but then Treilhard, Merlin de Douai and La Révellière-Lépeaux were forced out in rapid succession. This was serious, for Merlin and La Révellière had been the only true believers left among the Directors, whereas Sieyès, the perpetual dreamer of constitutions, was known to disapprove of that of 1795.

In an atmosphere of incipient military disaster and civil emergency reminiscent of the spring and the summer of 1792, a denouement was fast approaching. Despite all the administrative meddling, a sizeable minority of between 135 and 150 neo-Jacobin deputies had survived in the two Councils. With the support of others who *had* lost confidence in the regime, they were able to secure punitive laws against *émigrés* and former nobles and a 'forced loan' was imposed on the rich. The clubs revived and a motion was even put on 13 September 1799 to have 'the fatherland in danger' declared. The motion was defeated, for it prompted the deputies to take stock and to ask themselves whether their irritation with the Directors was worth risking a return to the Terror. The neo-Jacobin offensive ground to a halt amid a slight easing of tensions on receipt of news that General Masséna had decisively beaten the Austro-Russian army in the second battle of Zurich. The threat of a concerted counter-attack in the southwest and the west had receded by this time as well, although the *chouans* of Brittany and Normandy remained on a hostile footing. Nevertheless, these multi-pronged assaults prompted even the most sanguine supporters of the Directory to wonder how much longer it would be possible to steer a course between the extremes. Sieyès, who felt no compunction about discarding the Constitution, had already made contact with General Joubert, but he was killed at the battle of Novi on 15 August 1799. Bonaparte was by no means the politicians' first-choice instrument for the strengthening of executive authority, it should be said. In any case, he was in Egypt – or was he? On hearing of the disasters in the European theatre of war, he had abandoned his army and hurried back to France where he arrived on 9 October.

Opponents

The neo-Jacobin programme might or might not have offered a viable alternative to the *coup* of Brumaire if the Directory had been granted time and political space in which to evolve. By 1799, though, the revolution as a whole had generated a formidable list of opponents. First among the casualties had been Charles Alexandre de Calonne. Following his fall from grace as Controller General in April 1787, he was threatened with prosecution by the Parlement of Paris and withdrew to London. Hopes of a recall at the time of the Estates General were never realistic, and he would become the first of the servitors of absolute monarchy to join the emigration. Ministers such as Barentin and the Baron de Breteuil, who had conspired to oust Necker and overawe the infant National Assembly with a display of force in the summer of 1789, were the next to go. Most left the country soon after the fall of the Bastille. They included one of the king's brothers, the Comte d'Artois (future Charles X), the Princes de Condé and de Conti, the Duc de Bourbon and powerful courtier families such as the Polignacs. The Comte de Provence, the king's other sibling, would not depart until June 1791, whilst the king's aunts (Victoire and Adélaide) made a controversial journey out of the kingdom in February 1791. Like Louis they would be stopped on route by a vigilant municipality, but the Assembly could find no legal grounds on which to restrict their freedom to travel and they were allowed to go on their way unimpeded. All these men and women refugees formed nuclei of a political and physical emigration which would define itself as explicitly hostile to the revolution. Most would gather in European capitals such as London, Turin and Verona to await a turn of the political tide. Few could have imagined in 1789, 1790 or 1791 that their self-imposed exile would last a decade and more.

Not all opponents became *émigrés* of course. As early as the autumn of 1789 a trickle of deputies had chosen to absent themselves from the legislature on the ground that the pace of political events had outstripped what they, or their constituents, could tolerate. After the defeat of the *Monarchiens'* proposal for an upper house and an absolute veto, Jean-Joseph Mounier and the Marquis de Lally-Tollendal – their chief parliamentary spokesmen – quit in disgust. Many other deputies also sought passports in the aftermath of the October Days. Some, who did not leave, managed to live obscurely and safely by keeping their opinions to themselves and trusting neighbours not to expose them. The same is true of the aristocracy – or rather, the ex-aristocracy – since the legally enshrined status of noble had been abolished by the National Assembly. The majority did *not* emigrate. Instead, they lived quietly on their estates in the hope that the wheel of political fortune would one day turn again in their favour.

Until 1792 and the descent into war with the rest of Europe, it was not absolutely certain that France *had* gone past the point of no return in any case. A prudential attitude such as that adopted by the (ex-) Marquis de Ferrières therefore seemed justified. Although historians are apt to overstate the extent to which harmony and a sense of common purpose prevailed throughout the year 1790, the notion that the country faced malevolent opponents only began to take shape in the aftermath of the king's covert departure from the Tuileries Palace in June 1791. The Flight acted as a catalyst. It forced the Great Powers to act, albeit symbolically; it gave substance to conspiracy fears; it created an expectation of a war of intervention; and it triggered a renewed wave of despairing emigration when Louis appended his signature to the Constitution. For the first time ordinary men and women began to discuss the possibility of a 'counter-revolution'.

Once the deputies of the Legislative Assembly had got the political bit between their teeth, emigrant nobles really were put on the spot. The **Elector of Trier**, whose territories touched France's eastern border, was advised that he should stop sheltering *émigrés* in Koblenz, while the Comte de Provence was warned to return to France on pain of being excluded from the succession. When the essentially personal decision to express rejection of the train of events by leaving the country was made an offence punishable by law, the issue was clarified for many nobles: return and accept the revolution in all of its works, or stay abroad and pay the price. With loss of citizenship, seizure of property, imprisonment and perhaps even capital punishment the likely price, the decision to join an armed counter-revolution became an easier one to take.

Clerical opponents of the revolution were granted much less time in which to mull over their options. As early as 1791 the National Assembly forced the issue by insisting that all clergy swear an oath of loyalty. However, the result was more poignant since most parish priests had been conspicuous supporters of the new regime at the outset. The oath legislation split them into two roughly equal groups. Those who refused the oath generally became irreconcilable opponents of the revolution. Many fled the country in fear of arrest and imprisonment. Consequently, it became hard to distinguish them from a counter-revolution of courtiers and nobles who regretted the passing of the *ancien régime*. However, the requirement to swear successive oaths of allegiance made political hostages of the 'constitutional' or juring clergy as well. By the time of the Terror, the revolutionaries had lost interest in building a state church with a dedicated priesthood. Coerced into abandoning their spiritual vocation they were pushed onto the margins of public life, if not actively persecuted. Clerical celibacy had long been an object of attack, and in 1793–94 many ex-priests came under pressure to marry. Around 5,000 did so in that year alone (Cage, 2013: 602). It seems likely, then, that a number of constitutional clergy ended up in the opposition camp as well. In the event, the separation of church and state was promulgated formally early in 1795 and the Directory years would see an exuberant flowering of cults, not to mention 'do it yourself' religion pioneered in parishes with neither juring nor non-juring clergy to hand [**Doc. 28**]. The latter were frequently treated as outlaws by the authorities and were liable to deportation or worse if captured, but the former jurors were subjected to intermittent harassment as well.

Much, perhaps too much, has been made of counter-revolution by historians in recent years. As the decade of the 1790s drew to a close, most French men and women were still glad that the *ancien régime* had come to an end. The Directory's opponents, like the opponents of previous regimes, were not necessarily counter-revolutionaries. With the exception of well-defined areas, such as Brittany and the Vendée, there never seems to have been much support for counter-revolution inside the country. The repeated failure of outlaw clergy and roving emissaries of the Princes to trigger royalist insurrections acknowledges as much. Another such attempt occurred in the summer of 1799 when inhabitants of villages and small towns in the vicinity of Toulouse responded to a call to arms. But it is far from certain that the mobilization was inspired by a royalist agenda and, in any case, it soon fizzled out. No doubt many country dwellers had grown tired of the revolution by this date, but impatience at the reappearance of tax collectors, frustration at the absence of priests, and hostility to requisitions and military service would not turn them into counter-revolutionaries.

7   Consolidation, 1799–1804

Most survey histories of the French Revolution end in 1799; some even end in 1794 as we have noted. Why, then, do we continue the story until 1804 and Bonaparte's coronation as Emperor of the French? The question can be answered at several levels. For a start, the republic remained in being until 1804 and not until 1810 were all traces of its existence removed. It was, after all, a style of government that could accommodate hugely divergent interpretations of how power should be held. However, it could not accommodate the hereditary rule of one person. In 1799 France's young republic was continuing to evolve as we have seen, and to interrupt its life cycle purely on the grounds that another *coup* happened in that year would be arbitrary.

In any case there is little reason to suppose that the great mass of French men and women would have regarded the events of Brumaire as somehow out of the ordinary. They were informed that the intervention had happened so as to make the republic more secure. The sense of a new beginning – one associated indissolubly with the name of Bonaparte – only began to develop after the military victory at Marengo (14 June 1800) provided some ballast for the new regime. As for General Bonaparte personally (from 1802 official proclamations referred to him as Napoleon Bonaparte), his relationship to the recent revolutionary past may have been ambiguous, but it was not rooted in deep-seated hostility. Witness the manifesto to the public that accompanied the issuing of yet another constitution: 'Citizens, the Revolution is established on the principles which began it: it is finished' [**Doc. 27**].

Napoleon regarded himself not as the enemy of the revolution, but as its consolidator. The fact that others begged to differ (not least historians), simply tells us that the heritage of the revolution meant different things to different people by 1800. For Napoleon, the enduring legacy of the revolution lay in the victory over 'privilege' achieved in 1789, the institutional and administrative reforms initiated by the first two legislative Assemblies, and the social regrouping in the corridors of power that these achievements had made possible subsequently. He was scornful of the more radical schemes to recast society and regarded undiluted sovereignty of the people as tantamount to anarchy. Yet it is likely that most thinking people would have shared these views in 1799 – even while continuing to think of themselves as beneficiaries of the revolution.

DOI: 10.4324/9781003156185-9

Brumaire

Despite the annual drama of elections and electoral interventions, the Directory had, by the autumn of 1799, lasted longer than any of the previous governments put in place by the revolutionaries. The hustings held in March of that year had not added to the injuries inflicted in 1797 and 1798, and the regime might have continued to evolve had it not been destabilized by the military crisis of the summer. The news of Bonaparte's return from Egypt was taken to be a good omen; he would roll back the republic's external and internal enemies once more and quell all the alarmist talk insinuating that the nation's survival could only be guaranteed by a return to the politics of the Terror. His involvement in the proposals to strengthen executive authority being mooted by Sieyès and others was consistent with these expectations. The *coup*, when it came on 18 Brumaire, was not a determined bid for personal power. On the contrary, Bonaparte turned out to be a rather ham-fisted plotter and the assault launched against the Directory very nearly ended badly for him.

As in the case of all previous *coups* and insurrections, the aim was to achieve change by legal means if at all possible and to use force only as a last resort. Early on the morning of 9 November a number of deputies in the Council of Elders, who were no doubt privy to what was afoot, were advised of the discovery of a terrifying neo-Jacobin 'plot'. If plausible, the allegation was nevertheless entirely without foundation; its purpose was to induce the deputies to agree to the transfer of the legislative bodies to a place of 'safety' outside the capital. Bonaparte, meanwhile, was empowered to take charge of all the troops in the Paris military district, and three of the five Directors resigned (Sieyès, Ducos and Barras). To forestall any opposition, Bonaparte's brother Lucien, who had been elected president of the Council of Five Hundred only a couple of weeks earlier, cut short the discussion in his chamber; but no attempt was made to arrest any neo-Jacobin deputies at this stage.

The next day the legislative bodies reconvened in the former royal palace of Saint-Cloud, six miles distant from the capital. Realizing that they had been hoodwinked, some of the deputies began to show signs of a willingness to defend the regime – an eventuality that appears to have caught the plotters unprepared. Impatient at the delay, Bonaparte barged into the meeting place of the Elders and harangued the deputies in a manner that made it all too obvious that he was the instrument chosen to overthrow the government. But worse was to follow for he then entered the chamber of the Five Hundred accompanied by an escort of grenadiers, only to be greeted with shouts of 'Down with the dictator!' After some rough handling, he beat a retreat. This setback forced the conspirators into a life or death struggle, for a vote to outlaw Bonaparte and his collaborators would have caused the *coup* attempt to collapse. Lucien saved the day with remarkable presence of mind. Having also been ejected from the chamber, he harangued the waiting troops claiming that the majority of deputies were being held hostage by 'miserable offspring of the Terror' (Woloch, 2001: 22), adding that an attempt had been made to stab their commander to death. For good measure, he insisted that he would rather stab his brother himself than allow him to betray the nation's freedom. On this appeal from the president of the Five Hundred, the guards cleared the deputies from the hall with regular troops providing a back-up force. That evening a rump legislature voted to abolish the Directory and to substitute a three-man executive comprising Sieyès, Bonaparte and Ducos. Around 60 neo-Jacobin deputies were expelled from the Council of Five Hundred with immediate effect, and plans were put in hand to draw up a new constitution.

In the country at large, the events of Brumaire were rather poorly diagnosed on the whole. Public opinion in Rouen interpreted the news as simply another Directory *coup*, although decrees issued in the aftermath of the proroguing of the Councils made it clear that a provisional 'Consulate' had been set up. In Toulouse and Grenoble, the *coup* was perceived as having an anti-Jacobin thrust, even though Bonaparte issued an announcement insisting on the nonpartisan character of the action taken against the Directory. Paris remained non-committal at street level, a fact for which the plotters had reason to be grateful. Only in the department of the Jura in eastern France was an attempt made to concert armed resistance to the 'traitor' Bonaparte.

The stock exchange, on the other hand, rallied – presumably because the strengthened executive moved to abolish the 'forced loan' and the draconian legislation imposed on the families of *émigrés* the preceding summer. It would

Figure 7.1 James Gillray's depiction of the Brumaire *coup*
© Wikimedia Commons, public domain

be a year and more before the change of government brought to term the breakdown of law and order in the countryside, though. Highwaymen, draft-evaders and unruly priests generated a climate of insecurity which in the southeast of the country, particularly, had never seemed greater. Special tribunals with streamlined judicial procedures were set up to deal with offenders and by the end of 1802 over 2,300 capital punishments had been carried out (Brown, 2007: 1387). Only in the west did the authorities score an early success when the *chouans* agreed to an armistice. Like the Pretender (the self-styled Louis XVIII) and his *émigré* Court, they were watching closely in an effort to determine the political significance of the events of Brumaire. Elsewhere, in the non-insurgent regions, ordinary people dealt with the security issues spilling over from the Directory years on their own, without much help from the new government.

However, the speed with which the legislative commissions appointed immediately after the *coup* produced a constitution betrays the anxiety of all concerned to bring to an end the makeshift character of the new regime. Constitutions of the revolutionary era habitually took months, if not years, to draft, but the founding document of the Consulate was drawn up and issued in six weeks – that is to say, on 13 December 1799. In practice it was devised by Bonaparte himself who liked to do everything swiftly. As such, it was short, obscure and notably lacking in a preliminary statement of rights. Sieyès, whom everyone assumed would have a ready-made draft in his pocket, contributed general ideas including the proposition that 'confidence comes from below and authority from above' (Jainchill, 2008: 227), but he was ignored by the over-bearing General on the issue of power sharing. Bonaparte wanted to concentrate executive power rather than to divide and disperse it in order to achieve balance. Only by sublimating the freedom of all into a singular source of authority that would stand above party, he believed, could the revolution be brought to a successful conclusion. He therefore borrowed an idea from the lawyer-deputy Boulay de la Meurthe for a 'First Consul' who would exercise power for a ten-year term with the help of two other Consuls. Their role, however, would be consultative for the decision of the First Consul alone counted and the text of the Constitution specifically allocated the office of First Consul to Bonaparte. The problem of the Directory's weak executive – designed as such in reaction to the Terror – had been resolved.

Legislative arrangements under the Constitution of 1800 retained more traces of Sieyès's ideas, though. Two chambers came into being: a small body, known as the Tribunate, was empowered to discuss proposals put forward by the government, but could not vote on the measures, whereas a rather bigger Legislative Body (*Corps Législatif*) was entitled to vote on legislative proposals, but could not debate them beforehand. However, all bills were subject to prior scrutiny by a Senate acting as a kind of constitutional court. Members of the Senate were appointed, but not hereditary office holders. The right to initiate legislation was vested in the Consuls needless to say, and the First Consul alone had the power to submit amendments. To aid in the preparation of legislation, a Council of State was set up, the members of which would bring proposals before the Tribunate and the Legislative Body, and defend them as necessary. None of these bodies was directly elected – Bonaparte believed that direct elections nurtured factional strife – and neither the Consuls nor the ministers were responsible to the two-chamber legislature.

The Constitution as a whole should have been submitted to the outgoing Councils of the Directory for ratification. However, this would have invited comment on the very considerable powers now concentrated in the hands of one man. Instead, Bonaparte resorted to a plebiscite or referendum. In this respect he copied revolutionary practice (the Jacobin Constitution of 1793 had been endorsed in a similar fashion). A referendum would build a rampart of public support for the regime and de-legitimize expressions of criticism. In anticipation of such support, the Constitution was put into immediate effect. Voters scarcely had much of a choice in any case since both the *coup* and the extinction of the Directory were accomplished facts. According to the results announced on 7 February 1800, over 3 million accepted the new constitution and just 1,562 rejected it. In reality, the electoral returns were padded in the bureaux of the Interior Ministry which was controlled by Lucien Bonaparte: only about 1.6 million adult males out of a potential 7 million turned out to affirm their support for the regime.

Building afresh

If the *coup* of Brumaire was not intended to be a repudiation of the principles of the revolution, there was general agreement among supporters of the new regime that a certain amount of rebuilding would be required so as to remedy defects that had come to light since 1789. In many spheres, the Directory had already begun this work of course, although Bonapartist propaganda went to some pains to obscure the fact. Decisive action in the budgetary domain had largely sorted out the problem of financial insolvency which had hindered political actors ever since the time of Calonne. In the aftermath of the Fructidor *coup*, Ramel-Nogaret, the Finance Minister, reneged on two-thirds of the public debt, thereby cutting it at a stroke from about 250 million to 80 million *livres*. Converted into treasury bonds the remaining third soon lost value, with the result that the debt came to represent only about 10 per cent of annual income whereas in 1789 it had stood at 250 per cent. The experiment with a paper currency had also been brought to an end, which vastly increased the value of receipts from taxation. The Consulate was only too happy to build on these reforms and it built, too, on the trend towards a re-centralizing of tax collection. A law passed within days of Brumaire set up a specialist tax administration in each department. With the gradual return of law and order to the countryside, overhead costs went down and by 1801 it proved possible to collect tax liabilities in the year in which they fell. For much of the preceding decade taxes had been paid in arrears, often in depreciated paper notes and vouchers.

The Directory had also started to address some of the defects inherent in the devolved local government system put in place originally by the National

Constituent Assembly. Individual village municipalities – one of the prime sources of revolutionary activism – had been abolished in 1795 as we have seen; similarly, the District administrations which were replaced with consolidated or canton-based municipalities. The Constitution of 1795 had also made the first breach in the principle that local officials should be democratically accountable inasmuch as the Commissioners of the Executive Directory – the main cogs in the Directorial apparatus of local government – were appointed, not elected. Within months of taking office, however, the Consuls overhauled this system and resolved its ambiguities. Democratic accountability was no longer to be emphasized as part of the heritage of the revolution. The Bonapartist synthesis of liberty and authority required the initiative to come from above rather than below. Individual villages retrieved their mayors and municipal officers it is true, for power-holding at the level of the canton had not proved a satisfactory arrangement. But these local agents were now all appointed by, and answerable to, the government in the person of a 'prefect'. Opportunities for municipal councils to meet and deliberate were curtailed, too, for the First Consul considered assemblies and elections to be the twin sources of the party strife that had repeatedly prevented the consolidation of the achievements of the revolution.

The key figure in the post-1799 system of local government was the prefect, then. In each department the First Consul nominated an official whose responsibilities were all-embracing. With the help of sub-prefects residing in divisions of the departments known as *arrondissements*, he was to supervise police activities, village affairs, hospitals, public works, conscription, tax raising and much else besides. Vestigial assemblies reminiscent of the old Department and District councils set up in 1790 operated alongside the prefects and sub-prefects to be sure, but they had no powers of their own. The prefects are sometimes compared with those servitors of absolute monarchy, the intendants. Yet the prefects were far more powerful figures – if only because the abolition of corporate privilege had removed all rival sources of authority from the regions where they administered. They were also utterly loyal to central government and to a concept of law that placed them above and beyond the reach of factional politics.

The Consulate's greatest act of consolidation occurred in the religious domain. Despite the abandonment of the Civil Constitution of the Clergy in 1795 and the tentative moves towards toleration, the Directory had never felt at ease with the policy of religious pluralism. The link between the activities of the non-oath-swearing clergy, the *émigrés* and internal counter-revolution was too obvious to ignore. Besides, the regime had its own liturgy of civic festivals and adhered doggedly to the republican calendar that the Convention had introduced in 1793. When one of the first acts of the Brumaire plotters presupposed a reduction in the programme of secular feast days, exiled and outlawed clergy all over Europe pricked up their ears. Indeed, large numbers of non-jurors returned to their parishes during the winter months of 1799–1800 in the belief that a relaxation of the proscription laws was only a matter of time. However, the regime needed the kind of solidity and legitimacy that could only be earned on the field of battle before it felt able to contemplate a move in this direction.

On the eve of the decisive engagement at Marengo (14 June 1800), Bonaparte appeared to acknowledge that the goal of a reconciled civil society would prove illusory without the reinstatement of public religious worship and that this, in turn, would require a rapprochement with the pope. 'In religion', he later commented, 'I see not the mystery of the incarnation, but the mystery of the social order' (Ellis, 1997: 235).

Since the policy of clerical persecution (not to mention that of dechristianization) had manifestly failed, the advantages of a move towards pacification – if sincerely undertaken – were not difficult to identify. In all likelihood it would cut the tap-root of peasant resistance (in the Vendée; in Brittany); it would force those *ancien-régime* bishops who had spent ten years fishing in the troubled waters of the revolution from the safety of exile to choose between the interests of the monarchy and those of religion; it would make the future expansion of *'la grande nation'* into Catholic parts of Europe easier to accomplish; and, above all, it would bring to an end the clerical split of 1790–91, thus providing a further source of legitimacy for the regime in the making. In return Pope Pius VII would regain control over Europe's largest Catholic state, a chance to restore the fabric of the Church and the opportunity to rechristianize the population [**Doc. 28**]. To be sure, this 'control' would be offered at a price which many in the hierarchy considered excessive: Catholicism would not be the state religion, but merely 'the religion of the great majority of French citizens' (Buchez and Roux, 1834–38: vol. 38, 465), and the corporate privileges of the old Gallican Church would have to be given up without any hope of recovery. The abolition of the tithe would remain in place and the sales of Church property (***biens nationaux***) would not be reversed, nor compensation paid for losses.

A question mark hung over the future of the oath-swearing bishops and clergy, however, for the pope was most reluctant to have them back in the fold on a 'forgive and forget' basis. The constitutional Church was far from moribund and the treatment meted out to it represented a test of the government's commitment to whole-hearted reconciliation. Bonaparte would advise his Minister of Ecclesiastical Affairs to 'mix the constitutional priests with the others in such a way that no party seems to be triumphing at the expense of the other' (Lyons, 1994: 91). However, at the point the religious Concordat was signed on 15 July 1801, this issue was still not fully resolved.

Nor was that quite the end of the saga. The deal struck with the papacy remained secret for many months and Bonaparte used the pause to add further 'organic articles' to the outline agreement. These additional clauses enhanced the authority of the secular power in matters to do with the clergy, yet the authority of the bishops over the parish clergy was reinforced as well. Under the new regime, priests would be appointed by their ecclesiastical superiors rather than elected by the laity, and they could be moved at will. When the Concordat was finally made public in time for Easter Sunday 1802, the tolling of church bells was heard across the republic for the first time in eight years. Jacobin sympathisers who could remember the heady days of 1793 and 1794 were not impressed. At the solemn Mass held in the presence of the government and the diplomatic corps in Notre Dame cathedral, General Delmas is reported to have exclaimed: 'all we need are the 100,000 men who got themselves killed to be rid of all this' (Lyons, 1994: 88).

A new order

Although the resolution of the unfinished business of the revolution in matters of faith and conscience proved more robust than anyone could have anticipated, it was not the most enduring achievement of the Consulate. The Civil Code, which was promulgated in 1804, should be regarded as the supreme act of consolidation to emerge from the *coup* of Brumaire. Even at the time, this synthesis of *ancien régime* and revolutionary legal wisdom was hailed as the cornerstone of the new post-1799 social order. Bonaparte regarded it as a greater victory than any he had won on the battlefield. The Code became one of the primary instruments of French domination in Europe, and its clauses remain embedded in the constitutions of a number of states – France included – to this day. Diversity, and jurisdictional diversity in particular, had been one of the defining features of the corporate society of the *ancien régime* as we have seen. In fact, Lamoignon was preparing to tackle this legal tangle as Keeper of the Seals when he fell from power in 1788. The revolutionaries never doubted the need for a standardization of the law, but it had not been their top priority. In the meantime, another 30,000 decrees were committed to the statute book over the course of the decade.

Two legal problems had faced the legislators of the 1790s. They needed to decide among themselves which aspects of *ancien-régime* jurisprudence, if any, they wished to preserve and, having decided, they needed a powerful executive authority to push forward the work to fruition. Although the Thermidorian deputies did make some headway, the Directors lacked the authority to initiate legislation with the result that little was achieved. The task fell to the men of Brumaire, therefore, but opinions still differed as to how much of the legal wisdom of the revolution should be retained and how much discarded. An initial draft was criticized in the Tribunate and it was only after Bonaparte removed his opponents from that body in 1802 that the work of codification moved to a conclusion.

The Civil Code (or Napoleonic Code as it was known from 1807) gave legal expression to the social gains of the revolution [**Doc. 31**] – or at least to those gains that seemed, from the vantage point of 1804, to be the most important and the most worthy of preservation. Enshrined in the Code were statements guaranteeing the equality of all in the eyes of the law (and therefore the abolition of privilege); the inviolability of individual ownership (and therefore the validity of the sales of Church and *émigré* property); the freedom of contract; the freedom of careers; and the secular nature of the law. With its thoroughly modern conception of property rights and economic relationships, it should not surprise that the Code became a veritable charter for the liberal-bourgeois world of the nineteenth century. However, the document also laid out a systematic framework of law applicable to rights and obligations within households (dowries, divorce, adoption, wardship, etc.) and to inheritance, and in these areas it was more cautious and compromising. The authority of husbands and fathers within the family was reinforced in a manner that actually curtailed and even reversed some of the liberalizing impulses of the revolution.

Divorce, for example, was made harder to obtain, particularly for women. The remarkably egalitarian law of 1792 which had prompted Rosalie Jullien's quip to her husband 'you no longer have a wife' (Lockroy, 1881: 284) was repealed. Provisions were introduced which restricted divorce by mutual consent and imposed a 'double standard' test of adultery, to the advantage of husbands. In the city of Lyons, the frequency of divorces dropped from 87 annually prior to the implementation of the Code to seven after 1805 (Lyons, 1994: 100). The 1792 legislation had given adult women the legal right to bear witness as well, and we know that the majority of divorces were obtained by women. Watkin Tench claimed in letters written from France that in Nivôse of the Year Three (21 December 1794–19 January 1795) 198 of the 223 divorces in Paris had been obtained by women (Edwards ed., 2001: 121). But at least divorce was still possible after 1804 and in 1809 Napoleon made use of clauses in the Code to put away Joséphine de Beauharnais. In 1816 the restored Bourbons would remove the facility of divorce from the civil law altogether.

The Code also sounded the retreat from the strictly egalitarian inheritance legislation of the Terror years, which had drawn no distinction between the rights of siblings or the rights of legitimate and illegitimate offspring. In a nod towards the custom of male primogeniture in matters of inheritance, which was widely followed in the southern provinces of the kingdom prior to 1789, the drafters devised a solution that acknowledged the rights of the family group as well as those of the individual. Testators were allowed to will freely a portion of their assets, while the bulk had to be shared equally between (legitimate) heirs. Apart from anything else, this stipulation promised concrete political benefits as Bonaparte noted in a letter to his brother Joseph: 'at the end of a few years all the fortunes not attached to you will be destroyed, and any that you wish to preserve will be consolidated. That is the great advantage of the Civil Code' (Thompson, 2013: letter 119).

Many changes to the family law introduced in the 1790s were reversed in fact. Citizenship, moreover, became increasingly linked to position within the family group, the inference being that it should be identified with the status of head of household. As for foreigners, the route to citizenship via naturalization ceased to be semi-automatic as the residence qualification was gradually lengthened. But at least the citizenship taken away from emigrant nobles in 1793 was returned in Bonaparte's partial amnesty for *émigrés* of October 1800. Nevertheless, by 1804, virtually all that remained of citizenship as understood by the revolutionaries was the obligation to perform military service.

Napoleon Bonaparte understood better than most of his collaborators that the work of consolidation demanded the creation of a social elite whose loyalties were anchored firmly to the new status quo rather than to one or more of the failed regimes of France's recent past. In 1802, he declared that the reforms being undertaken by the Consulate would provide a 'granite substratum' (*masses de granit*) binding the nation together. Whether the social bedrock was made up of groups that had been rich and powerful under the *ancien régime* or groups that had risen to prominence during the revolution, did not much matter as long as their primary allegiance was focused on the regime. In a marked departure from previous republican practice, about 52,000 *émigrés* were enabled to return to France, although there was no question of them recovering possessions that had already been sold and they were required to swear the oath of allegiance to the Constitution. By 1803 all but the most notorious royalist exiles had been offered the chance to return, in fact. Jacobins of the 1793 vintage were encouraged to rally to the regime, too, providing that they had not been involved in subversive activity during the Directory years, or in the Opera Plot which nearly killed Bonaparte and his entire entourage in December 1800. Most old Jacobins kept their distance though: the governing bodies of the Consulate contained few regicides. In the country, meanwhile, the regime tried hard to nurture a class of 'notables' who would act as a pool of socially acceptable and non-partisan recruits for public office and positions in the bureaucracy. It is at this level that the re-alignment of former stalwarts of the Terror is most noticeable.

Whether the emerging new order in the metropole carried a positive charge in France's overseas territories is more open to question, though. The Convention's abrupt slave emancipation decree of 1794 had improved the republic's military position in Saint-Domingue even if it came too late to prevent the loss of Martinique to Britain for eight years (1794–1802). The Constitution of 1795 had re-affirmed, moreover, that France's colonies 'are integral parts of the republic and are subject to the same constitutional law' (Jainchill, 2008: 144). Bonaparte, however, had more flexible opinions on the slave issue and was feeling his way on colonial policy. In the event, the post-Brumaire constitution signalled a retreat from universalism inasmuch as it abandoned the principle that the colonies were to be governed by the same law as the metropole.

Following the successful conclusion of peace talks with Britain (October 1801), the strategic situation in the Caribbean altered fundamentally. It prompted the First Consul to envisage the recovery of Saint-Domingue in addition to Martinique (where slavery had never been abolished). A sizeable fleet, in fact a veritable armada, set sail with the remit to recapture the colony and thereby forestall a declaration of independence by the leading commander of the slave revolution **Toussaint Louverture**. Whether General Leclerc's instructions also included the restoration of slavery at this juncture is not clear: even in the planter lobby there were many who thought it futile to try to turn the clock back. On arriving in the Caribbean in February 1802 Leclerc disclaimed any intention to re-enslave the black population of Saint-Domingue. Back in Paris, however, a law would be passed on 27 April 1802 which maintained slavery where it already existed (i.e. in Martinique, Réunion and Mauritius) and reinstated the oceanic trade in slaves. The question of the future of Saint-Domingue and Guadeloupe was left open. But this was scarcely reassuring news for an insurgent black population which had experienced eight years of freedom. General Leclerc's forces were massively depleted in a brutal war for control of the colony and would eventually be defeated. In the autumn of 1803, the remnants of the expedition were repatriated and the following year the independence of Saint-Domingue was proclaimed under the new Amerindian name of Haiti. Historians disagree as to whether Bonaparte always aimed to reimpose the slave economy in the Caribbean (Girard, 2011: 3–28). The primary objective of the Leclerc expedition seems to have been to retrieve a valuable colonial asset and to ensure, once again, that it could only trade with the metropole. That being said, the episode certainly brought to a somber conclusion the story of citizenship in the French Caribbean, or for that matter in the Indian Ocean. By 1803 the politics of human improvement in the metropole had run its course. The goal was now to control citizens, not to transform them.

Towards dictatorship

For all the attempts to embed the regime, Bonaparte had no illusions as to its long-term future if statesmanship at home was not accompanied by generalship abroad. 'My power is dependent on my glory, and my glory on my victories', he later remarked, and 'my power would fall if I did not base it on still more glory and still more victories' (Brown and Miller eds, 2002: 32). The men of Brumaire would have emphatically agreed: it was the rather improbable victory at Marengo in Piedmont and the success of Moreau's Rhine Army at Hohenlinden (3 December 1800) that permitted the experiment of the Consulate to go ahead. Between the summer of 1799 and the spring of 1801, the balance of European warfare swung dramatically in France's favour once more. The left bank of the Rhine was recovered, as was northern and central Italy. At Lunéville (February 1801), the Austrians were brought to the conference table and obliged to accept French control over Venice and the Dalmatian coastline, the reinstatement of the sister republics and the annexation of Piedmont. The following year favourable terms were reached with Britain as well. At the Peace of Amiens, which was signed on 25 March 1802, France remained in possession of all of her continental conquests, although the British government withheld recognition of the satellite republics. For the first time since April 1792 military activity ceased in Europe.

  These foreign policy successes, together with the prospect of internal peace following the publication of the Concordat, brought the Napoleonic regime to a turning point in the spring of 1802. Intransigent royalists had already begun to ask themselves whether Bonaparte might not be persuaded to play the role of herald for a monarchical restoration. Indeed, the self-styled Louis XVIII had already raised the subject, only to be told: 'You must not hope for your return to France; you would have to walk over one hundred thousand corpses' (Lyons, 1994: 131). In fact, the nation's 'saviour' was more interested in perpetuating his own authority than in making way for someone else. Despite some expressions of unease as to the direction of government policy, the Tribunate was induced to make a suggestion that the powers of the Consuls be extended to ten years. But this was not quite what Bonaparte had in mind. Instead, he intervened – discreetly – to ensure that a rather different proposition be worded and placed before the electorate for ratification: 'Shall Napoleon Bonaparte be named First Consul for life?' This alarmed liberal republicans in the Tribunate, the Legislative Body and even the Senate, for it indicated that Bonaparte's authoritarian ambitions might extend beyond what was needed to consolidate the revolution. **Antoine Thibaudeau**, one of the deputies who had supported the Brumaire *coup*, demurred, observing: 'The impression of the revolution is still too fresh and this transition too abrupt' (Woloch, 2001: 94).

The willingness, notwithstanding, of long-serving revolutionaries like Thibaudeau to go along with what was happening requires some explanation. How did Napoleon Bonaparte manage to recruit so many able collaborators from their ranks? There are a number of possible answers to this question. For a start we should not underestimate what Bonaparte could offer: security, the rule of law, an end to political faction-fighting and perhaps also catharsis after a decade of undeliverable promises and gnawing, life-threatening fears. For all the seductive slogans of the revolution, the collaborators were principally men who had devoted their lives to the service of the state. Brumaire offered a chance to extend their careers and to mobilize their expertise in a mission to found a polity rooted in liberal institutions. True, the ultimate liberal value of representative government now appeared to be at risk. But who are we, they would reason, to raise objections when the people have been consulted and have given their consent? In any case, the 'saviour' of the revolution let it be known that service to the state and loyalty to his person would be rewarded most handsomely.

The results of the referendum on the Life Consulship of May 1802 proved to be highly satisfactory to its sponsor. A little over half of the electorate declared themselves in support of the proposition and on this occasion, there was no need to falsify the returns. The English social reformer Jeremy Bentham, who happened to be visiting Paris at the time, was able to use the citizenship conferred on him in 1792 to participate in the ballot. Voters were implicitly endorsing the reforms undertaken since 1799, but whether they were also giving Bonaparte a licence to transform the regime into a personal dictatorship is another matter. Still, the immediate consequence was to usher in a modification of the Constitution introduced only two years earlier. Napoleon Bonaparte as he was now styled, remained First Consul, but for life in common with the Second and Third Consuls. However, the latter were to be chosen by the First Consul (through the intermediary of the Senate) and he was empowered to appoint his own successor as well. Only the Senate, as guardian of the Constitution, could have hindered what amounted to quasi-prerogative authority vested in the person of the First Consul. Bonaparte therefore took steps to remove the doubters from this body; as for the Tribunate and the Legislative Body they could simply be put into abeyance. With the Senate now a docile tool, its power to issue decrees (*senatus consulta*) that bypassed the legislature fell into Bonaparte's hands as well.

Figure 7.2 Vote on the Life Consulate, 1802

In the aftermath of the constitutional revision of August 1802 few could have mistaken the direction in which the governance of France was now heading. Already in May an honours system had been established which would come to reward military valour rather than civic virtue (the Legion of Honour). Protesters in the Tribunate objected that it infringed the 'bedrock' principle of equality. The Constitution made provision, moreover, for Napoleon's effigy to appear on coins just like the kings of old, and an embryonic Court began to take shape in the Tuileries Palace – the First Consul's official residence. Slowly, the political culture of the revolution was receding from public memory, or rather from official public memory. Whilst the tricolour flag was retained, the red bonnet of the emancipated slave that had often accompanied it in 1793 and 1794 disappeared from view and was replaced with the image of an eagle. The Marseillaise was heard less often, the 14 July festival marked with less enthusiasm, and citizens reverted to the practice of addressing one another as 'Monsieur' and 'Madame'.

Political opposition from within the regime dwindled. On grounds of state security, censorship of the press had been re-imposed in the aftermath of Brumaire with the result that the number of political newspapers published in Paris dropped from 73 to thirteen. Both royalist and republican titles were targeted. 'Journals', a police report noted disdainfully, 'have always been the tocsin of revolutions' (Aulard ed., 1903–09: vol. 1, 96). Following an attempt to kill the

First Consul with a huge bomb (the Infernal Machine Plot) as he was making his way to the Paris opera, several street-level neo-Jacobins were executed and many more deported. These executions and deportations of alleged 'terrorists' without preliminary trial shocked men like Thibaudeau and were indicative of how the new government would play fast and loose with the rule of law. In fact, the attack had been the work of royalists and it was the continuing threat of plots and assassination attempts from this quarter that would set the stage for the ultimate transformation of the Consulate.

The peace signed at Amiens lasted barely fourteen months [**Doc. 30**] and with the return of Britain to the fray, royalist efforts to topple Bonaparte were renewed. **Georges Cadoudal,** the former *chouan* leader who had fled to England in order to escape the pacification of the west in 1801, played the key role. A plan was hatched for him to make contact – in Paris – with the royalist General Pichegru who had managed to return from deportation following the Fructidor *coup*, and General Moreau the conqueror of the Austrians at Hohenlinden. On a signal of the arrival in France of a Bourbon prince, the conspirators would kidnap or kill the First Consul. However, no royal prince seems to have been prepared to risk what would have been an extremely hazardous mission; Moreau's dislike of Bonaparte did not extend to co-operating in a Bourbon restoration; and in any case Cadoudal was betrayed. The government responded decisively and in the view of many, outrageously. The young Duke of Enghien (grandson of the Prince de Condé), who was assumed to be the princeling in question, was kidnapped on foreign territory, brought to Paris and court martialled. He met his end before a firing squad in the fortress of Vincennes on 21 March 1804, just a few days after the promulgation of the Civil Code.

The murder of Enghien, the suspicious 'suicide' of Pichegru in his prison cell and the exiling of Moreau formed part of Bonaparte's balancing act. Royalists had been warned that the road back to the *ancien régime* was definitely closed; sincere republicans were reassured, albeit temporarily, as to the fundamental character of the regime; and the generals were put on notice to stay out of politics. Yet the Cadoudal Plot also served notice, should any further demonstration be needed, of the willingness of Napoleon Bonaparte to resort to exceptional measures [**Doc. 29**]. It served as a timely reminder, too, of how much now depended on the survival of one man.

Unlike some of his collaborators, the First Consul did not view the abolition of the monarchy as an integral part of the revolution's legacy. He regarded it more as an accidental by-product of the embittered politics prevailing in 1792. Hereditary government was not an anathema, then. Indeed, in the conditions of 1804, it seemed to offer the robustness that would be required to withstand and overcome plots and threats of assassination. Even old revolutionaries who doubted whether hereditary power could ever be accommodated within the framework of a republic could see the dangers of anarchy. It is no coincidence, therefore, that shortly after Enghien's execution, a Senate rendered docile by rewards and bribes 'invited Napoleon Bonaparte to complete his work and make himself immortal like his glory'. A month or so later the Tribunate urged, quite explicitly, that he be proclaimed 'hereditary emperor of the French' (Boudon, 1997: 49). Only a handful of tribunes spoke against, among whom was Lazare Carnot, one-time member of the Committee of Public Safety who had voted against the Life Consulate two years earlier. But even Carnot stated that he would put to one side his reservations if the people voted to re-establish a monarchical system of government (Woloch, 2001: 106–07). Thereafter, events moved swiftly: the Senate drew up a modified constitution on 18 May and in keeping with the practice followed since 1800 the proposal to confer the dignity of hereditary emperor on Napoleon Bonaparte and his direct descendants was submitted to the electorate. A resounding vote in favour was recorded (3,572,329 'Yes' and 2,569 'No'), although analysis of the turnout figures suggests that support for the regime among ordinary voters may actually have fallen when compared with the ballot on the Life Consulate in 1802.

The revised Constitution of 1804 nowhere stated that the republic had been formally abolished. It simply declared that an Emperor would take over the reins of government and that the current First Consul would become Emperor ('Napoleon Bonaparte, present First Consul of the Republic, is Emperor of the French', title 1, article 2). However, the new incumbent was required to swear an oath to uphold, among other things, civil and political liberty, the freedom of religion and the irreversibility of the property transfers of the revolutionary era. He was also obliged to govern with a view solely to the happiness and glory of the French people. No question any longer of the division of powers; the various bodies of the state were to be activated by the will of Napoleon Bonaparte alone. The imperial coronation took place at the end of the year and it completed the metamorphosis of the Consulate into a dictatorship that was intended to be permanent. Yet this would be no ordinary political and military dictatorship: Bonaparte enjoyed a large measure of public support; he did not owe his elevation to the generals; and he could claim with some plausibility that his regime remained within the furrow ploughed by the revolution.

Part III

8 Assessment

The French Revolution can be visualized as a huge release of civic energy. The release started in 1787, reached a peak between 1789 and 1795, and then slowly faded. Only in a superficial sense is it accurate to describe this extraordinary phenomenon as a series of dramatic events. In reality the revolution was a drawn-out process which had at its core the realization among ordinary men and women that the human condition was not fixed until the end of time but could be altered. It could be altered if sufficient amounts of physical effort, human ingenuity and – yes – suffering were brought into play. For a decade and more the shock of this realization transfixed French society and held much of continental Europe spell-bound as well. Even in 1814–15 when throne and altar partnerships were restored in many countries, the effects were not entirely dispelled. Once the French Revolution had happened, no government could find safety merely in 'the length of its continuance' (Burke, 1790/1973: 149). The peoples of Europe were now poised to become actors in their own historical drama. In this sense, the French Revolution marks a dividing line between the medieval and modern epochs in the history of the western world. Along with the Industrial Revolution, it is linked indissolubly with the arrival of modernity.

What shape did this remarkable energy burst take? The revolution should be viewed as one of the key episodes in the history of representative government. What happened in France between 1787 and 1804 opened up a new range of possibilities as to how society might be organized, and at the forefront of these possibilities was the aspiration to achieve democracy. Before France's great revolution 'democracy' was an abstract concept; it had little purchase on the day-to-day practice of politics. No one would have ventured such a statement by the start of the nineteenth century, though. After the defeat of Napoleon Bonaparte in 1815 democracy was here to stay – never mind the talk among Europe's elder statesmen of turning the clock back. The word had entered common speech, both as a noun and as an adjective, and a whole generation of Europeans had grown to adulthood who understood the meaning of the verb to 'democratize' (Dunn, 2005: 16–17). Whether they would have approved of this seismic shift in the relationship between the state and society is another matter of course. The first trial of democracy had not been an auspicious one. An electoral system based on near universal voting rights for males did not

DOI: 10.4324/9781003156185-11

translate neatly into a happy, self-governing state as events between 1792 and 1794 had demonstrated. Many decades and many more revolutions would have to pass before this paradox could be resolved. Nevertheless, it is undeniable that the French Revolution gave the drive for democracy a motive force which it has never subsequently lost. In the process it expanded hugely the arena of achievable civil and political freedoms.

How, then, did this civic energy come to be released? Researchers have looked for the causes of the revolution in many quarters. Indeed, the question of causes can lead the student into a maze from which only the most clear-sighted stands any chance of emerging. Some historians have even asked whether the word itself has become a barrier to understanding. Better, perhaps, to think in terms of 'conditions' rather than of 'causes' (Maza, 2013: 43). For example, it is suggested that structural tensions within the *ancien-régime* economy created conditions of endemic crisis from around 1785 when disparate antagonisms began to merge into something more ominous and threatening (Jessenne, 2013: 38). But 'conditions' are necessarily less conclusive than 'causes': on their own they do not lend themselves to clear-cut answers.

The debate on the French Revolution as it is currently conducted reflects the preoccupation in the west with globalization and the extension around the world of 'rights'. One of the roots of this debate can be traced back to 2006 when the *Journal of Global History* was launched. In pursuit of an alternative 'grand narrative', historians removed the revolution from an exclusively domestic setting and put it into a broader geographical context. But should the outbreak of a revolution in France be attributed to trans-national forces and aspirations: to the struggle for military supremacy in Europe; the drive for colonies and 'empire'; the knock-on effects of aggressive commercial rivalries; the pressures imposed by international money markets; or the demand for human rights? There can be no doubt that these factors put France under a degree of strain in the decades after the Seven Years War. Some researchers, indeed, discern a world-wide 'age of revolution' between 1760 and 1840 (Armitage and Subrahmanyam eds, 2010: xii–xiv).

Whether it is helpful to insert the events taking place in France during the 1790s into such a scenario remains an open question. On close inspection the 'age of revolution' may only offer analogies produced by lumping together very different phenomena. A global perspective suggests connections and comparisons, but if it is to produce a new interpretation of the French Revolution historians will need to spell out precisely how the effects of trans-national capitalism catalyzed the domestic political tensions developing at the heart of the Bourbon monarchy in the 1770s and 1780s. So far this work of detailed comparative analysis has not made much progress (Desan, Hunt and Nelson, eds, 2013; Bell, 2014: 1–24). We know, for example, that France's colonial trade across the Atlantic was extraordinarily profitable and there is some evidence to suggest that plantation agriculture in the Indian Ocean islands generated good returns as well. However, it is not clear what role, if any, this wealth played in destabilizing the metropole as a revolution approached.

For most of the twentieth century historians restricted themselves to exploring social and economic explanations for the outbreak of revolution on a narrower front. A society organized around the legal fiction of 'orders' or 'estates', they argued, was being transformed into a society increasingly shaped around the emerging socio-economic reality of classes. Class formation was thus the remote control of revolution, and the frustrations and ambitions of an expanding bourgeoisie its immediate trigger (Soboul, 1988). In the ideas of the Enlightenment the middle class found all the arguments they needed to challenge the political structures of the *ancien régime*.

This interpretation drew its inspiration from the political philosophy of Karl Marx and it was buttressed by plentiful evidence to show that the largely agricultural economy of the *ancien régime* was also entering a phase of prolonged recession in the 1770s. One of the drawbacks of this diagnosis, however, is that it ignores a booming commercial economy rooted in overseas trade and assumes that the considerable diversity of eighteenth-century society can be marshalled into coherent groups or classes that were disputing for power in the state. It also invites the conclusion that the 'energy' responsible for wearing down the defences of absolute monarchy in 1787–88 emanated primarily from the bourgeoisie. These are not insuperable obstacles as some historians have demonstrated. We know, for instance, that the business community did try to make itself heard in the autumn of 1788. Big merchants in towns such as Nantes and Montpellier called for separate representation in the Estates General (Clay, 2015: 21–39). However, the traditional 'social interpretation' of the origins of the revolution nowadays tends to incur a more wide-ranging set of objections. By prioritizing the role of internal economic factors in bringing about the critical weakening of the regime, it deflects attention away from 'non-class' cultural and political explanations.

Since the 1990s, historians have been trying to redress this imbalance. In an effort to probe beyond the frame of analysis formulated by Marx, they have investigated closely the workings of the Bourbon state, the construction of platforms for political expression, the emergence of an ideology to counter absolutism and the impact of shifts in material culture during the second half of the eighteenth century. As a result, a largely political interpretation of how the revolution came about now exists to challenge the certainties of class-based economic analysis. In the literature on the revolution there are two main variants of this approach: one which still allows considerable scope for individual social actors and one which does not.

Now that the state – the machinery of government and its agents – has been freed, so to speak, from the essentially passive role allocated to it in the class-driven model of how change takes place, a number of historians have argued that the revolution was essentially the product of a breakdown in a system of government that tried repeatedly to reform itself, but failed to do so. Thus, the chronic fiscal embarrassments of the Bourbon monarchy become not a symptom, but a prime cause (Hunt and Censer, 2017: 3). If contemporary critics concentrated their fire on Court extravagance and pecuniary privilege, it can only have been because they knew little about the real condition of royal finances. A few historians might rest their case at this point, denying the instrumentality of any other factor in the collapse of the *ancien régime*. However, most would still find some grounds for economic causation, while insisting that the bleaker outlook of the later 1770s and 1780s would not have brought down the regime on its own. It is true that the historians who now identify the monarchy itself as the primary force for change do not always agree on how to depict that institution. Are we dealing with a proto-modern, bureaucratic and administrative state by the 1770s, or one still caught in a late medieval or Renaissance time-warp where the Court was the fulcrum of politics and every minister first and foremost its creature?

At least some sense of human agency and responsibility for the outbreak of the revolution is retained in this interpretation, even if we are now trying to make sense of the behaviour of Louis XVI and his reforming ministers rather than the collective stance of a thrusting and impatient bourgeoisie. The alternative is to discount the 'social' altogether and to seek agency in the autonomous interplay of ideas. This contribution to the debate about the origins of the revolution came from intellectual historians in the main, and it attracted considerable interest around the time of the bicentenary (1989). Rather than seeking to anatomize the society that gave birth to the revolution in the belief that it should be possible to uncover the signs of an incurable disease, they suggested that researchers might do better to start with the language and styles of discourse that became commonplace during the revolution and ask themselves where they came from. Language, after all, does help to shape social and political reality, even if the reverse is more often the case. Perhaps the process of revolution was somehow 'scripted' (Baker ed., 1990: 86–106) in the form of a language of resistance to the claims of absolute monarchy long before a crowd of angry Parisians managed to break into the inner courtyard of the Bastille.

Yet a proto-revolutionary language still requires real people to express it and to be influenced by it. Or, to put it another way, ideas, actors and events do not exist in separate, albeit parallel, compartments; they intersect and interact. The growth after 1750, or thereabouts, of a critical state of mind among educated men and women must surely have contributed to the outbreak and subsequent direction of the revolution. Such an intelligentsia might be called a middle class, but for the fact that the critical constituency included reform-minded clerics, liberal nobles, younger parlementaires and state bureaucrats as well. These were all individuals who took their intellectual nourishment from the Enlightenment – more from the higher works of literature than the street-level satire and smut attacking the monarchy (Burrows, 2015: 82–3). That said, though, it is not clear how a linguistic approach might replace a broad-based social interpretation and provide an explanation of revolution sufficient on its own. In any case, research carried out since the bicentenary has resulted in something of a retreat from the 'scripted' or purely ideological interpretation of the revolution's origins.

Historians exploring the routine of politics in the 1790s and in particular the way debates unfolded in the revolutionary Assemblies readily acknowledge the part played by improvisation and contingency. Indeed, there has been something of a revival of interest in individual agency. As the focus of research shifts away from ideology, a space has opened for consideration of the role of emotion, trauma and friendship in the forging and sustaining of revolutionary alignments (Linton, 2015: 475–76). All historians are familiar with the intense expressions of 'joy', 'anger', 'fear' and 'suspicion' that would become a staple of political discourse. However, it is not clear that this approach will succeed any better in explaining the dynamic of revolution than the approach which claims that the events of 1789 and thereafter only became possible because the writings of the Enlightenment made them thinkable. William Doyle points out that 'It took the Revolution itself to show how much revolution might achieve, and open people's minds to unthought-of possibilities' (Doyle, 2013: 97).

The energy that launched the revolution was by no means entirely masculine. Yet the contributions made by women are often treated as 'unscripted', either because the evidence tends to be overlooked, or because (male?) historians have failed to discover a meaningful pattern in the participatory activities of women. During the later *ancien-régime* decades, there can be no doubt that a few women were able to play a quasi-public role in the salons and masonic lodges to be found in Paris and the larger regional capitals. This has led some historians to judge that the French revolutionaries failed women on two counts: on the one hand they discouraged the promising developments of the late Enlightenment years; on the other they refused to admit the logic of their own universalistic rhetoric and extend political rights to female citizens. Yet, one might reasonably ask how far the Enlightenment really embodied a promise of liberation for women. There are methodological dangers in taking a handful of Parisian blue-stockings as representative of the position of women in general at the end of the *ancien régime* (Goodman, 1994).

As for developments after 1789, it is undeniable that women were never formally admitted to the public spaces of the revolution, though they were never formally excluded from them either. Their claims to citizenship were only acknowledged at the most informal level as we have seen. Women, though, did not wait on events in order to be told what to do: they participated in revolutionary politics willy-nilly. They marched to Versailles to seek bread and the king; they raided grocers' shops; they resisted the closure of churches; they raucously shouted down deputies whom they disapproved of from the spectator benches of the Assemblies; and they sued for divorce to escape from inadequate or politically suspect husbands. By the summer of 1792, moreover, there existed self-consciously female *sans-culottes* and, despite efforts to dismantle their club network, they played a significant role in promoting violence against perceived enemies and in sustaining the Terror. Indeed, there is evidence to suggest that the wives and partners of artisan militants spurred on their menfolk. An American witness to the events of the revolution concluded that 'one woman in this country is equal to 2 men' (Chew, 2012: 98). When the Thermidorian

Convention sounded the retreat from the controlled economy during the winter of 1794–95 the trigger for insurrection came not from the menfolk, but from ordinary Parisian women. The deputies obliquely acknowledged their role by excluding them from the galleries of the Convention and from the meetings of the Sections. This was the closest any of the revolutionary Assemblies came to legislating against women as such (Godineau, 1988: 319–31). It demonstrated that the revolution had indeed assisted in the empowerment of women.

Lest it be supposed that the revolutionary decade offered nothing concrete to adult women, we should not overlook either, the improvements in their legal status that took place in the 1790s. It is of course true that this trend came to a halt and was even put into partial reverse during the Consulate. The answer to the question: 'Did women have a revolution after 1789?' must be 'Yes', therefore. Some women such as nuns even had a revolution in spite of themselves. These religious women were given the opportunity to completely alter their identities (Gressang, 2020). Even as the provisions of the Civil Code took effect, more women enjoyed more freedom than they had ever possessed at the end of the *ancien régime*.

The character of the early revolution was coloured by the social tensions immediately preceding the surrender of absolute monarchy in the summer of 1788. Historians who find the class approach unpersuasive sometimes point to evidence that elites were on a convergence course by the end of the *ancien régime*. Aristocrats, bourgeois and the senior prelates of the Church were all growing more alike, whether in terms of economic status or cultural outlook. They therefore fight shy of expressions such as the 'aristocratic revolution' or the 'revolutionary bourgeoisie' – expressions that belong more properly to a class-based analysis of the origins and outbreak of the revolution. These labels do now seem redundant and have been used sparingly in this introductory survey. If the most aggressive destabilizing force of the late 1770s and 1780s was, in fact, the monarchy, it scarcely seems appropriate to schematize the resistance of the Parlements in 1787–88 as an 'aristocratic revolution'.

However, this approach is less successful when it is a question of accommodating what actually happened between 1789 and 1791. Although the structuring of the Estates General scarcely favoured a convergence of elites, the deputies seem to have been painfully aware of what divided them almost from the outset. Noble and bourgeois representatives kept their distance from one another. If the desire to punish the aristocracy as a caste was largely absent from debates before the summer of 1791, there was no real meeting of minds either. Commoner deputies continued to think of themselves as 'unprivileged' and of nobles as 'privileged', even though, objectively speaking, legally enshrined privilege no longer existed. This tension would disappear in subsequent legislatures, if only because the nation's representatives would be selected overwhelmingly from the ranks of the old Third Estate.

Were the deputies so unexpectedly brought together in 1789 political novices? The question is important to historians, because the answer has implications for our understanding of the Terror as well as the transition from reforming absolutism to constitutional monarchy. Some believe that educated Frenchmen did not have much of a political vocabulary before 1789 – a plausible hypothesis since political activity under absolute monarchy was largely confined to the king, his councillors and the Court. However, we know that the king and his advisors were ceasing to define the monarchy in this strict sense by the 1780s – in fact, they were actively casting around for a safe means of enlarging the sphere of consultation and participation. In the event, a sizeable minority of the Third Estate's nominees were able to bring some political experience to bear on debates in the Estates General and the National Assembly – thanks largely to the provincial assemblies' reforms pushed through the royal council by Necker, Calonne and Brienne. The elite thrust into power in the summer of 1789 may have been new to office, then, but they were scarcely untried enthusiasts. Nor, indeed, were their counterparts in the provinces; that is to say the men who would colonize the machinery of local government set up in 1790. Many could call upon experience gleaned in seigneurial courts or the lowest municipal tier of the assemblies set up by Brienne. Of course, the deputies and their collaborators liked to clothe their actions in 'new man' regenerationist rhetoric, but in this instance a focus on language is apt to mislead. The achievements of the National Assembly sprang from the spirit of pragmatism that animated its committees, not from an exchange of disembodied ideas culled from the Enlightenment.

Nevertheless, those historians who have renewed our understanding of the Terror place particular emphasis on the alleged political immaturity of the deputies who took over in 1789. Borrowing from the influential nineteenth-century study of the *ancien régime* by Alexis de Tocqueville, they depict these first-generation legislators as self-taught *philosophes* whose abstract modes of reasoning did not combine well with the realities of holding and sharing political power. As Rousseauist intellectuals, they supposed that the revolutionary nation had inherited the pretension to absolute authority of the old Bourbon monarchy and must therefore speak with one voice. This so-called discourse of the 'general will' (Baker ed., 1994: xix) could tolerate no opposition or dissent, and it leads to the conclusion that the potential for a future Terror was embedded in the language of the revolution from the very outset. Terror and violence were intrinsic components of the revolutionary mentality therefore, not aberrant by-products of military emergency and civil war. The relentless head-chopping of the Revolutionary Tribunal in the spring and summer of 1794 was prefigured in the prison lynchings of September 1792, which, in turn, were foreshadowed in the bestial violence which accompanied the seizure of the Bastille in July 1789.

Several objections can be raised against this line of argument, however. For a start, it seems unlikely that the deputies of the Third Estate in the Estates General – or any others for that matter – were particularly avid readers of the political writings of Jean-Jacques Rousseau and, as we have seen, they were scarcely without experience either. As for the appropriation of the absolutist proclivities of the unreconstructed monarchy, this is an idea whose semantic neatness is its chief defect. Absolutism is not the same as totalitarianism. In any case, the lessons that future revolutionaries might have absorbed from the later years of the reign of Louis XVI would have been lessons in quasi-constitutional, not absolutist practice. Historians who have examined closely the deputies' patterns of behaviour in the National Assembly also find little evidence of a Terror mind-set in embryo. On the contrary, they emphasise the restraining effect of the humanitarian ideas of 1789 (Fitzsimmons, 2015: 210–11). If the violent mentality can be located anywhere at this early date, it is to be found in the popular approach to justice and retribution pioneered in Paris and the departments. It has been suggested that the revolutionary crowd was not pathologically violent (Alpaugh, 2015: 37); nevertheless, it should be remembered that the Terror, when it finally came, was improvised from below before it was wielded from above.

Still, it is an undeniable fact that the deputies did have some trouble learning how to agree to disagree. Unanimity was prized in the belief that nobody could possibly *not* wish to participate in the regeneration of the kingdom. The line between 'loyal' opposition and 'subversive' disagreement was therefore hard to adhere to, and even harder to police. For as long as the revolutionaries showed themselves to be capable of resolving their political problems divergence of opinion did not matter too much, but with the religious schism (1791), the outbreak of war (1792) and the recourse to armed rebellion in the west (1793), dissension in the ranks became harder and harder to countenance. Most historians (like most contemporaries, indeed) would agree that a distinction ought to be drawn between the early 'liberal' revolution (say up to the summer of 1792), and the 'authoritarian' Jacobin republic of 1792–94, therefore. The war came to be perceived as a struggle for survival, if not exactly a 'total' war (Bell, 2007). This was particularly the case once the Vendée insurgency had turned into a full-scale military counter-revolution. Warfare progressively eroded the middle ground in domestic politics.

In these conditions political extremism began to develop a life of its own. Just as the rationale for a people's war began to fuse with France's traditional foreign policy objectives, so the reasons for Terror became confused with plot paranoia and the ambition to found a virtuous republic cleansed of all impure social elements. Mild expressions of anti-revolutionary sentiment that would have bothered no one in 1790 or 1791 became loaded with counter-revolutionary menace. Simple thefts of property would lead to accusations of treason now that a bell rope, a harness or a bit of metal left over from the demolition of a wayside cross could be construed as material of vital importance to the war effort. It is at this point that an enquiry into the logic of the Terror must begin.

If the Terror impulse can be detected first and foremost in the behaviour of the crowd, is it sufficient to explain this reflex as mindless bloodlust (Hardman, 2016: 332)? The judicial shedding of blood was as intrinsic to the old regime as it was to the new: there was nothing 'modern' about it. One has only to read the accounts of eighteenth-century travellers to know that mangled and broken corpses spread-eagled on cartwheels were a familiar and (for English travellers) a disturbing sight at road junctions. Crowd violence nearly always occurred in a judicial setting, too, albeit one that frequently bypassed the formal institutions of repression. The crowds of the 1790s were rarely 'mindless' in any of their activities in fact, and as the revolution developed, they became more and more 'purposive' (Lucas, 1988: 259) – that is to say, better organized and better able to determine the dosage of pressure or violence required to achieve their aims. Collective violence would be used in the name of the sovereign people to punish and to purify, but it would also be used to consolidate and defend the revolution.

The transient *sans-culotte* phenomenon can be understood in this context as the ultimate refinement of the purposive crowd. Indeed, the political sophistication with which militants in the crowd exploited its brute capacity for meting out violence and extra-legal justice alarmed the deputies almost as much as the violence itself. In a sense, therefore, the bureaucratization of the Terror following the consolidation of Revolutionary Government in the early months of 1794 amounted to an attempt to substitute measured state violence for the violence of unruly or independent-minded Parisians. A cycle of violence that had begun in 1789 with informal butchery and hangings from lamp posts ended with the tumbrels of the Revolutionary Tribunal being routed through the poorer districts of the capital for the edification of onlookers.

The disarray – not to say discomfiture – of historians when confronted with the issue of violence in the revolution may help to explain the renewal of interest in the period of the Directory. After all, the challenge of coming to terms with the Terror and then finding a way out of it fell to the deputies of the Thermidorian Convention and the Councils of the Directory. Agents and even institutions could be replaced or renewed, yet it proved immensely difficult to erase the mentality of 1793–94 with its characteristic ingredients: denunciations, plots, purges and the resort to exemplary punitive justice. That said, historians have tried hard to redeem the regime from its reputation as 'one of the most chaotic periods in modern French history' (Sutherland, 1985: 279) in the belief that, beneath the surface, it continued the work of consolidating and extending the revolution. After the interlude of the Terror, democratic political practice resumed its faltering progress; there were even a few signs that a public space large enough to accommodate modern political parties was starting to open up. In the country at large, the various splinters of the revolutionary elite began to bind together once more as personal animosities born of the early years blurred into an overarching recognition and acceptance of a common post-1789 heritage. Yet the Fructidor *coup* (4 September 1797) would expose the fact that the regime was still searching for the elusive path towards a politics of normality. In the view of some historians, therefore, the most important turning point of these years was not so much 1799 as 1797. With the benefit of hindsight, it is evident that Fructidor launched the republic on a new trajectory; that is to say, the quest for a means of combining liberty with authority. The solution would be found in the person of Napoleon Bonaparte.

The elite that was gradually acquiring a collective identity and vocation by the later 1790s was none other than the 'granite substratum' of the Consulate and the Empire. Thanks to research undertaken in the 1970s and 1980s, historians now agree on its composition, but tend to differ in how they label it. For some, the 'notables' are a vindication of the proposition that the revolution was both launched and consummated by the bourgeoisie or middle class. Others point out that the 'notables' resembled nothing so much as the parallel elites of the *ancien régime* whose imminent fusion had been so brusquely interrupted in 1789.

It is true that if we were to carry out an occupation and status analysis, the results would be rather surprising. The revolution did not wipe out the nobility, and titled – or formerly titled – families appear in some strength on the electoral lists of 'notabilities' drawn up during the Consulate. Although this is an area in which it is hard to generalize, it is likely that the majority of the wealthiest landowners in 1802 came from families which would have passed as 'noble' in 1789. Of course, many titled *émigrés* had been granted permission to return home by this date, but the real import of the finding lies in the fact that the revolution did not undermine irretrievably the economic strength of the old Second Estate. On current best estimates, provincial nobles may have lost about one-fifth of their lands and one-third of their income as a result of the events of 1789 and subsequent years. To give a concrete example, the nobility of the district of Bordeaux lost about 30 per cent of its property during the Terror (Figeac, 1995: 540–41). There had been 824 noble families in the district in 1789, of whom 102 were imprisoned and 397 fled abroad (thereby risking the forfeiture of their lands).

Yet the 'notables' were not the elites of the *ancien régime* simply reheated. For a start, the outworn social categories of the eighteenth century had been abandoned, or legislated out of existence. Landowners, whether noble or bourgeois, were now universally labelled 'proprietors'. Analysis of the electoral list for 1810 (totalling 66,735 individuals) shows that 25 per cent can be identified as owners of land, 34 per cent held administrative posts and 14 per cent were members of the liberal professions (attorney, advocate, medical practitioner, etc.). As far as we can judge, no more than 11 per cent made a living from commercial activity (Lyons, 1994: 162). A composite elite, then, but an open elite as well. The 'notables' of the Consulate and the Empire earned their admission to this rank not on the basis of birth and ancestry, but by virtue of their wealth and social utility. Moreover, they were no longer divided by fiscal 'privilege'.

The modest presence within this post-revolution elite of families engaged in trade and industry should come as no surprise. *Ancien-régime* France had been a land-based society – a fact that an intensely political revolution was not going to alter overnight. But the lists of 'notables' compiled during the Consulate do reveal that a much broader conception of the economic foundations of political authority had taken root. Whether we label this post-revolutionary elite a middle class is a matter for individual historians. Some would find no tension in the phrase 'the bourgeois revolution of property owners' (Lewis, 1993: 35), whereas others operate with stricter criteria as to what constitutes a fundamentally 'bourgeois revolution'. Yet there can be little doubt that the men who voted Napoleon Bonaparte into power and who worked the levers of his government machine at the local level had a radically different cast of mind from that of their *ancien-régime* predecessors – a cast of mind that it would not be inappropriate to describe as 'bourgeois'.

The mixed character of the power elite that was assuming an institutional form during the Consulate is only one of several phenomena that make Bonapartism extremely difficult to pigeonhole. A regime that managed to combine father-figure authority with outward respect for the principle of popular sovereignty necessarily points in two directions. Bonaparte and his officials could behave illiberally, even despotically, yet they worshipped the rule of law and pursued the rationalization of public administration unflinchingly – goals that liberals all over Europe admired and supported. These same officials dispatched armies across western Europe and the Near East in the name of self-determination, only to define freedom as the entitlement to furnish tax revenue and military manpower for the greater glory of a new French Empire. Feudal privilege and the corporate status of the Church were attacked nearly everywhere these armies marched, yet at home Bonaparte would strike a deal with the papacy, and take steps to recreate an alternative hierarchy based on honorific privilege.

Is it any wonder, therefore, that historians experience difficulty in deciding where to draw the line between the revolution and the regime that took visible shape from Brumaire onwards? Many would not stray beyond the year 1799 in their bid to survey comprehensively the French Revolution, whereas others regard the vote on the Life Consulship of 1802, or the founding of a dynastic empire in 1804 as the proper place to stop. But equally, an argument could be made in favour of 1808 (the creation of the Imperial nobility), 1810 (the Habsburg marriage) or 1812 (the Russian campaign). This introductory survey has opted for 1804 on the ground that the substitution of a hereditary empire in the place of an increasingly threadbare republic dispelled any illusions that Napoleon Bonaparte might not have been striving for personal dictatorship. Ever since the late summer of 1789 voices had been heard declaring that the revolution was now over. In 1791 the deputies officially stated as much, and again in 1795. In 1799 it was the turn of the Consuls to say so. By 1804 it really was at an end.

When the monarchy was toppled on the morning of 10 August 1792, Rosalie Jullien remarked in a letter to her husband that it seemed as though she had lived through centuries in just four days (Lockroy, 1881: 233). What, then, were the long-term consequences of this revolution that both inspired and traumatized an entire society? Was Robespierre right when he asserted that the revolutionaries had managed to achieve two millennia of progress in just five years (Bell, 2015: 655)? The psychological impact of the rituals of citizenship (oath-taking, voting, enrolment in the national guard, the wearing of a tricolor cockade or a liberty cap) is hard to specify. However, it would be unwise to assume that the impact was transient and that the aspiration for greater freedom of the individual had been snuffed out by 1804. The small amount of research undertaken in this area indicates that in the countryside a distinct weakening in the influence of the

Church and of established elites took place. After a period of prolonged cultural disruption, accentuated by dechristianization and a radical reimagining of property rights (Blaufarb, 2016), the assumptions and expectations of individual household members altered significantly. We know, for instance, that parents ceased to choose biblical names for their children as a matter of routine. And when those same children of revolution began to come of age in the second decade of the nineteenth century a distinct shift in outlook both within the family group and beyond can be detected (Daumas, 2002: 161–68).

The anæsthetic of Bonapartism wore off and as the Empire went into decline (1811–14), the language of popular sovereignty and national defence would be heard again. Napoleon Bonaparte soon followed the republic into oblivion, but the centralized and immensely powerful state that the revolutionaries had brought into being survived largely unscathed. The long-nurtured project of monarchs to bring their subjects under full administrative control had finally been accomplished. While the pedigree of the centralized state might be somewhat questionable, the restored Bourbons were certainly not going to repudiate this convenient legacy. They would not repudiate the economic, financial and fiscal changes that had occurred during the revolutionary years either. Louis XVIII went out of his way to guarantee the property transfers that had taken place in the 1790s, just like Napoleon Bonaparte before him, and there would be no return to *ancien-régime* inheritance practices either. Purchasers of church and *émigré* property could rest easily in their beds, then. In fact, less real estate had changed hands than was once assumed by historians (under 10 per cent of the total stock of land) (Bodinier and Teyssier, 2000: 8).

The revolution had some economic effects that no one anticipated, however. Civil turmoil, five years of inflation followed by two years of deflation, and 22 years of near-continuous warfare seriously dislocated commerce and industry. Economic growth was checked, some leading sectors of industry went into decline for a period and the centre of gravity of commercial activity moved from the south and southwest to the north and northeast – in line with the shift northwards of the international trading economy (Forrest, 2020: 287). Since much capital, including compensation for liquidated venal offices, had been re-routed to the land transfer operation and inflation had killed off the market for credit, France initially found herself rather ill-prepared to meet the challenges of the early industrial age. Not until around 1800 did industrial output return to the level recorded in 1789, while the volume of external trade by the end of the Empire was still only about half what it had been in the boom years of 1784–91. Yet new economic structures were emerging which, in the view of some historians, would facilitate the growth of a uniquely French form of capitalism (Horn, 2006). The Bourbons had been trying to bring about a structural transformation of the economy since the time of Controller General Calonne and had not wanted for businessmen and capable technicians. What had been lacking back in the 1780s was an entrepreneurial climate. Without anyone having anticipated or planned the outcome, a new partnership model between the state and the entrepreneur emerged from the Terror. The Directory, and then the

Consulate, would build on these foundations. It is true that Bonaparte's imperial ambitions halted and even undermined the move in this direction for a time. But France's characteristic state-led approach to industrial progress would reassert itself in the 1820s with the ending of the era of continental and oceanic warfare.

The macro-economic impact of the revolution does not tell us very much about how ordinary men and women computed their gains and losses, though. The ending of fiscal privilege meant that everybody was now taxed according to their wealth rather than their birth, occupation or place of residence – a huge gain, both material and psychological. But discrepancies in the fiscal 'load' between different regions of the country took much longer to iron out, and it is not at all certain that French people paid less tax overall as a result of the revolution. More likely, the brief sense of fiscal well-being derived from the fact that tax obligations to the state had been avoided altogether, or else settled in depreciated paper money between 1790 and 1798. Coupled to this is the fact that payments to the Church (the tithe) and to former overlords (seigneurial dues) had come to an end – a net benefit to owners of land. Working men and women had reason to feel grateful to the revolution inasmuch as real wages rose across the period, thanks mainly to labour shortages. On the other hand, the always precarious livelihood of the semi-destitute poor was jeopardised by the dwindling of alms consequent on the abolition of monastic vows and the selling of Church endowments. Farmers benefited not only from a run of good harvests in the later 1790s and early 1800s, but from improved access to land and from rents which stagnated and perhaps even dropped in real terms (Béaur, 2008: 229–30). On the other hand, requisitions (fat-stock, horses, fodder, metals, etc.) and the conscription of manpower for the armies had a braking effect on agricultural yields, particularly after 1804.

In France's colonies and ex-colonies, the effects of the revolution are hard to disentangle from the ongoing Great Power struggle for supremacy in the Atlantic and Indian Oceans. The metropole would eventually lose control of Saint-Domingue (Haiti) and Ile-de-France (Mauritius) on a permanent basis as we have seen. The inhabitants of Haiti, in particular, never allowed themselves to forget that they had fought and beaten the French: independence rallies featured slogans such as 'Haiti, tomb of the French' (Burnard and Garrigus, 2016: 20). But Paris was slow to forget as well and imposed a heavy financial burden on the new nation in return for trading privileges. In fact, the first black republic was only recognized diplomatically by France in 1826. Unsurprisingly, the prosperity of the *ancien-régime* plantation economy never revived: the ex-slave population practised subsistence not estate agriculture. In Guadeloupe, Martinique, French Guiana and Réunion, meanwhile, slavery would persist until 1848 (fourteen years beyond its abolition in Britain's colonies). Only then did the great mass of the population obtain citizenship rights.

The shipping of enslaved persons around the Indian Ocean seems actually to have increased during the Napoleonic years, the planters of Réunion and Mauritius having refused point blank to accept interference in their affairs which emanated from the metropole. But by the 1820s the estate agriculture of both islands was starting to rely more on indentured than slave labour. As for the territorial enclaves on the Indian sub-continent (Pondichéry, Yanam, Mahé, Karikal and Chandernagore), they were recovered from the British in 1815 and remained French until they were absorbed into India post-Independence. In the early nineteenth century some members of the Tamil community of Pondichéry continued the agitation for French citizenship, but in other respects it is hard to detect an impact of the revolution on the indigenous population.

If truth be told it is likely that the biggest gains for the ordinary people of the metropole were deeply personal ones. They concerned the way individuals assessed their life chances and viewed their relationships with one another. The inheritance legislation of the revolution which introduced strict equality between offspring must have affected attachments between brothers and sisters and between younger and eldest sons profoundly. Such changes can only be detected indirectly, though. The frequency of divorce in the 1790s we have already mentioned, but the practice of marriage accelerated as well. After all, parental consent was no longer required and parents could no longer choose an heir. The same applies to the habit of family limitation. In the words of one historian, young couples emerged from the revolution more 'egotistical and calculating' (Dupâquier, 1979: 118). Men, more-over, stopped going to church like sheep every Sunday – and these two cultural responses may well have been linked. Despite attempts at moral rearmament by the post-Concordat clergy, the Catholic Church had lost its capacity to compel. Now that a revolution had demonstrated that things really could change, men and women were exploiting the new freedoms they had experienced and quietly taking charge of their own lives.

Part IV

Documents

We are grateful to all those who have granted us permission to reproduce the extracts listed here. While every effort has been made to trace and acknowledge ownership of copyright material used in this volume, please advise the publisher of any errors or omissions and these will be corrected in subsequent editions.

DOI: 10.4324/9781003156185-12

Document 1

A royal reprimand

Louis XV had been offended by an unwarranted suggestion coming from the Parlement of Rouen that he had sworn an oath to the 'nation' at his coronation. The following extract is taken from a rebuke that the king caused to be read out before the Parlement of Paris on 3 March 1766. It became known as the Session of the Flagellation or the Scourging and would be treated almost as a doctrinal statement of absolutism for the remainder of his reign.

[...] to set about erecting into matters of principle such pernicious innovations is to do injury to the body of the magistrature, to betray its interests, and to mistake those laws that are really fundamental to the state. As if it could be overlooked that it is in my person alone that sovereign power resides, the true character of which is founded in conciliation, justice and reason; as if it could be overlooked that the courts owe their existence and authority to me alone; that this plenary authority, exercised in my name, remains forever attached to me and can never be turned against me; that legislative power is vested in me alone, without any subordination or subdivision; that the officers of my courts undertake not the fashioning of the laws but their registration and publication on my sole authority, albeit with permission to make remonstrance as befits good and loyal counsellors; that all public order stems from me and that I am its supreme custodian; that my people are at one with me; and that the rights and interests of the *nation*, which some have dared to constitute as a body separate from that of the monarch, are necessarily united with my rights and can only reside in my hands. The officers of my courts will, I am persuaded, never lose sight of these sacred and immutable maxims, which are inscribed in the hearts of all faithful subjects [...]

> Source: Antoine, M. 'La Monarchie absolue', in Baker, K.M. (ed.) *The French Revolution and the Creation of Modern Political Culture. Volume 1: The Political Culture of the Old Regime* (Pergamon Press, Oxford, 1987), p. 6. Copyright Elsevier 1987. Translated by Peter Jones.

Document 2

Imagining the ancien régime body politic

This description of French society is taken from a remonstrance of the Parlement of Paris dated 12 March 1776. It shows how vested interests within the kingdom chose to visualize the institution of absolute monarchy.

All of your subjects, Sire, are divided into as many different *corps* as there are different estates of the realm: the Clergy, the Nobility, the sovereign courts; the inferior courts, the officers attached to these tribunals, the universities, the academies, the companies of finance and of commerce; all present and existing throughout the State, these *corps* may be regarded as the links in a great chain of which the first is in the hands of Your Majesty, as chief and sovereign administrator of all that constitutes the *corps* of the Nation.

Source: Cavanaugh, G.J. 'Turgot: the Rejection of Enlightened Despotism',
French Historical Studies, vol. 6 (Spring 1969), p. 32, note 4.

Document 3

Fundamental laws according to the Parlement of Paris

The news that Lamoignon, Keeper of the Seals, was preparing a root-and-branch reform of the judiciary had leaked out in April 1788. Fearing the worst, the magistrates restate their understanding of what passed for the constitution of the kingdom.

The court, with all the chambers assembled and the peers present, amply warned by public knowledge and notorious fact of the coup d'état which threatens the nation by striking at the magistrature [...] and leaves the nation no other resource but a precise declaration by the court of the maxims it is charged with maintaining [...]

Declares that France is a monarchy governed by the king, in accordance with the laws. That of these laws several are fundamental and that these include:

> The right of the reigning house to succeed to the throne in the male line according to primogeniture with the exclusion of females and their descendants.
> The right of the nation to grant taxation freely in an Estates General regularly convoked and of fixed composition.
> The customs and capitulations of the provinces
> The irremovability of magistrates.
> The right of the courts in each province to verify the king's legislative volition and to proceed to its registration only in so far as it is conformable to the basic laws of the province as well as the Fundamental Laws of the state.
> The right of every citizen, whatever his offence, to appear only before his peers as defined by law.
> And the right, without which all the others are of no avail, to appear before the competent judge immediately after arrest, no matter on whose orders.
> The said court protests against any future violation of the above principles.

Source: Hardman, J. *The French Revolution: the Fall of the
Ancien Régime to the Thermidorian Reaction, 1785–1795*
(Arnold, London, 1981), p. 55.

Document 4

Defining the nation

*Penned by a clergyman, Emmanuel-Joseph Sieyès, around the time of the
Assembly of Notables, the pamphlet* What is the Third Estate? *was published
early in 1789. It was one of the most widely read contributions to the debate on
the composition of the forthcoming Estates General.*

The plan of this work is quite simple. There are three questions that we have to
ask ourselves:

1   What is the Third Estate? *Everything.*
2   What has it been until now in the existing political order? *Nothing.*
3   What does it want to be? *Something.*

[...]
First we will see whether these answers are correct [...]
Who would then dare to say that the Third Estate does not, within itself,
contain everything needed to form a complete nation? It resembles a strong,
robust man with one arm in chains. Subtract the privileged order and the
Nation would not be something less, but something more. What then is the
Third? Everything; but an everything that is fettered and oppressed. What
would it be without the privileged order? Everything, but an everything that
would be free and flourishing. Nothing can go well without the Third Estate,
but everything would go a great deal better without the two others.
[...]
It is pointless for the Third Estate to expect joint action by the three orders
to restore its *political* rights and all its civil rights in their full entirety. The fear
of seeing abuse reformed has inspired more of a feeling of alarm than a desire
for liberty among the aristocrats. Faced with a choice between liberty and a few
odious privileges, they have opted for the latter. The privileged soul has aligned
itself with the favours granted to servility. They are as afraid of the Estates
General today as they were once so vigorous in calling for them. As far as they are
concerned, everything is fine. Their only cause for complaint is the spirit of inno-
vation. Nothing, it seems, is now wanting. Fear has given them a constitution.
In the light of these changes in matters and moods, the Third Estate has to see
that it has to rely solely upon its own vision and courage. Reason and justice are on
its side. It ought to aim, at the least, to secure their full support. The time for
working for a conciliation between the parties is over. What hope of agreement
can there be between the energy of the oppressed and the fury of the oppressor? It
is they who now have dared to launch the word 'secession' and use it as a threat
against both the king and the people. Ah! dear God, how happy a day it would be
for the Nation if that great and desirable secession was to be accomplished and

made final. How easy it would be to do without the privileged orders! How difficult it will be to induce them to become citizens! [...]

Source: Sonenscher, M. (ed.) *Emmanuel Joseph Sieyès: Political Writings* (Hackett Publishing Company, Indianapolis, 2003), pp. 94, 96, 145.
Reprinted by permission of Hackett Publishing Company, Inc.

Document 5

Fixing a framework for the Estates General

Having returned in triumph to its courthouse, the Parlement of Paris declares on 25 September 1788 that the forthcoming Estates General should be convened in accordance with the precedents established in 1614.

The court, continuing in the principles which inspired its resolutions of 3 and 5 May last [...] orders that the said declaration be registered on the rolls of the court to be implemented according to its form and tenor but with the following provisos: that it cannot be argued from the preamble or any of the articles of the said declaration that the court needed to be restored in order to resume functions which violence alone had suspended; the court cannot be prevented, by the silence imposed on the king's *procureur-général* in matters relating to the execution of the **Ordonnances**, Edicts and Declarations of 8 May last, from taking cognizance of offences with which the court would have been obliged to deal; that it cannot be argued from articles 4 and 5 that the judgements mentioned there are not subject to appeal or that any of those who have not been examined and sworn in by the court, should be allowed to exercise the functions of judge in the lower tribunals. Finally the said court, in conformity with its resolution of 3 May last, maintains its insistence that the Estates General designated for next January be regularly convoked and composed, and that according to the forms observed in 1614.

Source: Hardman, J. (ed.) *The French Revolution: the Fall of the Ancien Régime to the Thermidorian Reaction, 1785–1795* (Arnold, London, 1981), p. 70.

Document 6

Swansong of the aristocracy?

With no end to the press debate on 'privilege' in sight and deadlock – or disarray – within the ministry as to how to respond to the demands being made by Third Estate pamphleteers, the Princes of the Blood become seriously alarmed. This Memorandum was sent to the king on 12 December 1788 by five of his brothers and cousins (the Comte d'Artois, the Prince de Condé, the Prince de

*Conti, the Duc de Bourbon and the Dud d'Enghien). Two, the Comte de
Provence and the Duc d'Orléans, refused to sign the protest.*

When Your Majesty forbade the Notables to discuss the memorandum submitted to them by the Prince de Conti, Your Majesty declared to the 'Princes of
the Blood that when they desired to communicate to him that which might be
useful to the good of his service and that of the state, they might address him'.

The Comte d'Artois, the Prince de Condé, the Duc de Bourbon, the Duc
d'Enghien and the Prince de Conti consider it their duty to respond to this
invitation from Your Majesty.

It particularly behoves the Princes of the Blood to tell you the truth: by rank,
they are the first of your subjects; by their condition, your natural advisors; by
their rights, most interested in defending yours; and they consider likewise that
they owe you an account of their feelings and of their thoughts.

Sire, the state is in peril. Your person is respected, the virtues of the monarch
assure him of the nation's homage. But, Sire, a revolution is being prepared in
the principles of government; it is being accomplished through the turmoil in
men's minds. Institutions which were considered sacred and which have
enabled this monarchy to flourish for so many centuries have been put into
question or even decried as unjust.

The writings which have appeared during the [second] Assembly of
Notables; the memoranda which have been submitted to the princely signatories, the demands formulated by various provinces, towns, *corps*; the
subject matter and style of these demands and memoranda all herald, all
prove that there is a deliberate plan of insubordination and of contempt for
the laws of the state. Every author sets himself up as a legislator; eloquence
or a facile pen – even devoid of study, knowledge or experience – seem
sufficient authorisation to regulate the constitution of empires. Whoever
advances a bold proposition, whoever proposes to change the laws is
assured of readers and sectaries.

So fast does this deplorable mania develop that opinions, which a short while
ago would have appeared most reprehensible, today seem reasonable and just
[...] Who can say where the audacity of opinions will stop? The rights of the
throne have been called into question; opinion is riven over the rights of the
two orders of the state; soon the rights of property will be attacked; inequality
of wealth will be presented as something which needs to be reformed; already it
has been proposed that feudal dues be abolished as representing a system of
oppression, a barbarous survival.

Derived from these new theories, from the intention to change rights and
laws, is the claim advanced by several sections of the Third Estate that their
order should have two votes in the Estates General whilst each of the two
leading orders continues to have but one.

The princely signatories will not repeat what has been developed by several
committees [of the Notables], namely the injustice and danger of innovations in
the composition of the Estates General; the host of resultant claims; the ease

with which, if votes were counted by head and not by order, the interests of the Third Estate – better defended by the existing arrangements – would be compromised by corrupting members of the Third Estate; the destruction of the equilibrium so wisely established between the three orders and of their mutual independence.

It has been demonstrated to Your Majesty how important it is to preserve the only method of convoking the Estates which is constitutional, the mode hallowed by law and custom: the distinction between the orders, the right to deliberate in separate chambers, equality of votes [between them] – these unchangeable foundations of the French monarchy

[...]

Signed: Charles-Philippe, Louis-Joseph de Bourbon, Louis-Henri-Joseph de Bourbon, Louis-Antoine-Henri de Bourbon, Louis-François-Joseph de Bourbon.

Source: Hardman, J. (ed.) *The French Revolution Sourcebook* (Arnold, London, 1999), pp. 69–70.

Document 7

Forward-looking nobles

Nobles could be as concerned about civil liberties as educated members of the Third Estate, a fact which serves to remind us that the liberal attack on arbitrary government had aristocratic roots.

Cahier of the nobility of the *bailliage* of Nemours

1   The wish of the nobility of the *bailliage* of Nemours is that places in the meeting hall of the Estates General be occupied without distinction of province or deputation, so as to avoid anything that might be interpreted as conferring pre-eminence on one province or another.
2   That the president of the order of the nobility in the Estates General be freely elected by and in his order, without distinction of province or rank.
3   That the persons of the members of the Estates General be declared inviolable and that in any case they may not answer for what they have said or done in the Estates General to any but the Estates General.
4   That the wish of the order of the nobility of the *bailliage* of Nemours is that the vote be by order.
5   But in the case that voting by order be absolutely rejected by the Estates General, and the deputies of the *bailliage* see that further resistance to voting by head would be useless, they will ask that voting by head be done in the separate chambers of each order and not in a general assembly of the three orders together.

That the Estates General decide how many votes beyond half will constitute a majority. Voting by head can never be allowed in matters concerning only one of the three orders.

6   That the nobility of the *bailliage* wishes to declare at the outset to the Estates General that its intention is that taxes be generally and equally divided among individuals of the three orders.

And that, always wishing to set an example of the most entire obedience to the laws of the realm, the nobility ask that criminal and civil laws which ought to protect all citizens equally should apply to everyone, without regard to rank or birth.

7   That the nation having come together in the assembly of the Estates General, it regains all its rights and, as a consequence, all taxes presently established must be declared null and void, as not having been voted by the nation, which alone has the power to do so.

[...]

9   That the wish of the nobility of the *bailliage* is that individual freedoms be guaranteed to every Frenchman, before any other matters are dealt with...

[...]

13 That freedom of the press be granted, with such exceptions as may be determined by the Estates General.

[...]

15 That agriculture, industry, arts and commerce enjoy the greatest freedom and be delivered from the monopoly resulting from excessive privileges.

[...]

17 That the Estates General be constituted according to just proportions among the three orders, and that legislative power be given them in its entirety. Therefore in order to have full force, this legislative power need only be sanctioned by the Royal Assent.

[...]

Source: Kaplow, J. *France on the Eve of Revolution: a Book of Readings* (John Wiley & Sons Inc. New York, Toronto, 1971), pp. 155–56. Translated by Susan Kaplow.

Document 8

Backward-looking nobles

The Cambrésis, a frontier province annexed to France in 1678, enjoyed substantial tax advantages, not to mention a royal tobacco monopoly. All social groups – not just the nobility – anticipate that they will be losers if privileged enclaves are asked to make sacrifices in the name of the common good.

Cahier of the nobility of Cambrai and the Cambrésis

[...]

1   That the Estates General attends first and foremost to the drawing up and passing, in collaboration with His Majesty, of a body of constitutional law

which will be recorded for ever more in a national statute book; no deliberations on taxes or loans until such time as all the elements of this code have been definitively drafted, approved and promulgated as constituting the foundation of the constitution of France.

2   That it shall be established as fundamental maxims that the government of the kingdom is monarchical; that the throne is hereditary; and that females may not succeed to it. The Estates General is requested also to rule immediately on the issue of the regency in case of an [unanticipated] event.

3   *[Concerning] constitutional laws; the forming of a national assembly, and the frequency of meetings.*
That it be declared that national assemblies are integral to government; and that in consequence they will always be made up of the three separate orders, and will be summoned invariably every three years.

4   *[Concerning] the summoning of national assemblies.*
That the manner of convocation of national assemblies, the number of deputies [allocated to] each province, and finally all matters relating to organisation be determined by the assemblies themselves – in the light of any injustices that the present meeting might throw up, and in accordance with whatever circumstances might dictate over time.

5   That no law take on the status of constitutional law without the consent of the nation.

6   *[Concerning] voting by order.*
That in all debates votes be counted by order and not by head.

7   *[Concerning] the renouncing of exemptions and privileges.*
These matters having been dealt with in outline, the nobility of the Cambrésis, while sacrificing its pecuniary interests and willingly submitting to the strictly equal distribution of taxes, confines itself to asking for the maintenance of the constitution and privileges of the province, as specified and endorsed by our monarchs.
[…]

16   *[Concerning] the new civil code.*
[…]

17   That seigneurial assize courts in the Cambrésis be confirmed as forming part of the [original] enfeoffment, with the power to judge definitively cases to the value of 500 *livres*, with appeal to the Parlement for cases in excess; all intermediate justices to be abolished in consequence.
[…]

38   That letters of nobility no longer be granted, save in the case of conspicuous service to the fatherland, and only then at the request, and on the attestation, of the *corps* of nobility of the Provincial Estates where the [candidate] resides.

Signed: Marquis d'Estourmel; Cordier de Caudry secretary.
Source: Marchand, P. (ed.) *Florilège des cahiers de doléances du Nord*
(Centre d'histoire de la région du nord et de l'Europe du nord-ouest,
Université Charles de Gaulle – Lille III, Lille, 1989), pp. 219–20; 223.
Translated by Peter Jones.

Document 9

Parish grievances

The choosing of the deputies and the drawing up of the cahiers de doléances *of the Third Estate took place in two stages. Villagers articulated their thoughts in parish assemblies, whereupon individuals were appointed to take these 'preliminary' grievance lists to the neighbouring town. There, a much larger assembly of delegates amalgamated the grievances into a single document and chose the deputies who were to carry it to Versailles.*

Grievances and complaints which the inhabitants of the *bourg* and *prévôté* seat of Chaumont-sur-Moselle humbly request His Majesty to address, and which they expect their deputies to the *bailliage* [assembly] of Vézelise and their representatives to the Estates General to place a firm emphasis upon.

1 They demand and will always demand [the setting up of] Provincial Estates with control over all branches of the administration;
2 That no taxes ever be established without the prior approval of the Estates General, and only then for a fixed duration;
3 That their representatives in the Estates General consent to no new taxes unless they judge them to be essential to the needs of the state, and then only after the subtraction of all useless and extravagant expenditures – excluding from this description those linked to the splendour and majesty of the throne – and only after the reduction in both the number and the scale of pensions, the arbitrariness of which has weighed down the state.
4 That all the pecuniary burdens known as taxes, subventions or subsidies – and under whatever label they might feature in the future – be distributed among all citizens, notwithstanding distinctions of order, or privilege, but in proportion to their property and ability to pay.
5 That the price of salt be cut by half, [since] its extreme dearness often forces the rural poor to do without; it is from this privation that many of the illnesses which frequently afflict them stem, and it makes it impossible for farmers to maintain and to increase their stock.
6 The abolition of [the offices of] valuers-and-auctioneers whose exorbitant charges and fees, which they alone know how to multiply, all too often swallow up the greater part of the inheritances falling to minors; and who keep the subjects of His Majesty in thraldom by virtue of their exclusive privilege to estimate the value of chattels and to carry out sales, whether forced or voluntary.
7 That all monopolies, and particularly that of the wine press, be abolished; or, at least, that owners of vines be allowed to have their own presses as is the case in territories belonging to the king, in return for a payment to the seigneurial overlord of 2 *francs* per *jour* of vines; this abolition would prevent the spoiling or loss of a large quantity of wine.

8 That the inhabitants be free to employ any competent distiller they please for the manufacture of their eau-de-vie, not those designated for the locality; on the ground that all exclusive privileges are contrary to the public interest. This demand is founded, moreover, on the Edict of 13 August 1782, article 3, which requires owners wishing to have distilled their wine and grape pressings to employ any suitable distiller, and not one designated for the locality in preference to another as the inspectors who supervise the production of eau-de-vie have claimed.

9 That they be relieved of the burden of contributing to the perquisites of the officers of the Parlement [of Nancy], on the ground that such a burden should be a matter solely for the litigants; that the intendants be abolished.

10 That those who tender successfully for timber from the communal forests be obliged to make payment directly to the **sindics** appointed for the purpose by the municipal assemblies so that the sums can be used to meet the needs of the community. The current practice of depositing the sums with the forestry receiver is just another pointless expense and burden for rural communities, not only because of the receivership duty that is debited, but also because of the difficulties and obstacles they have always encountered in trying to withdraw these monies when they are needed; not to mention the numberless journeys and efforts that the sindics are required to undertake for the purpose – all at the expense of their constituents.

11 That the stud farm set up in the province be abolished on the ground that its costs outweigh the meagre benefits it secures; besides, it would be much more preferable to distribute the stallions among substantial and well-regarded farmers who would be granted privileges in return for their upkeep: by this means costs would be reduced almost to nothing and farmers would no longer moan about the pointlessness of concentrating all the stallions at Rosières; instead they would become very useful under this new arrangement.

12 That their dwellings and cellars be exempted from the excavations of the saltpetre inspectors in conformity with the paternal intentions of His Majesty as clearly laid out in his *arrêts* of 8 August 1777 and 24 January 1778 [...]

13 That the royal Letters-Patent concerning the amalgamation and redistribution of land holdings in the territory of [the community of] Chaumont dated 15 December 1770 be withdrawn, and that the free grazing of the common flocks be restored, as we always understood was to be the case.

14 The abolition of the duty on hides which has pushed up their price to such an extent that farmers and country dwellers can no longer obtain what they need.

15 That tendering for the community's work stint on the highways be conducted before the municipal assembly, and that it be allowed to arrange for the work to be undertaken by *corvée* if it chooses while standing guarantee for the solidity of the workmanship, thereby retaining the value of the tax levied for this purpose.

16 The abolition of the *corvées* and *tailles* demanded repeatedly by our seigneurs.

17 Knowing as our representatives do that the high price of wood derives from sales abroad and the consumption of the salt-works, amounting to a double charge on this province since it is providing the means of obtaining its salt [...] there should be some indemnification. By reducing the cost of salt by half, sales would increase by a quarter; the resultant price should then be set against this double tax load, which brings enormous sums into the country [...]

18 That seigneurs who insist on maintaining forges, glass-works and other work-shops do so using their own wood; and that the majority of these enterprises be abolished.

The said inhabitants have given authority to their delegates to present and make known all the articles in this *cahier*, and any others they judge to be consonant with their interests, those of the state and the public good; to combine with the other parishes and jurisdictions of the *bailliage* of Vézelise in order to elect upright and capable individuals to participate in the Estates General of the kingdom scheduled to take place in Versailles on 27 April next.

Drawn up in the court-room of Chaumont-sur-Moselle, on the 11 March 1789, and signed by all those present who are so able. [Sixty-eight signatures, of which four illegible].

Endorsed by Lambert, seigneurial judge of Chaumont.

> Source: Etienne, C. *Cahiers de doléances des bailliages des généralités de Metz et de Nancy. Tome 3: Cahiers du bailliage de Vézelise* (Nancy, 1930), pp. 56–61. Translated by Peter Jones.

Document 10

The new doctrine of rights

Voted on 27 August 1789, this document was intended by the National Assembly to be a preliminary statement of the principles around which the constitution would be framed.

Declaration of the Rights of Man and of the Citizen.

The representatives of the French people, organized into a National Assembly, considering that ignorance, forgetfulness, or contempt of the rights of man are the sole causes of public misfortunes and of the corruption of government, have resolved to set forth, in a solemn declaration, the natural, inalienable and sacred rights of man, in order that such a declaration, continually before all members of the social body, may be a perpetual reminder of their rights and their duties; in order that the acts of the legislative and those of the executive power may constantly be compared with the aim of every political institution and may accordingly be more respected; in order that the demands of the citizens, founded henceforth upon simple and incontestable principles, may always be directed towards the maintenance of the Constitution and the welfare of all.

Accordingly, the National Assembly recognizes and proclaims, in the presence and under the auspices of the Supreme Being, the following rights of man and the citizen:

1 Men are born and remain free and equal in rights; social distinctions may be based only upon general usefulness.
2 The aim of every political association is the preservation of the natural and inalienable rights of man; these rights are liberty, property, security and resistance to oppression.
3 The source of all sovereignty resides essentially in the nation; no group, no individual may exercise authority not emanating expressly therefrom.
4 Liberty consists of the power to do whatever is not injurious to others; thus the enjoyment of the natural rights of every man has for its limits only those that assure other members of society the enjoyment of those same rights; such limits may be determined only by law.
5 The law has the right to forbid only actions which are injurious to society. Whatever is not forbidden by law may not be prevented, and no one may be constrained to do what it does not prescribe.
6 Law is the expression of the general will; all citizens have the right to concur personally, or through their representatives, in its formation; it must be the same for all, whether it protects or punishes. All citizens being equal before it, are equally admissible to all public offices, positions and employments, according to their capacity, and without other distinction than that of virtues and talents.
7 No man may be accused, arrested, or detained except in the cases determined by the law, and according to the forms prescribed thereby. Whoever solicit, expedite, or execute arbitrary orders, or have them executed, must be punished; but every citizen summoned or apprehended in pursuance of the law must obey immediately; he renders himself culpable by resistance.
8 The law is to establish only penalties that are absolutely and obviously necessary; and no one may be punished, but by virtue of a law established and promulgated prior to the offence and legally applied.
9 Since every man is presumed innocent until declared guilty, if arrest be deemed indispensable, all unnecessary severity for securing the person of the accused must be severely repressed by law.
10 No one is to be disquieted because of his opinions, even religious, provided their manifestation does not disturb the public order established by law.
11 Free communication of ideas and opinions is one of the most precious of the rights of man. Consequently, every citizen may speak, write and print freely, subject to responsibility for the abuse of such liberty in the cases determined by law.

12   The guarantee of the rights of man and the citizen necessitates a public force; such a force, therefore, is instituted for the advantage of all and not for the particular benefit of those to whom it is entrusted.

13   For the maintenance of the public force and for the expenses of administration a common tax is indispensable; it must be assessed equally on all citizens in proportion to their means.

14   Citizens have the right to ascertain, by themselves or through their representatives, the necessity of the public tax, to consent to it freely, to supervise its use, and to determine its quota, assessment, payment and duration.

15   Society has the right to require of every public agent an accounting of his administration.

16   Every society in which the guarantee of rights is not assured or the separation of powers not determined has no constitution at all.

17   Since property is a sacred and inviolable right, no one may be deprived thereof unless a legally established public necessity obviously requires it, and upon condition of a just and previous indemnity.

Source: Stewart, J.H. *A Documentary Survey of the French Revolution* (The Macmillan Company, New York, 1951), pp. 113–15.

Document 11

Gendered citizenship

While adult women were only occasionally admitted to the vote as individuals, married women and mothers sometimes argued that the key role they played in the household conferred on them special responsibilities and, by implication, rights. The rhetoric of the revolution depicting the nation as an extended 'family' strengthened this claim.

National Assembly, 29 March 1790

Address of the wife of a municipal officer of Lannion [Brittany], endorsed by several others, calling for women to be allowed to take the civic oath. The Assembly orders the printing of the letter which follows:

"Monsieur le Président,

Not a word is spoken about women in the constitution and I grant that they should not be meddling in public affairs, yet mothers with children can and should be citizens. What sort of woman will she be who does not imitate the example of our queen, who has pledged to raise her noble son according to the principles of the new constitution? Touched profoundly by this patriotic statement and a mother of ten children the youngest of whom is still being nursed, I gathered them around me and there, in the presence of their grandmother, I swore on my knees before God, to raise them in faith with the nation and with the king. My eldest daughter who is also a nursing mother swore the same oath. I should be sorry, Monsieur le Président, if this action were to displease the National Assembly. On the contrary I dare to flatter myself that [the Assembly] will issue a regulation permitting mothers to take this solemn oath in the presence of the municipal officers who we shall henceforward respect because they will be chosen by the people. I think that this estimable ceremony would dignify motherhood and instil civic responsibility in those who are the primary teachers of citizens".

[...]

Signed BRIGENT BAUDOUIN

Approved by and in the presence of Bernard Brigent, Baudouin Grimault.

Source: *Archives Parlementaires*, vol. 12, p. 402. Translated by Peter Jones.

Document 12

Church reform

Although the cahiers *had signalled the need for church reform, the debate on the issue in the National Assembly swiftly moved beyond concrete grievances and necessary adjustments to become all-embracing.*

The Civil Constitution of the Clergy, 12 July 1790

Chapter 1: ecclesiastical offices

Each department will form a single diocese and each diocese will have the same extent and the same limits as the department.

The seats of the bishoprics of the 83 departments of the kingdom will be fixed in accordance with the following table [...] All the other bishoprics present in the 83 departments of the kingdom which are not expressly mentioned in the present schedule are, and will remain, suppressed.

The kingdom will be divided into ten metropolitan provinces.

[...]

7   On the advice of the bishop and of the new district authorities immediate steps will be taken for a new division of all the parishes of the kingdom [...]

[...]

16 In towns where there are less than 6,000 souls, there will be only one parish; the other parishes will be suppressed and joined to the principal church.

Chapter 2: nomination to ecclesiastical offices

From the publication of the present decree there will be only one way of appointing to bishoprics and cures, namely election.

All elections will be conducted by ballot; the successful candidate will have an absolute majority of votes.

The election of bishops will be conducted in the form prescribed and by the electoral college provided for by the decree of 22 December 1789 for the nomination of members of the departmental administration.

[...]

19 The new bishop may not ask the Pope for confirmation; but he may write to him as the visible head of the Church Universal in token of the unity of faith and of communion he should maintain with him. [...]

21 Before the ceremony of consecration begins, the newly elected one, in the presence of municipal officers, the people and the clergy, will take a solemn oath to care for the faithful of the diocese which is entrusted to him, to be faithful to the nation, to the law and to the king and to maintain with all his power the constitution decreed by the National Assembly and accepted by the king.

Source: Hardman, J. *The French Revolution Sourcebook*
(Arnold, London, 1999), pp. 115–16.

Document 13

What the king really thought about the revolution

Plans for the escape from Paris had been in the making for months. Louis left this Déclaration *in the Tuileries Palace, where it was found on 21 June 1791.*

As long as the king could hope to see order and the welfare of the kingdom regenerated by the means employed by the National Assembly, and by his residence near that Assembly in the capital, no sacrifice mattered to him [...]; but today, when his sole recompense consists of seeing the monarchy destroyed, all powers disregarded, property violated, personal security everywhere endangered, crimes unpunished, and total anarchy taking the place of law, while the semblance of authority provided by the new Constitution is insufficient to repair a single one of the ills afflicting the kingdom, the king, having solemnly protested against all the acts issued during his captivity, deems it his duty to place before Frenchmen and the entire universe the picture of his conduct and that of the government which has established itself in the kingdom.

[...]

But the more sacrifices the king made for the welfare of his people, the more the rebels laboured to disparage the value thereof, and to present the monarchy under the most false and odious colours.

The convocation of the Estates General, the doubling of the deputies of the Third Estate, the king's efforts to eliminate all difficulties which might delay the meeting of the Estates General and those which arose after its opening, all the retrenchments which the king made in his personal expenses, all the sacrifices which he made for his people in the session of 23 June [1789], finally, the union of the orders, effected by the king's wish, a measure which His Majesty then deemed indispensable for the functioning of the Estates General, all his anxiety, all his efforts, all his generosity, all his devotion to his people – all have been misjudged, all have been misrepresented.

The time when the Estates General, assuming the name of National Assembly, began to occupy itself with the constitution of the kingdom, calls to mind the memoirs which the rebels were cunning enough to have sent from several provinces, and the movements of Paris to have the deputies disregard one of the principal clauses contained in their *cahiers*, namely that providing that *the making of the laws should be done in concert with the king*. In defiance of that clause, the Assembly placed the king entirely outside the Constitution by refusing him the right to grant or to withhold his sanction to articles which it regarded as constitutional, reserving to itself the right to include in that category those which it deemed suitable; and for those regarded as purely legislative, reducing the royal prerogative to a right of suspension until the third legislature, a purely illusory right as so many examples prove only too well.

What remains to the king other than the vain semblance of monarchy?

[...]

Signed Louis

Paris, 20 June 1791

> Source: Stewart, J.H. *A Documentary Survey of the French Revolution* (The Macmillan Company, New York, 1951), pp. 205–06 and 210.

Document 14

Parting of the ways in the Champ de Mars

Interrogation of a cook named Constance Evrard, who had been arrested on 17 July 1791 following an accusation that she had insulted the wife of a national guardsman.

QUESTION: Has she been to the Champ de Mars?

ANSWER: Yes, she had been there with Madame Léon and her daughter.

QUESTION: Why had she been there?

ANSWER: To sign a petition 'like all good patriots'.

QUESTION: What was the petition about?

ANSWER: She understood that its aim was 'to organise in a different manner the executive power'.

QUESTION: Did she often go to public meetings?

ANSWER: She had sometimes been to the Palais Royal and the Tuileries.

QUESTION: Did she belong to any club?

ANSWER: She had sometimes been to the Cordeliers Club, although not actually a member.

QUESTION: Had she been with any particular group in the Champ de Mars?

ANSWER: She had been on the 'altar to the fatherland' and signed the petition.

QUESTION: Had she thrown stones or seen any stones thrown?

ANSWER: No.

QUESTION: Who had invited her to sign the petition?

ANSWER: No one, but she had heard various people say that there was a petition to sign in the Champ de Mars.

QUESTION: Was it true that her name had appeared in the papers?

ANSWER: Yes, her name had appeared in *Les Révolutions de Paris*, because she had expressed grief at the death of Loustalot. Question: What papers did she read?

ANSWER: She read Marat, Audoin, Camille Desmoulins, and very often, *L'Orateur du Peuple*.

Source: Rudé, G. *The Crowd in the French Revolution*
(Clarendon Press, Oxford, 1959), pp. 86–87.

Document 15

Overthrow of the monarchy

From a letter sent by a national guardsman to a friend in Rennes.

Paris, 11 August 1792, Year Four of Liberty

We are all tired out, doubtless less from spending two nights under arms than from heartache. Men's spirits were stirred after the unfortunate decree which whitewashed Lafayette. Nevertheless, we had a quiet enough evening; a group of *fédérés* from Marseilles gaily chanted patriotic songs in the Beaucaire café, the refreshment room of the National Assembly. It was rumoured: 'Tonight the tocsin will ring, the alarm drum will be beaten. All the *faubourgs* will burst into insurrection, supported by 6,000 *fédérés*.' At 11 o'clock we go home, at the same instant the drums call us back to arms. We speed from our quarters and our battalion, headed by two pieces of artillery, marches to the palace. Hardly have we reached the garden of the Tuileries than we hear the alarm cannon. The alarm drum resounds through all the streets of Paris. People run for arms from all over the place. Soon the public squares, the Pont Neuf, the main thoroughfares, are covered with troops. The National Assembly, which had finished its debate early, was recalled to its duties. It only knew of some of the preparations that had been made for the *journée* of 10 August. First the commandant of the palace wishes to hold the mayor a hostage there, then he sends him to the mayor's office. The people fear a display of his talents! In the general council of the Commune it is decreed that, according to the wishes of the 48 Sections, it is no longer necessary to recognise the established authorities if dethronement is not immediately announced and the new municipal bodies, keeping Pétion and Manuel at their head, entrusted with popular authority. However, the *faubourgs* organised themselves into an army and place in their centre Bretons, Marseillais and Bordelais, and all the other *fédérés*. More than 20,000 men march across Paris, bristling with pikes and bayonets. Santerre had been obliged to take command of them. The National Assembly are told that the army has broken into the palace. All hearts are frozen. Discussion is provoked again by the question of the safety of the king, when it is learned that Louis XVI seeks refuge in the bosom of the Assembly.

Forty-eight delegates are sent to the palace. The royal family places itself in the middle of the deputation. The people fling bitter reproaches at the king and accuse him of being the author of his troubles. Hardly was the king safe than the noise of cannon-fire increased. The Breton *fédérés* beat a tattoo. Some officers suggested retreat to the commander of the Swiss guards. But he seemed prepared and soon, by a clever tactic, captured the artillery which the national guard held in the courtyard. These guns, now turned on the people, fire and strike them down. But soon the conflict is intensified everywhere. The Swiss, surrounded, overpowered, stricken, then run out of ammunition. They plead for mercy, but it is impossible to calm the people, furious at Helvetian treachery.

The Swiss are cut to pieces. Some were killed in the state-rooms, others in the garden. Many died on the Champs-Elysées. Heavens! That liberty should cost Frenchmen blood and tears! How many victims there were among both the people and the national guard! The total number of dead could run to 2,000. All the Swiss who had been taken prisoner were escorted to the Place de Grève. There they had their brains blown out. They were traitors sacrificed to vengeance. What vengeance! I shivered to the roots of my being. At least 47 heads were cut off. The Grève was littered with corpses, and heads were paraded on the ends of several pikes. The first heads to be severed were those of seven *chevaliers du poignard*, slain at 8 o'clock in the morning on the Place Vendôme. Many Marseillais perished in the *journée* of 10 August.

Source: Wright, D.G. *Revolution and Terror in France, 1789–1794* (Pearson Education Ltd, London, 1990), pp. 123–24.

Document 16

What is a sans-culotte?

A self-description. The Ami des lois *was a comedy fashionable in 1793 and* Chaste Suzanne *a light operetta. Gorsas was a Girondin journalist and the* Patriote françois *and* La Chronique *Girondin news sheets.*

Reply to an impertinent question: what is a sans-culotte?

A sans-culotte, you rogues? He is someone who always goes about on foot, who has not got the millions you would all like to have, who has no chateaux, no valets to wait on him, and who lives simply with his wife and children, if he has any, on the fourth or fifth floor. He is useful because he knows how to plough a field, to forge and file metal, to use a saw, to roof a house, to make shoes, and to spill his blood to the last drop for the safety of the republic. And because he is a worker, you are sure not to meet his person in the Café de Chartres, or in the gaming houses where others plot and wager, nor in the Theatre of the Nation, where *L'Ami des lois* is performed, nor in the Vaudeville Theatre at a performance of *Chaste Suzanne*, nor in the literary clubs where for two sous, which are so precious to him, you are offered Gorsas's muck, with *La Chronique* and the *Patriote françois*.

In the evening he goes to the meeting of his Section, not powdered and per-fumed and nattily booted in the hope of being noticed by the citizenesses in the galleries, but ready to support sound proposals with all his might and ready to pulverise those which come from the despised faction of politicians.

Finally, a sans-culotte always has his sabre and belt with him, ready to cut off the ears of all mischief makers; sometimes he carries his pike about with him; but as soon as the drum beats you see him leave for the Vendée, for the Army of the Alps, or for the Army of the North.

Source: Wright, D.G. *Revolution and Terror in France, 1789–1795* (Pearson Education Ltd, London, 1990), pp. 126–27.

Document 17

The popular programme

The Section des Sans-Culottes presents this petition to the Convention on 2 September 1793, just as frustration at the deputies' failure to address the social and economic grievances of ordinary people approaches boiling point.

Delegates of the people – for how much longer are you going to tolerate roy-alism, ambition, egotism, intrigue and avarice, each of them combined with fanaticism, surrendering to tyranny our frontiers whilst spreading devastation and death everywhere? How much longer are you going to suffer food hoarders spreading famine throughout the republic in the detestable hope of causing patriots to cut each other's throats and the restoration of the throne in the midst of bloody corpses and with the help of foreign despots? You must make haste for there is no time to lose [...] the whole universe is watching you: humanity reproaches you for the troubles that are laying waste the French republic. Posterity will condemn your names in centuries to come if you do not speedily find a remedy [...] Make haste, representatives of the people, to remove from the armies all former nobles; all priests, magistrates of the Parle-ments and financiers from all administrative and judicial posts; also to fix the price of basic foodstuffs, raw materials, wages, and the profits of industry and commerce. You have both the justification and the authority to do so [...] No doubt aristocrats, royalists, moderates and intriguers will retort that this is to compromise [rights of] property which should be sacred and inviolable [...] No doubt; but are these rogues unaware that property is constrained by physical need? Are they unaware that no one has the right to do anything that injures another? What is more injurious than the arbitrary power to attach to food a price that seven-eighths of citizens cannot possibly reach [...] Are they unaware, finally, that every individual making up the republic should employ his intelli-gence and the strength in his arms in the service of the republic, and should be prepared to spill his blood to the last drop for her? In return, the republic should guarantee to each one of its citizens the means of procuring sufficient basic necessities for his existence.

Have we not directed a fearsome law against hoarders, you will retort. But delegates of the people, do not be deceived [...] This decree, which forces those with large stocks of foodstuffs to make a declaration, tends to benefit hoarders more than it extinguishes hoarding: it puts all their stocks under the supervision of the nation, while leaving them to sell at whatever price their greed dictates. In consequence, the general assembly of the Section des Sans-Culottes, considering it to be the duty of all citizens to propose measures which seem calculated to bring about the return of plenty and public tranquillity, resolves to ask the Convention to decree the following:

1   That former nobles be barred from military careers and every kind of public office; that former *parlementaires*, priests and financiers be deprived of all administrative and judicial posts.
2   That the price of basic necessities be fixed at the levels prevailing in 1789–90, allowing for differences of quality.
3   That the price of raw materials, the level of wages and the profits of industry and commerce be also fixed, so that the working man, the farmer and the trader will be able to obtain not only the materials essential to their existence, but also the means of making the most of their life chances.
4   That all those farmers who, by some accident, have not been able to bring in their harvest be compensated from public funds.
5   That each department be allocated sufficient public money so as to ensure that the price of basic foodstuffs will be the same for all citizens of the republic.
6   That the sums of money allocated to the departments be used to eradicate variations in the price of foodstuffs caused by transport costs across the republic, so that everyone enjoys the same advantage.
7   That leases be abrogated and returned to the levels prevailing in average years; and that a uniform *maximum* be set for food and basic commodities.
8   That a *maximum* on wealth be fixed.
9   That no individual may possess more than one *maximum*.
10 That no one be allowed to lease more land than is required for a given number of plough-teams.
11 That no citizen shall be allowed to own more than one workshop, or boutique.
12 That all those with purely nominal title to goods or land be deemed proprietors.

The Section des Sans-Culottes believes that these measures will restore plenty and tranquility and will cause to disappear, bit by bit, the excessive disparity in wealth, and will multiply the number of proprietors.

Source: [with re-translations by Peter Jones] Wright, D.G. *Revolution and Terror in France, 1789–1795* (Pearson Education Ltd, London, 1990), pp. 128–30.

Document 18

Legislating Revolutionary Government

The law of 14 Frimaire II (4 December 1793) reasserted central control over the application of Terror.

Section II: Implementation of laws

1 The National Convention is the sole centre of impulsion of the government. [...]

9 All established authorities and all public functionaries are placed under the immediate supervision of the Committee of Public Safety for measures concerned with government and public safety, in conformity with the decree of 19 Vendémiaire [10 October]; and for everything relating to individuals and to general and internal police, this particular supervision belongs to the Convention's Committee of General Security, in accordance with the decree of 17 September last; these two committees are obliged to give an account of their operations to the National Convention at the end of each month. Each member of these two committees is personally responsible for the performance of this duty.

10 The execution of the laws is divided into surveillance and application. [...]

13 Surveillance over the execution of revolutionary laws and measures of government, general security and public safety in the departments is exclusively attributed to the Districts, who are obliged to give a faithful account of their operations every ten days to the Committee of Public Safety for matters of government and public safety, and to the Convention's Surveillance Committee for matters of general and internal police and for individuals. [...]

15 The application of revolutionary laws and measures of government and general security is entrusted to the municipalities and to the surveillance (or revolutionary) committees, who are likewise obliged to give an account every ten days of the execution of these laws to the District [administrations] of their area, to whom they are immediately subordinate. [...]

18 It is expressly forbidden for any authority or public functionary to issue proclamations or to take measures which extend, limit or contradict the literal meaning of the law, on the pretext of interpreting or expanding it. [...]

21 In the place of the procurator-sindics of the Districts and the procurators of the Communes and their deputies, posts which are abolished by this decree, there will be *agents nationaux* specially entrusted with requiring and enforcing the execution of the law and also with denouncing negligence in such execution and infringements which may be committed. These *agents*

nationaux are authorised to move from the seat of administration and to travel round the area of their jurisdiction to exercise surveillance and to assure themselves more positively that the laws are being implemented to the letter.

Section III: Competence of the established authorities

5 [...] The hierarchy which placed the Districts, municipalities or any other authority under the Department [administration] is abolished as regards revolutionary and military laws and measures of government, public safety and general security.
   [...]
10 All changes ordered by the present decree will be implemented within three days of its publication.
   [...]
20 No armed force, tax or loan (whether forced or voluntary) may be levied except in virtue of a decree. The revolutionary taxes of the representatives of the people will not be collected until they have been approved by the Convention, unless it be in enemy or rebel territory.

Source: Hardman, J. (ed.) *The French Revolution Sourcebook*
(Arnold, London, 1999), pp. 187–88.

Document 19

Dechristianization

Although the closing down of churches and the attempt to promote a new religion of reason started as early as October 1793 in some areas, in others these developments waited upon the organization of Revolutionary Government. In the department of the Ain, the secularization drive overlapped with calls for all links to the Christian past (first names and place names) to be broken.

Liberty, equality, fraternity or Death.

Montluel, 12 Ventôse Year Two of the one, indivisible and democratic Republic [2 March 1794]. The *sans-culottes* of the Jacobin Club of Montluel to representative of the people Albitte.

Citizen,

Having re-emerged from their prejudices, the French have just renounced an absurd and immoral religion which distracted the heart with false virtues and the intellect with mysterious fantasies.

You have taken steps to secure the removal of all signs of this nonsensical public worship and, *Long Live Reason*, you have done well. It is now necessary to ensure that the next generation finds not the least trace of it in the soil of freedom.

In this important matter the *sans-culottes* of Montluel anticipated your wise measures and long before your decrees no crosses, relics or phony evidence of so-called saints could be seen in this commune, or in the neighbourhood. However, all is not yet complete inasmuch as an impure off-shoot of the old superstition still has some roots. They must be eradicated for otherwise the religion of the priests will, like gangrene, germinate afresh from a single neglected seed, bringing back with it the monsters it once supported: aristocracy and despotism.

Citizen, we are referring to the saints' names which still serve as first names for regenerated Frenchmen. First names such as Blaise or Nicholas can remain if so desired as can others of this ilk which are carried by individuals; after all there might be some civil drawbacks involved in their removal. But we should no longer allow children to be given fantastic patron saints' names, or any names likely to perpetuate the memory of a demeaning religion. In this respect the club has done what it could. Through the organ of its president, it has invited all members to refrain from giving their children Christian names and to substitute either the names of great men, or the names of flowers and plants drawn from the new calendar, according to choice.

[...]

Certified copy

Signed ALBITTE

Source: Archives Nationales, DIV bis 80. Corrected and translated by Peter Jones.

Document 20

Scorched earth treatment for rebels

A letter of Turreau, one of the generals put in charge of crushing any remaining counter-revolutionary resistance in the Vendée, to the Minister of War, 19 January 1794.

My purpose is to burn everything, to leave nothing but what is essential to establish the necessary quarters for exterminating the rebels. This great measure is one which you should prescribe; you should also make an advance statement as to the fate of the women and children we will come across in this rebellious countryside. If they are all to be put to the sword, I cannot undertake such action without authorisation.

All brigands caught bearing arms, or convicted of having taken up arms to revolt against their country, will be bayoneted. The same will apply to girls, women and children in the same circumstances. Those who are merely under suspicion will not be spared either, but no execution may be carried out except by previous order of the general.

All villages, farms, woods, heath lands, generally anything which will burn, will be set on fire, although not until any perishable supplies found there have been removed. But, it must be repeated, these executions must not take place until so ordered by the general.

I hasten to describe to you the measures which I have put in hand for the extermination of all remaining rebels scattered about the interior of the Vendée. I was convinced that the only way to do this was by deploying a sufficient number of columns to spread right across the countryside and effect a general sweep, which would completely purge the cantons as they passed. Tomorrow, therefore, these twelve columns will set out simultaneously, moving from east to west. Each column commander has orders to search and burn forests, villages, market towns and farms, omitting, however, those places which I consider important posts and those which are essential for establishing communications.

Source: Cobb, R. and Jones, C. (eds) *The French Revolution: Voices from a Momentous Epoch, 1789–1795* (Simon and Schuster, London, 1988), p. 206.

Document 21

Celebrating the abolition of slavery

Marie-Thérèse Lucidor Corbin was born in Paris, but had a Caribbean background. Her mother had married a freed black slave (André known as Lucidor). By 1794 Marie-Thérèse was a well-connected revolutionary and her participation in the Festival for the Abolition of Slavery appears to be recorded in an engraving of the festival (see cover image). J.-P. Marat's book The Chains of Slavery *(1774) was republished in French just months before his murder.*

Speech of *Citoyenne* Lucidor F. Corbin, a republican creole woman, delivered at the Temple of Reason, Year Two of Liberty.

French people, the great day has arrived, the totem of feudalism has finally been shattered. Liberty [and] Equality rule over our hemisphere; all our afflictions have been brought to an end. The precious Decree passed by our legislators renders us equal to the rest of mankind; we are reunited by bonds of fraternity, our chains are broken, never to be put back. Yes, this we swear before our Goddess of Liberty, we will never adhere to other principles than those of Marat, who was put to the sacrifice by a monster of despotism. Oh! Marat, even if you are not present on this day, what joy would shine in your heart and in your eyes.

But you who were cherished in life as in death, be assured that our Hearts are so many altars for the preservation of your virtues. Through your writings, it was you who inspired in us the sacred love of Liberty for which we will be eternally grateful.

And you Ogée [*sic*], free man of colour, our brother and our friend who secured us the decree of 15 May 1790 [*sic*] and who died the first victim of assassination by the aristocracy in our islands, receive this feeble homage of our gratitude.

Frenchmen, what more beautiful a day is there for us to deploy this symbol of the coming together of three peoples [Europeans, Creoles and Africans], whom the insolent aristocracy sought to separate with a line of division. But it is at last broken into pieces, like the chains beneath our feet. We swear yet again to defend Liberty [and] Equality, and to uphold the one and indivisible Republic.

Source: Bibliothèque nationale de France Lb [41] 5315. Discours, de la Citoyenne LUCIDOR F. CORBIN, créole, républicaine. Prononcée [*sic*] par elle même au Temple de la Raison, l'An 2ᵉ de la Liberté.

Translated by Peter Jones.

Document 22

Implementing the abolition of slavery

The official communication of the Convention's decree of 16 Pluviôse II (4 February 1794) abolishing slavery took six months to reach Ile-de-France (Mauritius) in the Indian Ocean. It was accompanied by this inflammatory address penned in Paris, which greatly alarmed the established authorities on the island.

Brave fellow citizens we are sending to you the decree of 16 Pluviôse, this monument to French magnanimity. Make haste to put it into effect. No doubt landowners and the rich will be opposed to it [...] Well, in that case, pursue the rich and landowners as you would enemies of the public good.

Source: A. Marrier d'Unienville, *Statistique de l'Ile Maurice et ses dépendances*, vol. 2 (Gustave Barba Libraire, Paris, 1838), p. 199.

Translated by Peter Jones.

Document 23

Crisis in the Sections of Paris

The Committee of Public Safety and the Committee of General Security received regular briefings from police agents on the public mood at street level in the capital as the winter of 1794 gave way to spring.

2 Germinal II (22 March 1794)

It is imperative to speed up the trial of Citizen Hébert. There's a muffled ferment which is hard to define. However much one talks to people, makes enquiries, asks questions in order to try and ascertain public opinion, everybody is negative and responds vaguely.

Nonetheless, it's easy to judge that many have been affected [by the trial] and I firmly believe that it is important to proceed to sentencing as quickly as possible. In the meantime as much publicity as possible should be given to the conduct of Hébert so as to pre-empt stirrings among a section of the populace who are strongly disposed in his favour.

I even think it necessary to post up the justification of the sentence before his execution.

Source: Markov, W. and Soboul, A. *Die Sansculotten von Paris.*
Dokumente zur Geschichte des Volksbewegung 1793–1794 (Verlag, Berlin,
1957), p. 338. Translated by Peter Jones.

Document 24

Civic culture in the making?

Although both of these extracts come from official sources, they raise questions about the Directory's efforts to embed its particular vision of the political order in the population at large.

16 Ventôse IV / 6 March 1796

The Commissioner of the Executive Directory [of Neuviller] reported that the law of 3 Brumaire [25 October 1795] designated 10 Germinal [30 March 1796] for one of the seven annual festivals. The Municipal Administration deliberated on how to celebrate it, and resolved that nothing does more to strengthen and consolidate public-spiritedness than the gathering together of citizens in order to rejoice together at the conquest of liberty [...] It considered, moreover, that festivals should not only be days for relaxation and entertainment, but employed principally for the purpose of developing [public] behaviour and leading hearts towards fraternity [...] It was resolved that on the occasion of the 10 Germinal Festival of Youth, appropriate games would take place and that the organization of the national guard would be put in hand on the same day.

Source: Archives Départementales de Meurthe-et-Moselle L2943 *bis.*
Register of deliberations of the administration of the canton of Neuviller,
14 Nivôse IV–18 Floréal VIII. Translated by Peter Jones.

Ventôse VII / March 1799

National festivals have been set up, but I would not speak here of their celebration. Is there any sight more pathetic than a municipal body decked in its sashes of office and accompanied by four or five village urchins coarsely intoning around a dead [liberty] tree a few couplets which usually have nothing to do with the ceremony in question, before returning home in a similar procession? Yet this is what happens in three quarters of France. This way of celebrating festivals is an insult to the nation; to say the least it is manifestly contrary to the intentions of legislators.

Source: Report of the Commissioner of the Executive Directory [of
Leintrey, Meurthe et-Moselle]: Clémendot, P. *Le Département de la
Meurthe à l'époque du Directoire* (Raon L'Etape, 1966), pp. 293–94.
Translated by Peter Jones.

Document 25

Messaging the Directory: Bonaparte's victory banner

Bonaparte's diligence in conveying the spoils of war (cash reparations, paintings, statues, objets d'art, *manuscripts, etc.) to Paris granted him a freedom of action that no other General enjoyed.*

[...] before leaving [Milan, on 17 November 1797] he sent the Directory one of these monumental objects which might easily be considered far-fetched, but which, on this occasion, was nothing other than the truth. This object was THE BANNER OF THE ARMY OF ITALY; General Joubert was entrusted with the mission of presenting it to the heads of government. On one side of the flag could be read 'To the Army of Italy from a grateful Fatherland'; on the other side were listed all the battles fought, the towns taken and, in particular, the following succinct and glorious summary of the Italian campaign: 150,000 prisoners; 170 flags; 550 pieces of ordnance; 600 field guns; 5 pontoon trains; 9 vessels of 64 guns; 12 frigates of 32 guns; 12 corvettes; 18 galleys; armistice with the King of Sardinia; Convention with Genoa; armistice with the Duke of Parma; armistice with the King of Naples; armistice with the Pope; peace preliminaries of Leoben; Convention of Montebello with the Republic of Genoa; peace treaty with the Emperor at Campo-Formio.

Liberty bestowed upon the peoples of Bologna, Ferrara, Modena, Massa-Carrara, Romagna, Lombardy, Brescia, Bergamo, Mantua, Cremona, part of the Veronese, Chiavena, Bormio, the Valteline, the peoples of Genoa, the Imperial fiefdoms, the peoples of the departments of Corçyra, the Aegean Sea and Ithaca.

Sent to Paris all the masterpieces of Michael-Angelo, Guercino, Titian, Paolo Veronese, Correggio, Albano, the Carracci, Raphael and Leonardo da Vinci.

Here were summarized on a banner destined to embellish the public meeting chamber of the Directory the military exploits of the Italian Campaign, its political consequences and the confiscations of works of art.

Source: *Mémoires de M. de Bourienne, ministre d'état sur Napoléon, le Directoire, le Consulat, l'Empire et la Restauration* (Paris: chez Ladvocat, 1830), vol. 2, pp. 3–4.

Document 26

Managing 'une grande nation'

The conquests and territorial expansion of France between 1795 and 1799 raised fundamental questions in the minds of the policy makers of the Directory. These were resolved, in part, by setting up a number of 'sister' republics.

Treaty between France and the Cisalpine Republic, 3 Ventôse VI / 21 February 1798

The French Republic recognizes the Cisalpine Republic as a free and independent power; it guarantees its liberty, its independence, and the abolition of every government anterior to the one which now administers it.

There shall be peace, amity and good understanding between the French and the Cisalpine Republic in perpetuity.

The Cisalpine Republic pledges itself to take part in all wars which the French Republic might wage, when requisition thereto has been made upon it by the Executive Directory of the French Republic; as soon as such requisition is addressed to it, it shall be required to put all its forces and resources into action. By notification of the said same requisition, it will be constituted de facto in a state of war with the Powers against which it has been requisitioned, but until such notification has been made to it, it will remain in a state of neutrality. The French Republic shall be required to include the Cisalpine Republic in treaties of peace which follow wars which it has engaged in by virtue of the present article.

The Cisalpine Republic having requested of the French Republic an army corps sufficient to maintain its liberty, its independence, and its internal peace, as well as to preserve it from all aggression on the part of its neighbours, the two Republics have agreed upon the following articles.

Until otherwise agreed thereon, there shall be in the Cisalpine Republic a body of French troops amounting to 25,000 men, including the staff and administration. The said body shall be composed of 22,000 infantry, 2,500 cavalry, and 500 artillery, either horse or of the line.

The Cisalpine Republic will furnish annually to the French Republic, for payment and maintenance of the said troops, a sum of 18,000,000 [francs], which shall be paid, in twelve equal monthly instalments, into the funds of the army; and in case of war, the necessary supplement of supplies. [...]

The French Government may withdraw and replace the said troops at will.

The said troops, as well as those of the Cisalpine Republic, shall always be under the command of French generals

[...]

Separate articles

[...]

The Cisalpine Republic may not, without the consent of the French government, go to war with any Power friendly to, or allied with, the French Republic.

[...]

Source: Stewart, J.H. *A Documentary Survey of the French Revolution* (Macmillan, New York, 1951), pp. 721–24.

Document 27

The revolution is over

This statement was drawn up a month after the coup d'état *of Brumaire and printed for circulation to all the departments. The aim was to convey the message that the revolution was not just over; it was completed.*

Proclamation of the Consuls of the Republic of 24 Frimaire Year VIII [15 December 1799].

The Consuls of the Republic to the French:

A Constitution is presented to you.

It ends the indecisiveness the Provisional Government brought to external relations, to the internal and military situation of the Republic

It places in the institutions it establishes chief magistrates whose devotion is required for its activity.

The Constitution is founded on the true principles of representative government, on the sacred rights of property, equality and freedom.

The powers it institutes will be firm and stable, as they must be in order to guarantee the rights of citizens and the interests of the State.

Citizens, the Revolution is established on the principles which began it: it is finished.

> Source: *Proclamation des Consuls de la République. Du 24 Frimaire, an VIII de la République une et indivisible.* Translated by Peter Jones

Document 28

State of the country after Brumaire

These extracts are taken from reports commissioned by the First Consul a few months after the establishment of the Consulate in 1800. Theophilanthropy was a civic quasi-religion briefly fashionable during the Directory, whereas Jansenists, Molinists and Convulsionists were mutually antagonistic sects within the pre-1789 Catholic Church.

Report of state councillor Fourcroy on his mission to the departments of the 14th military division [Calvados, Manche, Orne] in the month of Floréal Year IX [April–May 1801].

V. Political, military and administrative situation of the three departments comprising the 14th military division.

[...] There exists a marked diversity of opinion among the inhabitants of the three departments. Some individuals express a wish for a return to the *ancien régime*; others would like the constitutional monarchy of 1791, and a few still hanker for the ochlocratic [democratic] government of 1793. There are those who regret [the passing of] the Constitution of the Year III [1795], but the great majority – friends of the revolution – have rallied with sincerity to the Constitution of the Year VIII [1800], which has provided France with internal peace and stable government.

These opinions are purely speculative. Among the avowed partisans of anarchy or royalty, no one wishes to run the risks of another revolution; and no one, above all, is inclined to take up arms or to foment disturbances in order to secure the victory of one or other of these parties. I have noticed merely that among the individuals currently employed in the prefecture of the Calvados who are attached to the Constitution of the Year III, some continuing hopes of appointing to posts all those who share their opinion. And in order to achieve this objective, they pursue the policy of informing and denunciation which proved successful so often during the time of revolutionary turmoils. The government should investigate this matter which breeds distrust between administrators and those whom they administer.

[...]

Mission in the Year IX [1800–1801] of General Lacuée, councillor of state in the 1st military division [Aisne, Eure-et-Loir, Loiret, Oise, Seine-et-Marne, Seine-et-Oise].

Sources of national and individual wealth.

Agriculture – before the revolution agriculture (in the six departments excluding the Seine) might have been in a flourishing state but for the tithe, the *champart* and the [problem of] game. It is estimated that game destroyed one-eighth of the sowings and one-tenth of the harvest; at least this was the case in the Seine-et-Oise.

Requisitions and the Maximum caused a lot of damage to agriculture during one period of the revolution, but these drawbacks have been more than compensated for by the subdivision of landholdings; the non-collection of taxes; the residence [on their estates] of landowners and the abolition of [exclusive] hunting [rights], the *champart* and the tithe. Thus appreciable steps towards a better state of affairs have occurred.

However, agriculture suffered badly during the Year VII [1798–99]. Apprehensive owners of national property farmed poorly and wastefully. But the 18th Brumaire rekindled hope, [the sowing of] fodder crops multiplied, land was cleared, trees planted, the quantity of stock increased, farm buildings repaired.

[...]

Religion – the needs of the people in this sphere seem at the moment to be limited, both in the towns and the countryside, to vain spectacles and ceremonies. Attendance at Mass, listening to the sermon, going to Vespers, that's good enough; but submitting to confession, taking communion, abstinence from meat, or fasting is nowhere commonplace, and practised only by a tiny number. In those parts of the countryside where there are no priests, a lay official (magister) officiates and everyone is well content. The priests in rural areas are mostly indifferent. In the towns this indifference can be found also, but it is less marked. Some prefer the constitutional [clergy], but only a few; those [priests] who have sworn the oath of loyalty have more adherents; however, it is those who have declined to swear any oath who are the most ardently followed.

The services of the constitutional clergy are the most basic, whereas those provided by clerics who have taken the oath of loyalty [to the regime] are more elaborate. The non-jurors operate clandestinely, and these latter are the only ones to complain about the obstacles posed by the laws. All the others are broadly content with the freedom they enjoy, particularly the clergy ministering to non-Catholics.

The Jews are few in number, and protestants can only be found in the [departments of] the Seine and the Loiret.

The Theophilanthropy cult is collapsing, or has collapsed, everywhere. There are still some Jansenists and Molinists around, and Convulsionists can even be found in Paris.

The constitutional clergy manage on their pensions and whatever surplice fees they can collect. All the rest get by on hand-outs and the yield of collections, although they are scarcely the poorer thereby – at least in the towns. The non-jurors brought money with them when they returned [to France], but most of it was spent on giving pomp to their services.

In the countryside the people prefer [the sound of] bells without priests, to priests without bells.

> Source: Rocquain, F. *L'Etat de la France au 18 Brumaire d'après les rapports des conseillers d'état chargés d'une enquête sur la situation de la République* (Didier et Cie, Paris, 1874), pp. 179–80; 237–8; 253–4.
>
> Translated by Peter Jones.

Document 29

Regaining internal control

The establishment of special criminal tribunals was part of the government's strategy to overcome brigandage, but in the eyes of some observers the measure risked undermining the principles of the system of justice set up at the start of the revolution.

Law of 19 Pluviôse IX / 29 January 1801
Title 1

A special tribunal will be established in departments where the government deems it appropriate for the repression of the crimes stipulated below.

This tribunal will consist of two criminal law judges, three military persons possessing the rank of captain or above and two citizens qualified to act as judges. Individuals in the last two categories will be appointed by the First Consul.

[...]
Title 2

6 The special tribunal will prosecute crimes and offences subject to corporal punishment or deprivation of civil rights committed by vagabonds, vagrants and convicts [...]
[...]
8 The special tribunal will take cognizance of highway robbery involving violence, assault or other aggravating circumstances by whomsoever it is committed.

It will likewise take cognizance of theft in the countryside and from rural dwellings and buildings where breaking and entering has taken place, or where the offence involved the carrying of weapons and was committed by two or more people.

It will also take cognizance, concurrently with the ordinary courts, of cases of premeditated murder by whomsoever committed.

[...]

24 On submission of an accusation, with supporting evidence [...] the tribunal will try cases within its competence without right of appeal
[...]

25 The verdict will be notified to the defendant within twenty-four hours. The Government Commissioner will likewise send to the Minister of Justice within twenty-hour hours a notification for onward dispatch to the court of appeal.
[...]

29 [Arguments for a stay of execution having been heard], the tribunal will sentence in the last instance and without appeal. Robberies of the type described in articles 9 and 10 will incur a death penalty. Threats and assaults directed against purchasers of national property will be liable to a punishment of imprisonment of not less than six months and not exceeding three years, but with the option of more severe penalties in aggravated cases
[...]

Source: *Gazette nationale ou Moniteur universel* (Paris, 1789–1810), an VIII, pp. 545–46. Translated by Peter Jones.

Document 30

War resumes

The Peace of Amiens broke down in May 1803, prompting the Royal Navy to re-start a blockade of French and French-controlled ports on the Continent from Toulon to the Texel. General Bonaparte, meanwhile, put in hand plans for an invasion of Great Britain. The economic impact of the naval blockade would only be really effective after the battle of Trafalgar (21 October 1805) gave Britain better command of the seas.

Citizen Prefect,

The British cabinet wishes for war. Not content with dominating Asia and America, England aspires to the mastery of Europe; she claims exclusive possession of the world's trade and dares to shut us out of the Levant. Invade everything, possess everything, make all peoples dependent, stifle industry everywhere; this is the policy and the aspiration of her government [...] England welcomes neither our commercial prosperity nor the standing that the nation has secured in Europe; she would prefer an abject nation, permanently dependent on her industry and subject to her laws of trade. But, citizen Prefect, our destiny is manifest in the population and the position of France, in the character of its inhabitants, in the strength of its government and the intelligence of its leader. Be in no doubt, England will in her delirium come to break herself against the bronze colossus at the feet of which the whole of Europe has laid down arms.

> Source: Archives Nationales F¹ᵃ24 circular of L.-A. Chaptal, Minister of the Interior to the Prefects, 12 Prairial XI (1 June 1803). Translated by Peter Jones.

Document 31

Marking out the new civil order

The Civil Code of 1804 sought to combine the Customary and the Roman law of ancien-régime *France with the legislation passed in the 1790s. It lays out unambiguously the rights and responsibilities of individuals within the family and in matters relating to inheritance. The statement on property expresses the consensus verdict as to what had been achieved after a decade and a half of revolution.*

CIVIL CODE
> *Preliminary title: on the publication, application and effects of general laws*
> [...]

2   The law applies to the future only; it has no retrospective effect.

> *Book One: on persons*
> Chapter One: on the enjoyment of civil rights
> [...]

8   Every Frenchman shall enjoy civil rights.

> Chapter Six: on the rights and responsibilities of married persons

212   Married persons owe to each other fidelity, succour and assistance.
213   The husband owes protection to his wife; the wife owes obedience to her husband.
214   The wife is obliged to live with her husband and to follow him wherever he may choose to reside; the husband is obliged to take her in, and to provide her with all of life's necessities, according to his means and his station.
215   The wife cannot plead in her own name without the authorisation of her husband, even though she should be a public trader, or not in community, or separate in property.
216   The authorisation of the husband is not required when the wife is prosecuted under criminal or police jurisprudence.

217   The wife, even though not in community or separate in property, cannot donate, give away, pledge or acquire, whether freely or at a cost, without the husband's agreement or written consent.

218   If the husband refuses to authorise the wife to plead in her own name, a judge can give such authorisation.
       [...]

Title Six: on divorce
Chapter One: on the causes of divorce

229   The husband may demand divorce because of the adultery of the wife.
       [...]

230   The wife may demand divorce because of adultery on the part of the husband where he has kept his mistress in the communal home.
       [...]

233   The mutual and sustained consent of the married persons, expressed as prescribed by the law and in accordance with the conditions and tests which the law lays down, will be considered sufficient proof that communal living is no longer tolerable to the parties, thereby constituting a conclusive ground for divorce.
       [...]

Chapter Four: on the consequences of divorce

297   In the case of divorce by mutual consent, neither of the parties shall be permitted to contract a new marriage until three years have elapsed from the date of the divorce.

298   In the case of divorce admitted by law on the ground of adultery, the guilty party shall never be permitted to marry his/her accomplice. The adulterous wife shall be condemned by the same judgement, and at the behest of the public prosecutor, to confinement in a house of correction for a fixed period not exceeding two years and not less than three months.
       [...]

Book Two: on property and the various modifications to which it is subject
Title One: on the characteristics of property
Chapter Three: on property in relation to possession

537   Individuals are free to dispose of property belonging to them, subject to the modifications laid down by the law.
       [...]

542   Communal possessions are properties, the ownership or usufruct of which, the inhabitants of one or several communes have an established title to.

Title Two: on property

544 Property is the faculty to enjoy the use of, and to dispose of, things in the most absolute manner, provided that no use of them is made which is forbidden by law or by regulations.

545 No one can be obliged to give up his property unless it be in the public interest, and only then on condition of a previous just indemnity.

546 Property in a thing, whether movable or immovable, confers entitlement to all that it produces [...]

Book Three: on the various ways in which property is acquired
Title Five: on marriage contracts and the respective rights of married persons
Chapter Two: on the regime of community

1421 The husband alone administers property held in community.

1422 He can sell it, dispose of it, or pledge it without the agreement of the wife.
[...]

1428 The husband administers all the personal possessions of the wife [...] He may not dispose of real estate owned personally by the wife without her consent.

Source: Bourguignon, M. *Conférence des cinq codes* (Corby, libraire, rue St-André-des-Arts, Paris, 1823), pp. 2–3; 42–43; 45–46; 55; 94–95; 237.

Translated by Peter Jones.

Glossary

agents nationaux   Chief executive officers of the Districts and the municipalities during the Terror.

aides   Indirect taxes on articles of consumption.

ancien régime   [Literally, 'former regime']. The term was invented soon after the start of the revolution. It is used to describe the structure of government and society before 1789.

appel au peuple   A popular referendum to decide on the punishment of Louis XVI.

Assembly of Notables   A gathering of eminent individuals called into being by the monarch; convened in February 1787, and again in November 1788.

assignats   Interest-bearing bonds exchangeable for nationalized Church lands; would eventually become a paper currency.

bailliage   A judicial and administrative subdivision.

biens nationaux   Confiscated property formerly belonging to the Church and to individuals who had fled the revolution, which was put up for sale.

Bourbon   The first Bourbon king was Henry IV, who came to the throne in 1589 following the extinction of the Valois line. The last would be Louis-Philippe I, who abdicated in 1848.

bourg   A large village; often possessing a market.

Brumaire   Shorthand for the *coup* of 1799 that would bring Napoleon Bonaparte to power.

Brunswick Manifesto   The threatening declaration of 25 July 1792 issued by the commander-in-chief of the Austrian and Prussian invading forces.

cahiers de doléances   Grievance lists drawn up by all three orders for submission to the king on the occasion of the Estates General.

capitation   A universal and graduated poll tax originally introduced in 1695.

chambres des comptes   'Sovereign' courts entrusted with the task of scrutinizing the returns of royal accountants.

champart   A seigneurial harvest due.

chevaliers du poignard   Young noblemen who occupied the Tuileries Palace in February 1791 in a gesture of support for Louis XVI.

chouans   Royalist insurgents; chiefly to be found in Brittany between 1793 and 1802.

DOI: 10.4324/9781003156185-13

Compte rendu au roi Necker's controversial budgetary statement; published in 1781.

conciliar monarchy A system of rule according to which the monarch is dependent upon the advice of the royal council in which the aristocracy have a preponderant voice.

contribution foncière The new net land tax introduced in place of the *taille* and the *vingtièmes* in 1791.

contribution patriotique A one-off tax introduced in 1789 to stem the deficit.

Contrôle Général [*des Finances*] A rambling ministry with multiple administrative responsibilities. Headquarters of the Controller General.

corps An order, estate or body of individuals with collective privileges.

corvée [*royale*] Labour service performed by commoners for road maintenance; converted into a monetary tax in 1787.

cours des aides 'Sovereign' courts heading the fiscal judiciary; equipped with auditing powers.

'dead hand' [of the Church]. Non-transferable property owned by monasteries, hospitals, etc.

décadi A division of time; the tenth day (and the rest day) in the revolutionary calendar.

dechristianization The policy of closing down churches, defrocking priests and imposing the worship of secular abstractions such as 'reason' and the 'supreme being'.

Declaration of Pillnitz The statement jointly issued on 27 August 1791 by the Habsburg Emperor and the King of Prussia urging the Powers to intervene in support of Louis XVI.

déclassé An individual occupying a position lower than that accorded by his status.

don gratuit A subsidy offered by the Assembly of the Clergy in lieu of direct taxation.

Elector of Trier The ruler with territory to the west of the river Rhine who provided shelter to *émigrés*.

émigrés Individuals opposed to the revolution who left France and often joined the counter-revolution.

enragés The pejorative label attached to militants in the Sections who called for government action to legislate the 'popular programme'.

Estates General The body of representatives of the three orders of state; convened by the monarch at intervals since 1302.

'factories' Trading posts enabling contact between foreign merchants and local inhabitants.

faubourgs Working-class neighbourhoods on the periphery of the capital.

Federalism The resistance of dissident republicans in the spring and summer of 1793.

fédérés Militants and enthusiasts who were despatched to Paris for the Fête de la Fédération of July 1790, and again in 1792 when they were involved in the overthrow of Louis XVI.

Feuillants   Constitutional monarchists who quit the Jacobin Club in July 1791 and founded their own political club in the monastery of the Strict Bernardines (*feuillants*).

First Estate   The functional category to which all clergy belonged.

fouage   Hearth tax.

gabelle   Salt tax.

Gallican Church   The Catholic Church of France as controlled after 1682 by the reigning monarch rather than the Holy See.

gens de couleur   [Literally, 'people of colour']. The free blacks in France's Caribbean territories.

Girondins   [Literally, from the Gironde department]. Deputies who grouped around Jacques-Pierre Brissot; expelled from the National Convention in June 1793.

Hôtel de Ville   [Literally, 'town hall']. Seat of the Paris city government, which helped the Crown to raise money via bonds issued on the security of its revenues.

indulgents   Deputies who, late in 1793, called for a relaxation of the Terror.

intendant [de province]   Royal executive agent in charge of a province before 1789.

jacqueries   Peasant insurrections.

jour   An area measurement (0.4 hectare) in use in the province of Lorraine.

journée   [Literally, 'day']. The occasion of a popular demonstration or uprising.

levée en masse   Proclamation of a 'mass levy' of able-bodied men to rush to the defence of the revolution.

lit de justice   [Literally, 'bed of justice']. An enforced registration of laws by a Parlement in the presence of the monarch.

livre   [*tournois*]. The money of France until displaced by the *franc* in the later 1790s.

Marseillaise   A patriotic song composed on the outbreak of war by Rouget de Lisle; adopted by the *fédérés* of Marseilles as they marched to Paris in 1792.

Martial Law   Decree of 21 October 1789 empowering the new municipal authorities to use force against crowds that refused to disperse.

masses de granit   The social sub-stratum of 'notables' upon which Napoleon Bonaparte set out to secure his regime.

Maximum   State-imposed price controls, first introduced in May 1793 and generalized in September of that year.

metropolitan   Archbishop in charge of an ecclesiastical province.

Monarchiens   Deputies located on the moderate wing of the patriot party in the National Assembly, who favoured a two-chamber legislature and an 'absolute' veto for the monarch.

Montagnards   [Literally, 'mountaineers']. Deputies in the National Convention who challenged the Girondins and took power during the Terror.

national guard   Civic militia originating in Paris in July 1789 and subsequently replicated in towns and villages throughout the country.

October Days Events surrounding the march to Versailles by the women of Paris on 5 October 1789 and the return of the royal family to the capital the following day.

octrois Municipal tolls levied on goods entering towns.

ordonnances Edicts.

parlementaires Magistrates of the Parlements.

Parlements Appeal courts with important administrative powers in addition. There were thirteen of these 'sovereign' courts at the end of the *ancien régime*.

pays d'états Regions governed by **Provincial Estates**.

philosophes [Literally, 'philosophers']. The term is used to describe free-thinking intellectuals and writers in the eighteenth century.

pourris A group of deputies and their racketeer backers who peddled influence and blackmailed bankers and trading companies in the summer and autumn of 1793.

Princes of the Blood Male blood relatives of the monarch who were not members of the royal family, but entitled to attend royal councils.

Provincial Assemblies Consultative councils introduced by reforming ministers between 1778 and 1787.

Provincial Estates Historic representative bodies with powers to distribute and collect royal taxes in the regions.

représentants en mission Deputies who were commissioned by the National Convention to tour the departments and enforce government policy.

sans-culottes [Literally, 'those without knee-breeches']. Militants in the Sections of Paris who depicted themselves as hard-working, plebeian revolutionaries.

Second Estate The legal category to which all nobles belonged.

Sections [of Paris]. Wards or electoral subdivisions of the municipal government of Paris created in May 1790.

senatus consulta 'Consultations' or decisions equivalent to laws issued by the Senate.

sénéchaussée A judicial and administrative subdivision.

sindic Delegated person.

sous [or *sols*]. Twentieths of a *livre*.

subvention territoriale A universal land tax proposed by Controllers General Bertin and Calonne among others.

taille The principal direct tax; confined overwhelmingly to commoners.

taxation populaire The fixing of the prices of food commodities by means of crowd pressure.

Thermidor Shorthand for the *coup* against Robespierre in 1794 that resulted in the ending of the Terror.

'third' Prior to its dissolution, the Convention passed electoral laws to ensure a degree of political continuity. Voters were required to select two-thirds of the new deputies from the ranks of those who had served in the Convention. Thereafter, these deputies would stand down, a third at a time, each year.

Third Estate [*Tiers Etat*] The legal or functional category to which all non-clerics and non-nobles belonged.

tithe   A payment made by owners of land towards the upkeep of the clergy.

topas   Free men of mixed parentage (Portuguese and Indian) in Pondichéry.

venality of office   The monarchical practice of selling offices, jobs, or titles, for money.

Vendée   The department that became the epicentre of the royalist rebellion of the west.

vingtièmes   (twentieths). Proportional taxes applicable to all sources of income and paid by privileged and unprivileged alike; first introduced in 1750.

Further reading

The literature on the French Revolution is enormous and expands all the time. What follows is a selection from the material available in English. The selection draws attention to books and articles used in the preparation of this 'Seminar Study' which are accessible to school sixth-form and undergraduate readers. No attempt has been made to provide a comprehensive bibliography, or one that will satisfy more advanced final-year and postgraduate students.

Translated documents

There are a number of such compilations, of which the following can be recommended:

Dwyer, P.G. and McPhee, P. (eds) (2002) *The French Revolution and Napoleon: A Source Book*. London and New York: Routledge.

Hardman, J. (ed.) (1998) *The French Revolution Sourcebook*. London: Arnold.

Levy, D.G., Applewhite, H.B. and Johnson, M.D. (eds) (1980) *Women in Revolutionary Paris, 1789–1795*. Urbana, IL: University of Illinois Press.

Mason, L. and Rizzo, T. (1999) *The French Revolution: A Document Collection*. Boston: Haughton Mifflin.

Stewart, J.H. (1951) *A Documentary History of the French Revolution*. New York: The Macmillan Company.

Readers

These are volumes containing articles of seminal or historiographical importance. They can provide a quick route to material that might otherwise prove difficult to locate. The best readers also contain a 'state of play' account of the subject and commentaries on the articles chosen for inclusion. The following can be recommended:

Blanning, T.C.W. (ed.) (1996) *The Rise and Fall of the French Revolution*. Chicago, IL and London: University of Chicago Press.

Censer, J.R. (ed.) (1989) *The French Revolution and Intellectual History*. Chicago, IL: The Dorsey Press.

Jones, P.M. (ed.) (1996) *The French Revolution in Social and Political Perspective*. London: Arnold.

Handbooks and manuals

These volumes contain authoritative overviews of the latest thinking on a wide range of issues relating to the ancien régime and the revolution.

Andress, D. (ed.) (2015) *The Oxford Handbook of the French Revolution.* Oxford: Oxford University Press.

Doyle, W. (ed.) (2012) *The Oxford Handbook of the Ancien Régime.* Oxford: Oxford University Press.

Forrest, A. and Middell, M. (eds) (2016) *The Routledge Companion to the French Revolution in World History.* London and New York: Routledge.

McPhee, P. (ed.) (2013) *A Companion to the French Revolution.* Chichester: Wiley-Blackwell.

Introductory accounts

For the student who has little or no prior knowledge of the French Revolution, the short survey is the place to begin. There are plenty to choose from, but chronological coverage varies from volume to volume. For an uncomplicated and sure-footed narrative, Goodwin, A. (5th edn, 1986) The French Revolution. London: Hutchinson is hard to beat. However, this book is no longer in print. The following can be recommended:

Campbell, P.R. (1988) *The Ancien Régime in France.* Oxford: Basil Blackwell.

Crook, M. (1998) *Napoleon Comes to Power: Democracy and Dictatorship in Revolutionary France, 1795–1804.* Cardiff: University of Wales Press.

Doyle, W. (2001) *The French Revolution: A Very Short Introduction.* Oxford: Oxford University Press.

Ellis, G. (2003) *The Napoleonic Empire.* London: Palgrave Macmillan.

Emsley, C. (2014) *Napoleon: Conquest, Reform and Reorganization.* London: Taylor & Francis Ltd.

Gough, H. (2010) *The Terror in the French Revolution.* London: Palgrave Macmillan.

Hunt, L. and Censer, J.R. (2017) *The French Revolution and Napoleon: Crucible of the Modern World.* London: Bloomsbury.

Popkin, J.D. (2020) *A Short History of the French Revolution.* New York: Routledge.

Temple, N. (1992) *The Road to 1789: from Reform to Revolution in France.* Cardiff: University of Wales Press.

Rather longer, but highly readable are:

Forrest, A. (1995) *The French Revolution.* Oxford: Basil Blackwell.

Lyons, M. (1994) *Napoleon Bonaparte and the Legacy of the French Revolution.* London: Palgrave Macmillan.

McPhee, P. (2002) *The French Revolution, 1789–1799.* Oxford: Oxford University Press.

Sutherland, D.M.G. (1985) *France 1789–1815: Revolution and Counterrevolution.* London: Fontana Press.

Sutherland, D.M.G. (2003) *The French Revolution and Empire: The Quest for a Civic Order.* Oxford: Blackwell Publishing.

Historiography

A minefield! Students are strongly advised to gather information before plunging into the controversies generated by the events of 1789. That being done, they should consult:

Bell, D.A. (2014) 'Questioning the Global Turn: the Case of the French Revolution', *French Historical Studies*, 37:1, 1–24.

Desan, S., Hunt, L. and Nelson, W.M. (eds) (2013) *French Revolution in Global Perspective*. Ithaca, NY and London: Cornell University Press.

Furet, F. (1981) *Interpreting the French Revolution*. Cambridge: Cambridge University Press.

Lewis, G. (2002) *The French Revolution: Rethinking the Debate*. London: Taylor & Francis Ltd.

Soboul, A. (1988) *Understanding the French Revolution*. London: The Merlin Press.

Themes

Origins

The origins of the revolution are best tackled via:

Baker, K.M. (1990) *Inventing the French Revolution: Essays on French Political Culture in the Eighteenth Century*. Cambridge: Cambridge University Press.

Campbell, P.R. (2013) 'Rethinking the Origins of the French Revolution' in P. McPhee (ed.) *A Companion to the French Revolution*. Chichester: Wiley-Blackwell, pp. 3–23.

Doyle, W. (2001) *Origins of the French Revolution*. Oxford: Oxford University Press.

Lefebvre, G. (2015) *The Coming of the French Revolution*. Princeton, NJ: Princeton University Press.

Soboul, A. (1989) *French Revolution, 1787–1799: From the Storming of the Bastille to Napoleon*. London: Unwin Hyman.

Stone, B. (1994) *The Genesis of the French Revolution*. Cambridge: Cambridge University Press.

Swann, J. and Félix, J. (eds) (2013) *The Crisis of Absolute Monarchy: From the Old Regime to the French Revolution*. Oxford: Oxford University Press.

Country dwellers

Jones, P.M. (1988) *The Peasantry in the French Revolution*. Cambridge: Cambridge University Press.

Markoff, J. (1996) *The Abolition of Feudalism: Peasants, Lords and Legislators in the French Revolution*. University Park, PA: Pennsylvania University Press.

The transition of 1787–89

Blackman, R.H. (2019) *1789: The French Revolution Begins*. Cambridge: Cambridge University Press.

Jones, P.M. (1995) *Reform and Revolution in France: The Politics of Transition, 1774–1791*. Cambridge: Cambridge University Press.

Price, M. (1990) 'The "Ministry of the Hundred Hours": a Reappraisal', *French History*, 4:3317–338.

Tackett, T. (1996) *Becoming a Revolutionary*. Princeton, NJ: Princeton University Press.

Religion

Aston, N. (2000) *Religion and Revolution in France, 1789–1804.* London: Palgrave Macmillan.

Cage, C. (2015) *Unnatural Frenchmen: The Politics of Priestly Celibacy and Marriage, 1720–1813.* Charlottesville, VA: University of Virginia Press.

McManners, J. (1999) 'Church and Society in Eighteenth-Century France', vol. 2: *The Religion of the People and the Politics of Religion.* Oxford: Oxford University Press.

The clerical oath

Tackett, T. (1986) *Religion, Revolution and Regional Culture in Eighteenth-Century France: the Ecclesiastical Oath of 1791.* Princeton, NJ: Princeton University Press.

Rural revolution

Jones, P.M. (2003) *Liberty and Locality in Revolutionary France: Six Villages Compared, 1760–1820.* Cambridge: Cambridge University Press.

Plack, N. (2013) 'The Peasantry, Feudalism, and the Environment, 1789–93' in P. McPhee (ed.) *A Companion to the French Revolution.* Chichester: Wiley-Blackwell, pp. 212–227.

The press

Gough, H. (1988) *The Newspaper Press in the French Revolution.* London: Routledge & Kegan Paul.

Clubs

Kennedy, M. (1982–88) *The Jacobin Clubs in the French Revolution* (2 vols). Princeton, NJ: Princeton University Press.

Women

Desan, S. (2019) 'Recent Historiography on the French Revolution and Gender', *Journal of Social History*, 52:3, 566–574.

Godineau, D. (1998) *The Women of Paris and their French Revolution.* Berkeley, CA: University of California Press.

Goodman, D. (1994) *The Republic of Letters: A Cultural History of the French Enlightenment.* Ithaca, NY and London: Cornell University Press.

Hufton, O. (1992) *Women and the Limits of Citizenship in the French Revolution.* Toronto: University of Toronto Press.

Colonies, slavery and race

Dubois, L. (2004) *A Colony of Citizens: Revolution and Slave Emancipation in the French Caribbean, 1787–1804.* Chapel Hill and London: University of North Carolina Press.

Hazareesingh, S. (2020) *Black Spartacus: the Epic Life of Toussaint Louverture.* Harmondsworth: Allen Lane.

Popkin, J. (2007) *Facing Racial Revolution: Eyewitness Accounts of the Haitian Insurrection*. Chicago and London: University of Chicago Press.

Elections

Crook, M. (1996) *Elections in the French Revolution*. Cambridge: Cambridge University Press.
Edelstein, M. (2014) *The French Revolution and the Birth of Electoral Democracy*. Farnham: Ashgate.

Citizenship

Certon, A. (2008) '"Shades of Fraternity": Creolization and the Making of Citizenship in French India, 1790–1792', *French Historical Studies*, 31:4, 581–607.
Heuer, J.N. (2005) *The Family and the Nation: Gender and Citizenship in Revolutionary France, 1789–1830*. Ithaca, NY and London: Cornell University Press.
Rapport, M. (2000) *Nationality and Citizenship in Revolutionary France: The Treatment of Foreigners, 1789–1799*. Oxford: Oxford University Press.
Sahlins, P. (2004) *Unnaturally French. Foreign Citizens in the Old Regime and After*. Ithaca, NY and London: Cornell University Press.

The King, Queen and the Court

Caiani, A.A. (2012) *Louis XVI and the French Revolution, 1789–1792*. Cambridge: Cambridge University Press.
Hardman, J. (2016) *The Life of Louis XVI*. New Haven, CT and London: Yale University Press.
Hardman, J. (2019) *Marie-Antoinette*. New Haven, CT and London: Yale University Press.

The revolutionary wars

Blanning, T.C.W. (1986) *The Origins of the Revolutionary Wars*. London: Longman.
Esdale, C.J. (2001) *The French Wars, 1792–1815*. London: Routledge.
Hayworth, J.R. (2019) *Revolutionary France's War of Conquest in the Rhineland: Conquering the Natural Frontier, 1792–1797*. Cambridge and New York: Cambridge University Press.

Counter-revolution, the emigrés and the Vendée

Carpenter, K. and Mansel, P. (eds) (1999) *The French Emigrés in Europe and the Struggle against Revolution, 1789–1814*. New York: St. Martin's Press.
Martin, J.-C. (2013) 'The Vendée, Chouannerie, and the State, 1791–99', in P. McPhee (ed.) *A Companion to the French Revolution*. Chichester: Wiley-Blackwell, pp. 246–259.
Petitfrère, C. (1988) 'The Origins of the Civil War in the Vendée', *French History*, 2:2, 187–207.
Sutherland, D.M.G. (1982) *The Chouans: The Social Origins of Popular Counter-Revolution in Upper Brittany, 1770–1796*. Oxford: Clarendon Press.

Jacobins and Girondins

Whaley, L. (2000) *Radicals, Politics and Republicanism in the French Revolution.* Stroud: Sutton Publishing.

Federalism

Forrest, A. (1988) 'Federalism' in C. Lucas (ed.) *The French Revolution and the Creation of Modern Political Culture*, vol. 2, The Political Culture of the French Revolution. Oxford: Pergamon Press, pp. 309–328.

Terror

Andress, D. (2005) *The Terror: The Merciless War for Freedom in Revolutionary France.* New York: Farrar, Straus and Giroux.

Baczko, B. (1994) *Ending the Terror: The French Revolution after Robespierre.* Cambridge: Cambridge University Press.

Gough, H. (2010) *The Terror in the French Revolution.* London: Palgrave Macmillan.

Linton, M. (2013) *Choosing Terror: Virtue, Friendship and Authenticity in the French Revolution.* Oxford: Oxford University Press.

Tackett, T. (2015) *The Coming of the Terror in the French Revolution.* Cambridge, MA: Belknap / Harvard University Press.

The sans-culottes

Andress, D. (2015) 'Politics and Insurrection: the Sans-Culottes, the "Popular Movement", and the People of Paris', in D. Andress (ed.) *The Oxford Handbook of the French Revolution.* Oxford: Oxford University Press, pp. 401–417.

Lewis, G. (1964) *The Parisian Sans-Culottes and the French Revolution.* Oxford: Oxford University Press.

Rose, R.B. (1983) *The Making of the Sans-culottes.* Manchester: Manchester University Press.

Robespierre

Hampson, N. (1974) *The Life and Opinions of Maximilien Robespierre.* London: Duckworth.

Haydon, C. and Doyle, W. (eds) (1999) *Robespierre.* Cambridge: Cambridge University Press.

McPhee, P. (2012) *Robespierre: A Revolutionary Life.* New Haven, CT: Yale University Press.

Danton

Hampson, N. (1978) *Danton.* Oxford: Basil Blackwell.

Dechristianization

Smyth, J. (2016) *Robespierre and the Festival of the Supreme Being: the Search for a Republican Morality.* Manchester: Manchester University Press.

Tallett, F. (1991) 'Dechristianizing France: the Year II and the Revolutionary Experience', in F. Tallett and N. Atkin (eds) *Religion, Society and Politics in France since1789.* London: Hambledon Press, pp. 1–28.

Vovelle, M. (1991) *The Revolution against the Church.* Cambridge: Polity Press.

Thermidor

Jones, C. (2021) *The Fall of Robespierre: 24 Hours in Revolutionary Paris*. Oxford: Oxford University Press.

Lyons, M. (1975) 'The 9 Thermidor, Motives and Effects', *European Studies Review*, 5, 123–146.

The armies

Bertaud, J.P. (1989) *The Army of the French Revolution*. Princeton, NJ: Princeton University Press.

Forrest, A. (1989) *Soldiers of the French Revolution*. Durham, NC and London: Duke University Press.

The Directory

Brown, H.G. (2006) *Ending the Revolution: Violence, Justice, and Repression from the Terror to Napoleon*. Charlottesville and London: University of Virginia Press.

Lyons, M. (1975) *France under the Directory*. Cambridge: Cambridge University Press.

The Babeuf conspiracy

Rose, R.B. (1978) *Gracchus Babeuf, the First Revolutionary Communist*. Stanford, CA: University of Stanford Press.

Thomson, D. (1947) *The Babeuf Plot: The Making of a Republican Legend*. London: Kegan Paul.

Royalism

Fryer, W.R. (1965) *Republic and Restoration in France, 1794–1797*. Manchester: Manchester University Press.

The transition of 1799

Brown, H.G. and Miller, J.A. (2002) *Taking Liberties: Problems of a New Order from the French Revolution to Napoleon*. Manchester: Manchester University Press.

Napoleon Bonaparte and the Bonapartist regime

Doyle, W. (2015) *Napoleon Bonaparte*. Stroud: The History Press.

Dwyer, P.G. (2004) 'Napoleon Bonaparte as Hero and Saviour: Image, Rhetoric and Behaviour in the Construction of a Legend', *French History*, 18:4, 379–403.

Emsley, C. (2014) *Napoleon: Conquest, Reform and Reorganisation*. London: Taylor & Francis Ltd.

Lyons, M. (1994) *Napoleon Bonaparte and the Legacy of the French Revolution*. London: Macmillan.

Woloch, I. (2001) *Napoleon and his Collaborators: The Making of a Dictatorship*. New York: Norton.

Economic impacts

Forrest, A. (2020) *The Death of the French Atlantic: Trade, War, and Slavery in the Age of Revolution.* Oxford: Oxford University Press.
Horn, J. (2006) *The Path Not Taken: French Industrialisation in the Age of Revolution, 1750–1830.* Cambridge, MA: MIT Press.

Reference works

The key book for the period up to 1799 is Jones, C. (2013) The Longman Companion to the French Revolution. London: Routledge. For the period after 1800 there is no comprehensive volume providing coverage of both domestic and foreign affairs, but see:

Emsley, C. (1993) *The Longman Companion to Napoleonic Europe.* London: Longman.

Websites

British Newspaper Coverage of the French Revolution: https://oldsite.english.ucsb.edu
Euro Docs: 1789–1871: https://eudocs.lib.byu.edu
Fordham University: Primary Sources on the French Revolution: https://sourcebooks.fordham.edu
French Revolution Images: Iconography from the Collections of the Bibliothèque Nationale de France: https://exhibits.stanford.edu
French Revolution Digital Archive: https://frda.stanford.edu
Liberty, Equality, Fraternity: Exploring the French Revolution: https://revolution.chnm.org
Napoleon.org: www.napoleon.org
Project Gutenberg: www.gutenberg.org
The Napoleon Series: www.napoleon-series.org

References

Allen, R.B. (2015) *European Slave Trading in the Indian Ocean, 1500–1850*. Athens: Ohio University Press.

Alpaugh, M. (2015) *Non-Violence and the French Revolution: Political Demonstrations in Paris, 1787–1795*. Cambridge: Cambridge University Press.

Andress, D. (2000) *Massacre at the Champ de Mars: Popular Dissent and Political Culture in the French Revolution*. Bury St Edmunds: The Royal Historical Society.

Armitage, D. and Subrahmanyam, S. (eds) (2010) *The Age of Revolutions in Global Context, c. 1760–1840*. New York: Palgrave Macmillan.

Aubert, R. (ed.) (1974) *Journal de Célestin Guittard de Floriban, bourgeois de Paris sous la Révolution*. Paris: Editions France-Empire.

Aulard, A. (ed.) (1903–09) *Paris sous le Consulat* (4 vols). Paris: Cerf.

Babelon, J.-P. (1965) 'Les maquettes et les pierres de la Bastille. Récolement des souvenirs lapidaires provenant de l'activité du patriote Palloy', *La Gazette des Archives*, 51, 217–230.

Bacourt, A. de (ed.) (1851) *Correspondance entre le Comte de Mirabeau et le Comte de La Marck pendant les années 1789, 1790 et 1791* (3 vols). Paris: Librairie Ve Le Normant.

Baker, K.M. (ed.) (1987) *The French Revolution and the Creation of Modern Political Culture*, vol. 1, *The Political Culture of the Old Regime*. Oxford: Pergamon Press.

Baker, K.M. (ed.) (1990) *Inventing the French Revolution: Essays on French Political Culture in the Eighteenth Century*. Cambridge: Cambridge University Press.

Baker, K.M. (ed.) (1994) *The French Revolution and the Creation of Modern Political Culture*, vol. 4, *The Terror*. Oxford: Pergamon Press.

Banks, B.A. (2017) 'Real and Imaginary Friends in Revolutionary France: Quakers, Political Culture and the Atlantic World', *Eighteenth Century Studies*, 50:4, 361–379.

Béaur, G. (2008) 'Révolution et redistribution des richesses dans les campagnes: mythe ou réalité?', *Annales historiques de la Révolution française*, 352:2, 209–239.

Bell, D.A. (2007) *The First Total War: Napoleon's Europe and the Birth of Warfare as We Know It*. Boston: Houghton Mifflin.

Bell, D.A. (2014) 'Questioning the Global Turn: the Case of the French Revolution', *French Historical Studies*, 37:1, 1–24.

Bell, D.A. (2015) 'Global Conceptual Legacies' in D. Andress (ed.) *The Oxford Handbook of the French Revolution*. Oxford: Oxford University Press, pp. 642–655.

Biggs, C. (1797) *A Residence in France during the Years 1792, 1793, 1794, and 1795; Described in a Series of Letters from an English Lady* (2 vols). London: Longman.

Blaufarb, R. (2016) *The Great Demarcation: the French Revolution and the Invention of Modern Property.* Oxford: Oxford University Press.

Bodinier, B. and Teyssier, E. (2000) *L'Evénement le plus important de la Révolution: la vente des biens nationaux.* Paris: Editions du Cths.

Bond, E.A. (2021) *The Writing Public: Participatory Knowledge Production in Enlightenment and Revolutionary France.* Ithaca, NY: Cornell University Press.

Boudon, J.O. (1997) *Le Consulat et l'Empire.* Paris: Monchrestien.

Boutanquoi, O. (1928) *Les souvenirs d'une femme du peuple, Marie-Victoire Monnard, de Creil 1777–1802.* Senlis: Imprimeries réunies de Senlis.

Boutier, J., Boutry, P. and Bonin, S. (eds) (1992) *Atlas de la Révolution française,* vol. 6, *Les sociétés politiques.* Paris: Editions de l'Ecole des Hautes Etudes en Sciences Sociales.

Boyd, J.P. (ed.) (1956) *The Papers of Thomas Jefferson,* vol. 13, *March to 7 October 1788.* Princeton, NJ: Princeton University Press.

Boyd, J.P. (ed.) (1958) *The Papers of Thomas Jefferson,* vol. 14, *8 October 1788–26 March 1789.* Princeton, NJ: Princeton University Press.

Boyd, J.P. (ed.) (1958) *The Papers of Thomas Jefferson,* vol. 15, *27 March 1789–30 November 1789.* Princeton, NJ: Princeton University Press.

Brassart, L. (2013) *Gouverner le local en Révolution: Etat, pouvoirs et mouvements collectifs dans l'Aisne (1790–1795).* Paris: Société des études robespierristes.

Brette, A. (1894–1915) *Recueil de documents relatifs à la convocation des Etats Généraux de 1789* (4 vols). Paris: Imprimerie Nationale.

Brown, H.G. (2007) 'Napoleon Bonaparte, Political Prodigy', *History Compass,* 5:4, 1382–1398.

Brown, H.G. and Miller, J.A. (eds) (2002) *Taking Liberties: Problems of a New Order from the French Revolution to Napoleon.* Manchester: Manchester University Press.

Browning, O. (ed.) (1909) *Despatches from Paris,* vol. 1, *1784–1787.* London: Historical Association of Great Britain.

Browning, O. (ed.) (1910) *Despatches from Paris,* vol. 2, *1788–1790.* London: Historical Association of Great Britain.

Buchez, P.-J.-B. and Roux, P.-C. (1834–38) *Histoire parlementaire de la Révolution française* (40 vols). Paris: Paulin.

Burke, E. (1790/1973) *Reflections on the Revolution in France and on the Proceedings in certain Societies in London relative to that Event* (Conor Cruise O'Brien edn). Harmondsworth: Penguin Books.

Burnard, T. and Garrigus, J. (2016) *The Plantation Machine: Atlantic Capitalism in French Saint-Domingue and British Jamaica.* Philadelphia: University of Pennsylvania Press.

Burrows, S. (2015) 'Books, Philosophy, Enlightenment', in D. Andress (ed.) *The Oxford Handbook of the French Revolution.* Oxford: Oxford University Press, pp. 74–91.

Cage, C. (2013) '"Celibacy is a social crime": The Politics of Clerical Marriage, 1793–1797', *French Historical Studies,* 36:4, 601–628.

Campbell, P.R. (2013) 'Rethinking the Origins of the French Revolution' in P. McPhee (ed.) *A Companion to the French Revolution.* Chichester: Wiley-Blackwell, pp. 3–23.

Carpenter, K. (2015) 'Emigration in Politics and Imagination' in D. Andress (ed.) *The Oxford Handbook of the French Revolution.* Oxford: Oxford University Press, pp. 330–345.

Carré, H. (ed.) (1932) *Marquis de Ferrières: correspondance inédite, 1789, 1790, 1791.* Paris: A. Colin.

Carré, H. and Boissonnade, P. (eds) (1898) *Correspondance inédite du Constituant Thibaudeau, 1789–1791*. Paris: Honoré Champion.

Carton, A. (2008) 'Shades of Fraternity: Creolization and the Making of Citizenship in French India, 1790–1792', *French Historical Studies*, 31:4, 581–607.

Chappey, J.-L. (2015) 'The New Elites. Questions about Political, Social and Cultural Reconstruction after the Terror' in D. Andress (ed.) *The Oxford Handbook of the French Revolution*. Oxford: Oxford University Press, pp. 556–572.

Chew, S.C. (1912) 'Diary of a Baltimorean of the Eighteenth Century', *Maryland Historical Magazine*, 7:4, 356–374.

Chew III, W.L. (2012) 'The Journée du Dix Août as Witnessed by a Yankee Merchant', *Journal of American Studies*, 46, 89–101.

Clay, L.R. (2015) 'The Bourgeoisie, Capitalism and the Origins of the French Revolution' in D. Andress (ed.) *The Oxford Handbook of the French Revolution*. Oxford: Oxford University Press, pp. 21–39.

Cobb, R. and Jones, C. (1988) *The French Revolution: Voices from a Momentous Epoch, 1789–1795*. London: Simon and Schuster.

Crubaugh, A. (2001) *Balancing the Scales of Justice: Local Courts and Rural Society in Southwest France, 1750–1800*. University Park, PA: Pennsylvania State University Press.

Daudin, G. (2011) *Commerce et prosperité. La France au XVIIIe siècle*. Paris: Presses de l'Université de Paris-Sorbonne.

Daumas, P. (2002) 'Familles en révolution (1775–1825). Recherches sur les comportements familiaux des populations rurales d'Ile-de-France, de l'Ancien Régime à la Restauration', *Résumé in Annales historiques de la Révolution française* 329 (July–Sept.), 161–168.

Desan, S., Hunt, L. and Nelson, W. M. (eds) (2013) *The French Revolution in Global Perspective*. Ithaca, NY: Cornell University Press.

Dewald, J. (2019) 'Rethinking the 1 Percent: the Failure of the Nobility in Old Regime France', *American Historical Review*, 124:3, 911–932.

Doyle, W. (1999) *Origins of the French Revolution*. Oxford: Oxford University Press.

Doyle, W. (2013) *France and the Age of Revolution: Regimes Old and New from Louis XIV to Napoleon Bonaparte*. London: I. B. Tauris.

Dunn, J. (2005) *Setting the People Free: the Story of Democracy*. London: Atlantic Books.

Dupâquier, J. (1979) *La Population française au XVIIe et XVIIIe siècles*. Paris: Que sais-je?

Edelstein, M. (2014) *The French Revolution and the Birth of Electoral Democracy*. Farnham: Ashgate.

Edwards, G. (ed.) (2001) *Letters from Revolutionary France. Letters written in France to a Friend in London between the Month of November 1794, and the Month of May 1795. Watkin Tench*. Cardiff: University of Wales Press.

Ellis, G. (1997) 'Religion according to Napoleon: the Limitations of Pragmatism', in Aston, N. (ed.) *Religious Change in Europe, 1650–1914*. Oxford: Clarendon Press, pp. 235–255.

Evans, C. (ed.) (1990) *The Letterbook of Richard Crawshay 1788–1797 with an introduction by G. G. L. Hayes*. Cardiff: South Wales Record Society.

Farge, A. (1994) *Subversive Words: Public Opinion in Eighteenth-Century France*. London: Polity Press.

Félix, J. (1999) *Finances et politique au siècle des lumières: le ministère L'Averdy, 1763–1768*. Paris: Comité pour l'histoire économique et financière de la France.

Félix, J. (2015) 'Monarchy', in D. Andress (ed.) *The Oxford Handbook of the French Revolution*. Oxford: Oxford University Press, pp. 56–73.

Figeac, M. (1995) 'Destins de la noblesse bordelaise, 1770–1830' (Thèse de Doctorat, Université de Paris-IV Sorbonne) reviewed in *Annales du Midi*, 108 (Oct.–Dec. 1996), 540–541.

Firges, P. (2017) *French Revolutionaries in the Ottoman Empire: Diplomacy, Political Culture and the Limiting of Universal Revolution, 1792–1798*. Oxford: Oxford University Press.

Fitzmaurice, E. (ed.) (1898) *Lettres de l'abbé Morellet à Lord Shelburne, depuis Marquis de Lansdowne, 1772–1803*. Paris: Plon.

Fitzsimmons, M.P. (2015) 'Sovereignty and Constitutional Power' in D. Andress (ed.) *The Oxford Handbook of the French Revolution*. Oxford: Oxford University Press, pp. 201–217.

Forrest, A. (2015) 'Military Trauma' in D. Andress (ed.) *The Oxford Handbook of the French Revolution*. Oxford: Oxford University Press, pp. 382–400.

Forrest, A. (2020) *The Death of the French Atlantic: Trade, War, and Slavery in the Age of Revolution*. Oxford: Oxford University Press.

Furet, F. (1981) *Interpreting the French Revolution*. Cambridge: Cambridge University Press.

Gainot, B. (2001) *1799, un nouveau Jacobinisme? La démocratie représentative, une alternative à Brumaire*. Paris: Editions du Cths.

Garrett, M.B. (1959) *The Estates General of 1789: the Problems of Composition and Organisation*. New York: American Historical Association.

Girard, P. (2011) 'Napoléon voulait-il retablir l'esclavage en Haïti?' *Bulletin de la Société d'histoire de la Guadeloupe*, 159, 3–28.

Gobalakichenane, M. (1996–97) 'La Révolution française des Tamouls de Pondichéry, 1790–1793', Mémoire de D.E.A., Université de Nantes.

Godineau, D. (1988) *Citoyennes tricoteuses: les femmes du peuple à Paris pendant la Révolution française*. Aix-en-Provence: Alinéa.

Goodman, D. (1994) *The Republic of Letters: a Cultural History of the French Enlightenment*. Ithaca, NY and London: Cornell University Press.

Goodwin, A. (1959) *The French Revolution*. London: Harper Collins.

Gressang, C. (2020) 'Breaking Habits: Identity and the Dissolution of Convents in France, 1789–1808', Doctoral dissertation, University of Kentucky.

Gruder, V.R. (2007) *The Notables and the Nation. The Political Schooling of the French, 1787–1788*. Cambridge, MA: Harvard University Press.

Hankin, C.C. (ed.) (1858) *Life of Mary Anne Schimmelpenninck*. Vol. I. London: Longman.

Hampson, N. (1974) *The Life and Opinions of Maximilien Robespierre*. London: Duckworth.

Hardman, J. (1993) *Louis XVI*. New Haven, CT and London: Yale University Press.

Hardman, J. (2016) *The Life of Louis XVI*. New Haven, CT and London: Yale University Press.

Hesse, C.H. (1991) *Publishing and Cultural Politics in Revolutionary Paris, 1789–1810*. Berkeley, CA: University of California Press.

Hincker, F. (1971) *Les Français devant l'impôt sous l'Ancien Régime*. Paris: Flammarion.

Horn, J. (2006) *The Path Not Taken: French Industrialization in the Age of Revolution, 1750–1830*. Cambridge, MA: MIT Press.

Horn, J. (2015) *Economic Development in Early Modern France: The Privilege of Liberty, 1650–1820*. Cambridge, MA: Cambridge University Press.

Hunt, L. (2013) 'The Global Financial Origins of 1789', in S. Desan, L. Hunt and W.M. Nelson (eds) *French Revolution in Global Perspective*. Ithaca, NY: Cornell University Press, pp. 32–43.

Hunt, L. and Censer, J. (2017) *The French Revolution and Napoleon: Crucible of the Modern World*. London: Bloomsbury.

Jainchill, A. (2008) *Reimagining Politics after Thermidor: the Republican Origins of French Liberalism*. Ithaca, NY and London: Cornell University Press.

Jessenne, J.P. (2013) 'The Social and Economic Crisis in France at the End of the Ancien Régime' in P. McPhee (ed.) *A Companion to the French Revolution*. Chichester: Wiley-Blackwell, pp. 24–41.

Jessenne, J.P. and Le May, E.H. (eds) (1998) *Député-paysan et fermière de Flandre en 1789. La correspondance des Lepoutre*. Villeneuve d'Asq: Centre d'histoire de l'Europe du Nord-Ouest.

Jeyes, S.H. (1911) *The Russells of Birmingham in the French Revolution and in America, 1791–1814*. London: George Allen.

Jones, P.M. (1988) *The Peasantry in the French Revolution*. Cambridge: Cambridge University Press.

Jones, P.M. (1995) *Reform and Revolution in France: the Politics of Transition, 1774–1791*. Cambridge: Cambridge University Press.

Jones, P.M. (2003) *Liberty and Locality in Revolutionary France: Six Villages Compared, 1760–1820*. Cambridge: Cambridge University Press.

Jones, P.M. (2013) 'Choosing Revolution and Counter-Revolution', in P. McPhee (ed.) *A Companion to the French Revolution*. Chichester: Wiley-Blackwell, pp. 278–292.

Kwass, M. (1994) 'Liberté, Egalité, Fiscalité: Taxation, Privilege, and Political Culture in Eighteenth-Century France'. Doctoral dissertation, University of Michigan.

Lefebvre, G. (1947) *The Coming of the French Revolution*. Translated by R.R. Palmer. Princeton: Princeton University Press.

Lewis, G. (1993) *The French Revolution: Rethinking the Debate*. London and New York: Routledge.

Linton, M. (2015) 'Terror and Politics' in D. Andress (ed.) *The Oxford Handbook of the French Revolution*. Oxford: Oxford University Press, pp. 471–486.

Llorca, M.-L. (ed.) (1994) *Lettres parisiennes d'un révolutionnaire poitevin: Pierre Dubreuil-Chambardel*. Tours: Presses universitaires François-Rabelais.

Lockroy, E. (1881) *Journal d'une bourgeoise pendant la Révolution, 1791–1793*. Paris: Calmann Lévy.

Louchet, L. (1792–94) 'Correspondance de Louis Louchet'. MS letters in Bibliothèque Municipale, Rodez, France.

Lough, J. (1987) *France on the Eve of the Revolution: British Travellers' Observations, 1763–1788*. London: Croom Helm.

Lucas, C. (1988) 'The Crowd and Politics' in C. Lucas (ed.) *The French Revolution and the Creation of Modern Political Culture*, vol. 2, *The Political Culture of the Revolution*. Oxford: Pergamon Press, pp. 259–285.

Lyons, M. (1994) *Napoleon Bonaparte and the Legacy of the French Revolution*. London: Macmillan.

Margadant, T.W. (1992) *Urban Rivalries in the French Revolution.* Princeton, NJ: Princeton University Press.

Martin, J.-C. (2006) *Violence et révolution. Essai sur la naissance d'un mythe national.* Paris: Seuil.

Maugras, G. (1910) *Journal d'un étudiant (Edmond Géraud) pendant la Révolution 1789–1793.* Paris: Plon.

Maza, S. (2013) 'The Cultural Origins of the French Revolution' in P. McPhee (ed.) *A Companion to the French Revolution.* Chichester: Wiley-Blackwell, pp. 42–56.

Miller, S.J. (2020) *Feudalism, Venality, and Revolution: Provincial Assemblies in Late-Old Regime France.* Manchester: Manchester University Press.

Morris, G. (1939) *A Diary of the French Revolution* (2 vols). London: Harrap.

Mousset, A. (1924) *Un Témoin ignoré de la Révolution: le Comte de Fernan Nuñez, ambassadeur d'Espagne à Paris, 1787–1791.* Paris: Champion.

Murphy, O.T. (1998) *The Diplomatic Retreat of France and Public Opinion on the Eve of the French Revolution, 1783–1789.* Washington: The Catholic University of America Press.

Norberg, K. (1994) 'The French Fiscal Crisis of 1788 and the Financial Origins of the Revolution of 1789', in Hoffman, P.T. and Norberg, K. (eds), *Fiscal Crises, Liberty and Representative Government, 1450–1789.* Stanford, CA: Stanford University Press, pp. 253–298.

Perović, S. (2012) *The Calendar in Revolutionary France: Perceptions of Time in Literature, Culture, Politics.* Cambridge: Cambridge University Press.

Phillips, R. (1981) *Family Breakdown in Late Eighteenth-Century France: Divorce in Rouen, 1792–1803.* Oxford: Clarendon Press.

Popkin, J. (2007) *Facing Racial Revolution: Eyewitness Accounts of the Haitian Insurrection.* Chicago and London: University of Chicago Press.

Price, M. (1990) 'The "Ministry of the Hundred Hours": a Reappraisal', *French History,* 4:3, 317–338.

Régent, F. (2015) 'Préjugé de couleur, esclavage et citoyennetés dans les colonies françaises (1789–1848)', *Cahiers de l'Institut d'histoire de la Révolution française,* 9.

Rougé, O. de (1910) *Histoire généalogique de la maison de Rougé.* Vendôme: H. Chartier éditeur.

Ruault, N. (1976) *Gazette d'un Parisien sous la Révolution. Lettres à son frère, 1783–1796.* Paris: Perrin.

Sahlins, P. (2004) *Unnaturally French: Foreign Citizens in the Old Regime and After.* Ithaca, NY and London: Cornell University Press.

Schopenhauer, J. (1847) *My Youthful Life and Pictures of Travel* (2 vols). London: Longman.

Soboul, A. (1974) *The French Revolution, 1787–1799: from the Storming of the Bastille to Napoleon.* Translated by A. Forrest and C. Jones. London: NLB.

Soboul, A. (1988) *Understanding the French Revolution.* London: The Merlin Press.

Spang, R. (2015) *Stuff and Money in the Time of the French Revolution.* Cambridge, MA: Cambridge University Press.

Stone, B. (1986) *The French Parlements and the Crisis of the Old Regime.* Chapel Hill and London: University of North Carolina Press.

Stone, B. (1994) *The Genesis of the French Revolution: a Global-Historical Interpretation.* Cambridge: Cambridge University Press.

Sutherland, D.M.G. (1985) *France 1789–1815: Revolution and Counterrevolution.* London: Fontana Press.

Tackett, T. (2009) 'Paths to Revolution: the Old Regime Correspondence of Five Future Revolutionaries', *French Historical Studies*, 32:4, 531–554.

Tarrade, J. (1972) *Le commerce colonial de France à la fin de l'Ancien régime: l'évolution du régime de 'l'Exclusif' de 1763 à 1789* (2 vols). Paris: PUF.

Thompson, J.M. (2013) *Letters of Napoleon*. Redditch: Read Books Limited.

Tocqueville, A. de (1969) *L'Ancien Régime* (Headlam edn). Oxford: Clarendon Press.

Whaley, L. (2000) *Radicals, Politics and Republicanism in the French Revolution*. Stroud: Sutton Publishing.

Woloch, I. (2001) *Napoleon and his Collaborators: the Making of a Dictatorship*. New York: Norton.

Young, A. (1794/1900) *Arthur Young's Travels in France* (Betham-Edwards edn). London: George Bell and Sons.

Index

Page numbers in **bold** refer to maps and figures. Pages numbers referring to a document are followed by 'd' and the document number, e.g. 131d1.